Are They Being Served?

QUALITY CONSCIOUSNESS
IN SERVICE INDUSTRIES

Edited by

BRIAN MOORES

*Cardiff Business School,
University of Wales Institute of Science and Technology*

Philip Allan

First published 1986 by
PHILIP ALLAN PUBLISHERS LIMITED
MARKET PLACE
DEDDINGTON
OXFORD
OX5 4SE

British Library Cataloguing in Publication Data
Moores, Brian
    Are they being served?
    1. Customer service——Great Britain——
    Management
    I. Title
658.8'12   HF5415.5

ISBN 0-86003-545-X
ISBN 0-86003-647-2 Pbk

Typeset by Dentset, Oxford
Printed in Great Britain by the Bocardo Press Ltd., Oxford

Dedicated to the Chief Nursing Officer
at the Welsh Office who is
doing her damnedest to
ensure that the nursing service
in Wales is second to none

Contents

1

Introduction

'Come give us a taste of your quality.'

Hamlet
William Shakespeare

I have vivid recollections of a December day back in 1974 when this book was originally conceived. Being one of those awfully tedious people who object to inhaling other people's smoke I had requested two soldiers to move from the non-smoking section of an InterCity train which was about to depart from London's Euston station. The request fell on deaf ears and the pulling of the communication cord served no useful purpose other than that of delaying the journey by several minutes.

I then found myself on the receiving end of a series of assaults, the accuracy and strength of which, fortunately, were in inverse proportion to the increasingly drunken state of my assailants who were, in fact, removed by the police at Crewe. Upon arrival at my ultimate destination I was concerned to discover whether it was just my pride which had been hurt; or was the awful pain in my jaw a more significant legacy of my battle for the rights of the individual? Naturally, I took off for the accident and emergency department of that town's teaching hospital.

For many years I had been conducting research on the management of the NHS, but over that same period I had never actually been a customer. What a shock I was in for! I found it distasteful to find someone else's dried blood on the X-ray plate. I was even more concerned that a young girl's bawling went unheeded while staff concentrated on hanging up the Christmas decorations. But what was most difficult to cope with was discovering that the loo boasted no toilet paper when it was already too late!

This particular episode was shortly followed by the account of one of my tutorial students, an Orthodox Jew, of some of the difficulties he had experienced as an inpatient over the Christmas vacation. I then got to wondering how, if at all, hospitals set about determining what customers felt about the service. It struck me then, and still does now, that being a virtual monopoly the NHS ought to be even more inclined to determine and improve customer service. The eventual

1

outcome of this ruminating was the production of a tool for assessing patient satisfaction which is described in Chapter 9. It is of more than passing interest to record that it has taken the trenchant observations of Sir Roy Griffiths, the chief executive of Sainsbury's, to alert NHS staff to an almost total lack of obvious concern for quality assessment.

Since the incident on the train my interest in the NHS has not waned. Indeed, if anything, it has intensified. One direct consequence of this growing interest was a four-day symposium in December 1984 on the theme of Quality. The audience comprised over 140 top British nurses who attended in the expectation of hearing of quality-related developments from which they might possibly benefit. The symposium featured a handful of contributions from other service industries and, far from being seen to be totally irrelevant, these external inputs were judged to be particularly valuable. The problems of dealing with customers in banks, holidaymakers and hotel guests were *not* seen to be a whole world removed from those enountered in dealing with patients.

From all accounts, that symposium was judged a great success and for a while I toyed with the idea of publishing the proceedings. I eventually decided against targeting only health care staff and decided instead to see whether it would be possible to secure contributions from experienced individuals from a range of service industries who had something worth saying to their opposite numbers in other service industries. The theme would be quality determination, but there would also be reference to how such assessments were used to bring about improvements. A few early tentative overtures to potential contributors suggested that there were indeed people who would not only be prepared to communicate but would be delighted to be so involved.

Phase II saw me putting together a synopsis of what I judged to be an appropriate spread of topics. In that document the names of several individuals and organisations featured in anticipation of their eventual agreement to contribute should a suitable publisher be found. Philip Allan, with whom I had previously collaborated, wrote back immediately with a contract having decided that such a text would not only fill a gap in the market but could conceivably sell in sufficient numbers to warrant a high-quality production.

Phase III then required me to approach those individuals whose names I had taken in vain with a request for a contribution. In only five cases did I meet with a rejection; it would be invidious to identify those who felt unable to participate. In two cases the reason for the refusal was a genuine concern about revealing to competitors just how the company set about measuring customer satisfaction. This was a very real pity as I do know what those two companies actually do on this front is very exciting. Nonetheless, I could not, in all conscience, push too hard. A couple of very large organisations, one recently privatised, gave me what I can only label as a 'bum's rush'. What was particularly depressing was their observation that how they measured customer satisfaction was of no concern to customers! As a citizen I was deeply disturbed, as both operate in a monopoly situation. The final rejection was the crudest. I was assured by one large fast-food chain that they were so dedicated to the gentle art of increasing the numbers eating their particular bovine product that, clearly, they could not afford the time nor, indeed, had they the inclination, to put pen to paper to tell other people how they did it.

On the positive side the response was most encouraging. In addition to agreeing to constraints on deadline and word counts (which most contributors subsequently met) other possible topics were suggested. The inclusion of these more than made up for the loss of the original five and, if anything, provided a better balance.

I hope that all readers will find something in the text which they will judge to be of value. Naturally, most will be tempted to turn to that chapter which appears to be of the greatest relevance to their particular industry. If, for example, you work for British Caledonian, doubtless you will immediately flip to page 77 to find out how British Airways has successfully introduced the 'customer first' concept throughout the airline. On the other hand, Tesco employees can be virtually guaranteed to direct their immediate attention to Chapter 14, as it contains details of Sainsbury's approach to customer satisfaction which quite clearly finds favour with the British public. NHS or BUPA employees will presumably look first at the chapters concerned with health care, and so on. My hope and expectation is that careful reading of the remaining chapters, or even a series of casual dips, will serve to convince you that *all* the contributors have something relevant and valuable to say if your line of business is in the delivery of a service, be it in the public or private sector.

The obvious point that arises is why both Philip Allan and I, and indeed the many contributors, feel that there is a gap to be plugged. Why should a text which brings together quality assurance and service industries be held to be timely? The naive and simple answer is that this is the reality of the situation. For a variety of reasons, many of which are touched on in the following chapters, there is an almost explosive current concern with quality, and nowhere is this more evident than in the service sector. In what is left of this introduction I will touch on what I see as the forces leading to this concern.

A visitor from another planet or even from another country could well be excused if, after being here for several weeks, he concluded that those employed in parts of the service sector were some strange form of parasite. Hardly a day passes without some personage or other publicly proposing that any chance that Britain has of digging itself out of its current economic demise crucially depends upon the improved performance of our manufacturing sector. Where is the money to come from to fund the various social services if not but from the proceeds of selling the fruits of our manufacture? Some even go so far as to suggest that North Sea oil, far from being a bonanza, has served to inhibit manufacturing. It was only two years ago, for example, that the then Chairman of British Leyland opined that, if we could not cope with the economic consequences of the windfall, perhaps we might be better off leaving it in Neptune's safe hands.

In fact, if one examines the figures, we have not been performing at all badly on the manufacturing front. It is, for example, a little known and strangely unpublicised fact that as a nation we still export one third more per individual than does Japan. While a substantial part of the increased unemployment can be attributable to a reduction in public sector expenditure, or at least a slowing down of the increase, a large part can be put down to companies genuinely becoming very much leaner. One has only to examine the performance of several large industries to see evidence of this. British Steel, for example, now produces more than twice the tonnage of steel per man than they did five years ago. Jaguar's output of vehicles in 1984 was 142 per cent greater than in 1980 and this increased level of output was achieved with a slightly reduced labour force. British Airways has not reduced its level of movements since 1981 but it has shed 23,000 of its 57,000 staff while at the same time, apparently, enhancing the quality of service. Some companies can record productivity increases well in excess of 1,000 per cent. People have been writing on the potential order of magnitude of such productivity improvements for years. Article upon article and book after book has carried an almost masochistic recital of how poor our economic performance has been when compared to that of our competitors who have progressively changed from the Americans to the Germans to the Japanese, and on to the countries of the Pacific Basin.

The recent dramatic and unfortunate explosion in the level of unemployment could be interpreted as the price we have paid for burying our heads in the sand in the face of a mass of evidence that we would be unable to continue to compete internationally at our previous levels of performance. Certainly, a large part of it can be interpreted as a cruel exposure of the soft underbelly of British industry. Not only have we begun to eat away at that fat but this is going hand in glove with the inevitable consequences of the so-called new technology. 'New' is something of a misnomer as technology has always been providing, and will continue to provide, improved ratios of outputs to inputs. The man-hours involved in the production of a motor car can be guaranteed to reduce over time. It is when the man-hours are replaced with robot-hours that the transition is seen in starker terms.

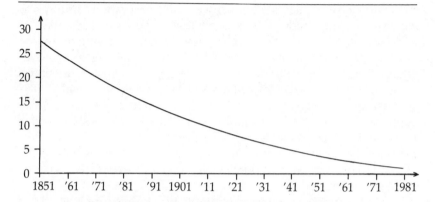

Figure 1.1 *Percentage of Male Working Population Involved in Agriculture, Horticulture and Forestry*

Consider what has happened in agriculture which was once so heavily labour-intensive. In Figure 1.1 we see how the proportion of the labour force involved in agriculture has inexorably declined over the past century. Presumably, at the turn of the century noises were made about the undesirable consequences of people moving from the land. We are now not only self-sufficient in foodstuffs but we make substantial contributions to the thoroughly unwholesome, and some would say unnecessary, EEC surpluses, be they lakes or mountains. It is hard to conceive of any product which will not be seen to be associated with a similar decline of labour content. Motor vehicles obviously are moving in this direction, as are computers, shirts, television sets and virtually anything else you would care to name. As there is a finite limit to how many cars we can drive, how many shirts we can wear and how many television sets we can watch, it is self-evident that labour resources will be increasingly directed towards the provision of services. Even reduced hours of work, increased holiday entitlements or reduced working lives will not keep pace with the diminution of the labour needed in the production of goods.

When we look at service industries it does not take a genius to appreciate that changes in the input/output ratio are not going to be of the same order of magnitude. Maybe, in such sectors as the fast-food industry, the quantity of calories served per employee will go on increasing, but it is difficult to envisage that robots will take over from nurses or chambermaids, at least in the foreseeable future.

Lest this sounds a trifle futuristic, consider the material in Table 1.1 which reveals that such an extrapolation is but a continuation of a clear trend. It has to be very clearly understood that not only are service industries here to stay, but the proportion of the labour force engaged in these service industries will inexorably continue to increase. It could indeed be argued that, when we talk about an increased standard of living, we are now talking of having more and more things done for us in return for having a greater choice over which things we want to do for ourselves. Some people write books so as to afford a decorator; others see decorating as a hobby. It is surprising how many supposedly well-informed observers seem to suppose that this trend can be bucked. Back in the 1960s Selective Employment Tax was quite patently introduced as some Canute-like measure aimed at stemming movements in the composition of the labour force which were as predictable as the return of Halley's comet and as irreversible.

Although my own interest in the topic sprang originally from involvement in the health service which is all too readily placed in the 'parasitic' category along with social services, the BBC, etc., there are other service industries which do, of course, have a direct and very tangible influence on our balance of payments. Britain has always featured a strong 'below-the-line' positive balance stemming from the provision of financial services. There is, though, another burgeoning service sector which is having an ever-increasing impact on our economic performance, namely, that which brings in tourist income. It has been estimated that Britain currently earns around £5 billion from this source which provides direct employment for over 900,000 individuals and generates around 50,000 extra new jobs each year.

It is sobering for someone writing from Cardiff to realise that tourism generates a revenue of approximately one billion pounds for the Principality each year. The Welsh Tourist Board has further estimated that some 90,000 full-time equivalent jobs are dependent directly or indirectly on this level of activity and this is double the combined employment in the coal and steel industries.

Organisations operating in the hospitality sector have long recognised that they have to compete increasingly on the strength of the quality of service they provide. Greatly enhanced net disposable income for those fortunate enough to be in employment has guaranteed that price, while remaining in the equation, has become a less dominant element. The post-war emergence of independent assessors of quality and the subsequent publication of the ratings

Table 1.1 *Labour Market Employment in the United Kingdom 1950–1983 (000s)*

Year	Agriculture, forestry and fishing	Mining and quarrying	Manufac- turing	Construction	Gas, electricity and water	Transport and communi- cation	Distributive trades	Services	Public administra- tion and defence	Self- employed
1950	806	857	8,520	1,325	360	1,769	2,130	3,573	1,402	1,802
1961	712	707	8,535	1,482	389	1,678	2,767	4,629	1,310	1,760
1972	427	379	7,779	1,300	356	1,543	2,640	6,144	1,553	1,997
1983	349		5,641	1,016	662	1,452	2,987	9,222	1,600	2,260

have had an impact on customers who themselves are now more discriminating. The only way in which a restaurant or hotel could hope to compete in the face of poor reviews would be via unrealistically large price differentials which would guarantee its demise. The future has to lie in enhanced levels of service. A more discerning public now demands nothing less and will be satisfied with nothing less. As we will see from many of the contributions, some of our leading companies have already recognised the economic desirability of putting the customer first and some have even formally instituted 'customer first' programmes. It was also an editorial decision to include contributions from a selection of outside agencies which, no-one can deny, have had an expanding impact on what the public has come to expect.

Increasingly, these hospitality industries will be confronted with international competition. It is not entirely unreasonable to postulate that the increased provision of private bathrooms in British hotels and guest houses stemmed directly from British holidaymakers being dissatisfied with anything less than what they had experienced on the Costa Blanca. Whether or not that was the pressure, it is almost certainly the case that the growth in the influx of international tourists to these islands has not been harmed by this improvement to our plumbing.

Some years ago Hertzberg came up with an appealing idea as to what were the factors which contributed to or detracted from satisfaction at work. It was based on the earlier work of the psychologist Maslow, who had argued that humans had a hierarchy of needs, starting with the basic ones of eating and heating and culminating with those that are termed 'self-actualisation'. These twin concepts provide a useful framework against which to see increased service sector employment and enhanced quality as natural developments.

We moved out of caves, and increasingly our food intake came from domesticated beasts rather than from those which had been hunted. While society now might well be experiencing a reaction against the ultimate and horrific forms of factory farming, this reaction could itself actually be interpreted as a manifestation of man's higher order needs. As our basic needs have increasingly been satisfied at lower costs, so we have had more time available to savour the products of our energy. Whatever the hunting of animals represents today, it is most certainly not the satisfaction of man's basic needs, at least in developed countries. An improved standard of living equates with the enjoyment of an ever-increasing number of a whole range of services. While we quite reasonably do not expect the National Health Service to guarantee immortality, we do expect to be able to avail ourselves of a hip replacement should the need arise. We do expect to take more holidays or short breaks and we do expect to get to whatever the destination might be in ever greater comfort. Our expectations gradually change. A colour TV can now be found in 83 per cent of British homes, 61 per cent of which also boast one or more cars. What is now considered a minimum level of existence would, not many years ago, have been judged quite luxurious.

Hand in hand with these enhanced expectations goes a growing sophistication on the part of consumers. Hertzberg argued that there are some features of work which by their nature can cause dissatisfaction. He termed these *hygiene* factors. In contrast, his so-called *motivation* factors are those which by their nature can occasion greater satisfaction. The important point is that one set is not the opposite side of the coin to the other. Pay and conditions (both hygiene factors) just have to be right to establish a baseline. To create improved satisfaction, and hence greater worker motivation, attention has to be directed to the other set of factors. Rightly or wrongly, Hertzberg felt these were related to the nature of the job, hence the title of his best-selling book *Work and the Nature of Man* (1966). It was, in fact, Hertzberg's ideas which led to the emergence of the quest for job enrichment in the late 1960s and early 1970s.

Whether or not the dichotomy was well founded or even sensibly pursued is not of relevance. What is of interest, though, is to consider quality issues in the service sector within this same context. To this writer, at least, it seems eminently reasonable to believe that the forces that are at work in generating an increased level of service activity are similar in kind to those that are bringing about more discerning customers. People's expectations increase with the result that yesterday's luxury is today's necessity. If these minimum standards are not met business will simply evaporate or may never even materialise. They could be thought of as analogous to the hygiene factors, and indeed at a prosaic level it could be argued that the label has a good deal more obvious relevance in the service sector. To take up Hertzberg's analogy, companies cannot compete on these factors. They simply have to be there, or their absence produces such gross dissatisfaction that not only are customers dissatisfied, but they just stop coming. Future competition will be fought over those factors which can bring about enhanced satisfaction; and, to continue with the Hertzberg analogy, these are *not* the converse of the dissatisfiers. Talk to the large hotel chains and you will see that while, quite sensibly, they might not have structured their thinking along these lines, they have come around to the view that a potential guest has a whole series of taken-for-granted expectations. If these are not provided, gross dissatisfaction can and does ensue, and a good deal of effort is required to ensure that this does not result in such a disaffected guest that never again will he darken your doorstep. Read the Sheraton contribution in Chapter 16 or that of British Rail (Chapter 6) or British Airways (Chapter 8), and you will realise that they have the situation pretty well sized up. It is the personal touch which will count for more and more and will be used for discriminating between alternative providers of service. This means that there will be an ever greater pressure or need to measure intangibles, and much of what follows naturally relates to attempts to capture and quantify this tricky 'will-o'-the-wisp'.

That said, we still would like to know which airline performs better at getting you there on time (or alive!) and I would certainly prefer to be operated on by a surgeon who boasts the best batting average. Much of what follows is to do with these 'harder' measures.

It is now time for me to sit back and for you to discover something of the variety of approaches to quality improvement using hard or soft measures. Some relate to internal activities undertaken by a selection of our blue-chip companies. Others relate to external monitoring. Obviously, I have had a chance to read all the contributions at least twice and have actually meddled with a few. I certainly found the material enthralling, as did Kath Hollister, my secretary, who diligently transcribed it onto her word processor. Word processors were, I suspect, invented for the likes of Kath who, on any index of quality of performance, has to rate as a ten. The contributors also deserve commendations for meeting deadlines and allowing me editorial licence. All of them, I'm sure, can expect to be on the receiving end of telephone calls requesting further information.

What was particularly agreeable about this whole venture was discovering just how willing people and organisations are to talk about what they are doing on the quality front. I have convinced myself that it is not on account of a desire to parade their name in front of the public. Sainsbury's does not need to, nor does the Sheraton chain, nor do any of the other companies involved. No, it does seem that this quality 'thing' is genuinely infectious. Staff get all fired up about helping to improve the company's product, service or image. They want to be so much a part of a winning team that I am personally convinced that the quality circle or 'customer first' team approach is not some passing management fad of the 1980s, but is a very real manifestation of this desire.

QUALITY CONSIDERATIONS

2

Quality in the Boardroom

'Example is the school of mankind, and they will
learn at no other.'

Letters on a Regicide Peace
Edmund Burke

RON MORTIBOYS, Quality Management Consultant.

Conscious of a need to take on board a concern for quality, many
organisations appear to labour under a delusion that this is best
achieved through the appointment or designation of a single individual
or group. That individual or group is then expected to spearhead an
initiative which is to bring about a revolution in quality related issues
throughout the company. Based on a considerable experience in a wide
range of industries Ron is convinced that right from the outset this
concern has to assume a company-wide perspective and needs to be
driven from the top.

Before setting up as a quality management consultant he had held a
number of senior management positions in production engineering,
procurement, metallurgy, materials management and quality management. His current assignments involve companies based at home and
overseas and he is also a member of various British Standard and
International Standard Organisations' Quality Management Committees. In addition to assignments with individual companies across a
range of industries, he has also undertaken projects for the Department
of Trade and Industry and is currently a consultant to their National
Quality Campaign. Other clients have included the National House
Building Council, the Open University, the National Health Service
and several of the Industry Training Boards.

★ ★ ★

'Quality' is defined, in British Standard 4778, as 'The totality of features and characteristics of a product or service which bear on its ability to satisfy a given need'. The effective executive of the 1980s and 90s will add 'from the customer's viewpoint'. Quality is synonymous with meeting customer needs and expectations.

In discussions in clubs and boardrooms all over the Western world, it is generally assumed that business is about the twin objectives of making a profit and continuing to do so. In the non-profit-making organisations or service industries it is generally assumed that their raison d'être is the provision and maintenance of a service. When an organisation has been created, it takes on an existence and momentum of its own, and social and moral obligations to provide products or services which actually meet the customers' needs and expectations do not figure prominently in its corporate policies and objectives. The desire to be self-perpetuating is regarded as being more important. In the Western industrialised countries it was possible to sustain this philosophy because we were creating wealth and fuelling the world economy. We led, others followed.

Companies and organisations adhering to this philosophy have come under pressure from external social and economic developments and internally from declining profits and increasing difficulties in obtaining the resources necessary for continued operation. These developments and how we reacted to them nationally will be discussed in more detail in Chapter 3. Here we are concerned only with the effect of those developments on boardroom thinking and attitudes. The first such development was the emergence, in the USA, of 'consumerism' as a force which brought about a change of emphasis in boardroom thinking. Product liability laws and the resultant litigation and very high damages awarded in the American courts gave teeth to the consumers' desire for products and services which would neither kill nor maim them. This was the first real pressure on companies and organisations to consider what the customer needed instead of simply considering what the customer could be persuaded to buy!

The second development to have a major effect on boardroom thinking and attitudes was the environmental movement which sought, and still seeks, to prevent companies, organisations and governments from polluting and destroying the environment and wasting natural resources. Again, the effect on boardroom thinking was to make executives take more account of the customers' needs and expectations. The customers' needs and expectations were beginning to be regarded as matters for the boardroom rather than being delegated, or perhaps more appositely 'relegated', to the quality control, marketing or design departments.

It is perhaps worth noting that, in terms of achieving consumer satisfaction, there is little difference, in the underlying principles of managing quality, between the manufacture of products and the provision of services. In both cases, the management of quality simply means providing products or services which satisfy the customers' needs and expectations. Someone has to design the product in such a way that these are met, at least to the extent that the customer can be persuaded to buy the product. Service organisations do not have design departments as such but, nonetheless, someone 'designs' the service. If companies and organisations fail to regard the achievement of customer satisfaction in their products and services as a matter of corporate policy, on a par with profit making and continued existence, they will fail to achieve customer satisfaction and put their profits and their very existence at risk.

The increasing realisation in the boardroom of the necessity to take account of customers' needs and expectations was boosted by the third development, which was concurrent with the other two, namely, the emergence of Japan and other Far Eastern countries as industrial nations able to compete on equal terms with those in the West. A major element of Japan's drive to become a major industrial nation was its policy of achieving a market share of at least 50 per cent in various geographical and product sectors. The strategy for achieving these targets relied heavily on the management of quality, i.e. on meeting customers' needs and expectations. Quality features prominently in the corporate philosophy of Japanese companies and organisations. Soon this philosophy began to permeate American companies, both through direct contact and indirectly through loss of market share. Even the Playboy club in Tokyo operates quality circles and IBM Japan has renamed its 'Quality Department' the 'Customer Satisfaction Department'.

The pressure on Western companies to change their boardroom attitudes and policies increased as a consequence of the arrival of Japan in the top division of the Northern industrialised countries. Not only were customers offered more choice than ever before, they were also able to choose from a new range of products which satisfied their needs and expectations better than many of the products which had previously been available to them.

Although Western manufacturing industries have been affected much more than Western service industries—because the Japanese have concentrated upon the development of their manufacturing industries—service industries must not be complacent. The under-lying principles of quality management are exactly the same for service as for manufacturing industries, and service sector companies and organisations will necessarily soon adopt them. It has already

happened in Japan; it is now happening elsewhere and it will happen
here, too. Executives must realise that the identification and satisfaction of customer needs and expectations is a prerequisite of
profit-making and the continued existence of the organisation. Even
those organisations which are non-profit-making will find it difficult
to attract the funds they need if they do not adopt customer
satisfaction as boardroom policy. Their costs will eventually prove to
be unacceptably high in contrast to other ways of securing the
services and they will simply not be seen to provide value for money.

Cost-Effective Quality Management

In order to help manufacturing and service companies realise the
importance of quality at the corporate level, the Department of Trade
and Industry has recently published a booklet titled *Quality
Management—A Guide for Chief Executives*. It draws attention, not only
to the necessity of understanding and satisfying customers' needs
and expectations, but also to the cost effectiveness of implementing
the principle company-wide, starting with the Chief Executive and
the Board. Because this approach is indeed so very cost-effective the
Department of Trade and Industry has coined the term 'Cost-
Effective Quality Management'. The key to Cost-Effective Quality
Management is to make it possible for *every* employee to perform his
or her job right first time. One must understand just what it is that
each employee needs and expects in order for him to do his job
right first time, and then satisfy those needs and expectations. This is
simply a logical extension of the quality management principle of
satisfying customer needs and expectations. For each person in the
company or organisation, the next individual to use his or her work
becomes the customer.

Cost-Effective Quality Management starts with the Chief Executive, then spreads to all parts of the company. The benefits to be
obtained are:

- Increased market share
- Increased productivity
- Increased competitiveness
- Increased profits
- Enhanced employee morale
- Reduced material wastage
- Reduced time wastage
- Reduced rectification or reworking
- Reduced stock
- Reduced customer complaints

- Reduced costs
- Improved communications
- Better relationships with suppliers and sub-contractors

How Does One Start?

The only way to start is at board level or the management committee in those satellite operations which have sufficient autonomy to be able to choose how they manage themselves. A good deal of work needs to be done by the executives before any attempt is made to introduce Cost-Effective Quality Management throughout the company. Firstly, they themselves must be helped to gain an understanding of the fundamental principles and how these can be applied in practice.

Secondly, executives must be helped to rid themselves of the traditional assumptions and conventions on which their attitudes and actions are based. These include such old chestnuts as:

- 'our employees aren't interested in doing a good job'
- 'we can't afford better quality'
- 'we can't do it because of circumstances beyond our control'
- 'it might work elsewhere, but not in our industry'
- 'we have a quality manager to manage quality'
- 'we will become competitive by reducing our prices, not by improving our quality—there is nothing wrong with our quality'
- 'we honour our guarantee and put things right if the customer complains'
- 'well, it isn't right, but let it go this time'
- 'we must be doing OK because we don't get many complaints'

Every director and manager must be included in this re-orientation. It takes only one executive—who doesn't believe that he has to make it possible for all of his employees' needs and expectations to be met so that all jobs will be done right first time and customers' needs and expectations will be cost-effectively met—to jeopardise the programme.

Thirdly, executives must be helped to change their management style from personal control and firefighting to planning. There are only three types of action a director or manager can take: he or she is either planning, applying personal control, or firefighting.

Planning

The manager identifies what has to be achieved and plans how to achieve it. Planning includes identifying and providing the necessary resources, communicating the plan, obtaining the commitment of all concerned, implementing the plan, and monitoring its progress and achievement. If the plan is not producing the required results, the manager will need to take corrective action, either by helping people to perform better, or by modifying the plan, or, in the extreme, by changing the objectives. In planning mode, the manager causes events to happen as he or she wants them to happen.

Personal control

The manager operating in personal control mode does not cause events to happen as he or she wants them to to happen. Rather, he or she reacts to events as and when they happen. Such managers generally have poorly defined objectives and enjoy seeing things about to go wrong because they can then shine by being seen to be dynamic troubleshooters. They revel in crisis management. Quality cannot be managed effectively, and certainly not efficiently, by directors or managers operating in personal control mode. Their subordinates will almost invariably also need to manage by personal control as they will not have had time to plan: the situation in which their managers will have involved them will be well beyond the possibility of any effective planning. It will require immediate personal control if the situation is not to deteriorate into firefighting.

Firefighting

All but the smallest and simplest organisations are so complex in the multiplicity and variety of decisions and actions taken each day that personal control usually degenerates into firefighting. Firefighting is the situation which pertains when the manager operating in personal control mode loses control! Instead of working productively, the manager is now forever trying to rectify what has gone wrong, to make good defective work, to limit the extent of delivery overshoot, to placate irate customers, to limit the costs of doing so—all terribly wasteful and disruptive.

The Chief Executive must find ways to help his directors and managers to get out of personal control and firefighting into planning mode. He will usually be met with the cry 'but we haven't the time to do anything extra'. Of course they haven't the time. They are too busy trying to prevent situations from getting out of control, or firefighting when they have got out of control. This situation requires that the Chief Executive must help them identify aspects of their work which can be changed from personal control and firefighting relatively easily to planning mode. All organisations have work routines which can be changed to planning mode relatively easily. The management time released by making these changes can be used very profitably for changing other aspects of the manager's work into planning mode.

As well as looking at the manager's work routines, one should also look at the problems caused by other people which absorb his time. If supplies of products or services, for example, do not meet the operational manager's needs and expectations in order for him to do his job right first time, he will be forced into personal control or even firefighting mode. The Chief Executive should act to ensure that his company or organisation does not accept defective supplies or services.

The first aspect of planning for quality that the Chief Executive should deal with is that of defining and communicating corporate policies and objectives. Because the understanding and satisfaction of customer needs and expectations must now be regarded as one of the fundamental reasons for the existence of the organisation, the Chief Executive must build this requirement into the corporate policies and objectives. In too many organisations these are either far too vague or are not documented. Even if they have been documented, have they been communicated effectively? Could the Chief Executive ask each of his directors and managers to explain the company's corporate policies and objectives and receive explanations that accord with his own understanding?

The author is in no way suggesting that directors or managers are not competent. Most directors and managers he has encountered over many years in organisations of very different types have been very competent indeed. However, we are in a period of rapid change and our management styles and methods must change to meet the new challenges confronting us.

Quality Management vs Quality Assurance

Before proceeding further, the board should understand the difference between quality management and quality assurance. The latter is the system which enables suppliers of products and services to assure their customers that they will meet their specified requirements, within the operational standards agreed by the supplier and customer, or implied by the supplier through his promotional material or statements. The essential difference between quality assurance and Cost-Effective Quality Management is the extent to which employees are able to participate actively in the management of quality. Quality assurance attempts to control employees' actions and workmanship through the operation of the quality assurance system. Unfortunately for anyone who puts his faith in this technique, employees are intelligent and are likely to do one of two things, or both. Firstly, they will find ways around the system or, worse, ignore it. Secondly, they will make the manager think that the system is working, because that will occasion them less trouble. Quality management makes it possible for employees to do their jobs right first time, encourages them to do so and enables them to participate in the management of quality.

Quality management embraces quality assurance but goes much further. The board must decide whether to aim for quality assurance or quality management. If it decides to go for quality management, how cost-effective the results will be will depend almost entirely on the level of commitment given by the board and on the level of employee participation it is able to generate. The costs of mismanaging quality, by not doing jobs right first time, are typically of the order of 15–40 per cent of turnover. Quality assurance can lower this by reducing the amount of rectification. Cost-Effective Quality Management can lower it much further by reducing the waste of time and effort involved in not doing jobs right first time throughout the organisation. In aiming for Cost-Effective Quality Management the board is creating a culture in which it is anathema for anyone not to do his or her job right first time. It is a company-wide culture, which makes it possible for them to do their jobs right first time, not merely a technique or system.

It is possible for an organisation to implement a quality assurance system and then, if it so desires, to develop this into a full-blown quality management culture. On the other hand, this approach can waste a considerable amount of time and effort because, in most cases, it is entirely feasible for the company to go directly to the Cost-Effective Quality Management culture. A quality assurance system can be implemented and made fully operational in six to twelve months. The development of a Cost-Effective Quality Management culture typically involves twelve months of foundation laying and as long as four years fully to nurture the culture and obtain the full financial benefits. In the author's opinion, because quality management can be so very cost-effective, it is preferable for any company or organisation to aim for Cost-Effective Quality Management right from the outset even though it takes longer to implement. Many organisations will be required by their customers to implement quality assurance systems of the BS 5750[1] type or equivalent. There is

---

1. BS 5750 is a three-part British Standard for quality assurance systems.

no conflict between aiming for a Cost-Effective Quality Management culture from the outset and implementing a quality assurance system at the same time.

Having stated that it is preferable to aim for Cost-Effective Quality Management rather than quality assurance, it would have to be admitted that, although there are hundreds of consultants operating in the UK who can assist companies to implement quality assurance systems, there are very few with the ability and experience to assist them to develop Cost-Effective Quality Management cultures. The reason is that such consultants need a wide experience of company management complemented by an in-depth understanding of the management of quality, including employee participation. This has led a number of companies to think that, because they have implemented a quality assurance system, possibly with the addition of some of the techniques of employee participation (e.g. quality circles), they have done all that needs to be done in terms of quality management.

A Quality Improvement Programme

As a first step in extending the management of quality to embrace the whole company, some companies appoint a Quality Manager. There is a danger in doing this. A so-called quality manager cannot manage quality. Every decision and every action taken by anyone anywhere in the company which affects the quality of the product or service in any way impacts upon the management of quality. Whether these decisions and actions positively or adversely contribute to the management of quality will be influenced far more by the company's management style and the culture created (intentionally or inadvertently) by the board, than by anything that the quality manager can do. It is, therefore, essential that any programme to improve the management of quality must be launched and led by the board—not by a quality manager. The role of a quality manager, if the company has one, is to help departments understand the principles and practice of quality management and provide assistance in monitoring their performance. It is probably wiser to designate such a person by some other title, for example Quality Co-ordinator. Any quality improvement programme must be led by the board if it is to achieve significant and lasting results.

The board should most certainly appoint a programme management team. This team, with the board's delegated authority, will define the programme objectives and plan the actions, responsibilities and timescales. Employees will have to be informed of the programme objectives and the roles they are expected to play in the programme. They, too, will have to be trained to understand the basics of Cost-Effective Quality Management. It will also be necessary to train employees in some of the techniques which are the tools of quality management, including, among others, job analysis and planning, problem solving, quality circles, interdisciplinary action groups and statistical quality control.

Communication is a particularly important feature of any quality improvement programme. Not only must appropriate information be passed down through the organisational structure as is the vogue at present, but employees must be encouraged to pass information up through the structure. It must also be possible for employees to pass comments and queries up through the structure and to expect to receive answers. But even this is not enough. Better lateral communications between sections, departments, divisions and between individual employees must be encouraged on all matters pertaining to the management of quality. As the quality improvement programme proceeds, the improvement in methods and performance must be carefully monitored and the results reported not only to the board but to all employees, although the form of the reports may very well need to be tailored to the different groups.

Finally, it almost goes without saying that an important feature of any quality improvement programme is the showing of due recognition for improved performance by any individual, section, department or division within the company or organisation.

Monitoring Factors

Improvements in the management of quality should be real, not imaginary, and substantiated by facts rather than opinions. Directors and managers, with or without the participation of other employees, should, for each section, department or division, identify factors in their operations which are important indicators of their quality performance. The most effective way of doing this is for each employee, section, department or division to ask themselves what are the needs and expectations of those who will be on the receiving end of their work in order that they can do their jobs right first time. A sales department might, for example, identify *legibility* and *freedom from typing errors in initial paperwork* as two of its monitoring factors. A personnel department might identify *vacancies filled on time*. A despatch department could identify *labelling errors*. The board might identify *meetings started late* or *information required for meetings not distributed* or *customer complaints not dealt with within a defined time* as three of its monitoring factors. It is generally most effective for each person or organisational unit to be monitored primarily on about five factors.

A key factor against which the whole company or organisation should be monitored is what is generally known as 'the cost of quality'. Perhaps this might more appropriately be labelled 'the cost of mismanaging quality' as quality, properly managed, is highly cost-effective. If the quality improvement programme has been well planned, improvement activity will be directed primarily at those areas or operations which will lead to the greatest overall improvement in customer satisfaction and quality mismanagement costs. The aim should be to reduce the figure of quality mismanagement costs from 15–40 per cent of turnover to about 3–5 per cent. Such improvements can be achieved and indeed have been achieved across a range of industries.

Operational Standards

There is just one other item that is deserving of mention and that is the operational standard to be achieved throughout the company. The prime question to be asked is, 'are any errors or defects to be tolerated?' Is it good enough for employees to do their jobs right first time most of the time, and for the service provided to meet customer needs and expectations most of the time? It is perfectly possible for all jobs to be completed without defects or errors. For that to happen, the board must clearly state that the operational standard it requires of itself and all other employees is 'no errors, no defects'. The Chief Executive and the board must be prepared to stand by this requirement. If, having specified the requirement, a director or manager says, 'Well, it's not right, but it will do', the employee to whom the remark was addressed will, in turn, adopt as his operational standard, 'Well, it's not right, but it will do'.

It will take some time to achieve the highly cost-effective situation in which all jobs are done right first time and in this period the directors and managers must keep firmly to the principle of no defects, no errors, and such resolution will be rewarded. Even when the ideal of error- and defect-free work has been achieved, and the service and related products offered meet all of the customer's current expectations, the organisation should still strive for continuous improvement and thus show the customer that he or she can reasonably expect greater value for money. For example, a travel agency or tour operator who has achieved a service free from booking errors, missed departures, over-crowded hotels, etc. can still aim to provide better value for money by offering the customer the same or an improved service at a lower price achieved through more efficient operations.

Summary

In the current situation of intense global competition for orders, profits and jobs, and for the resources needed to sustain a company or organisation, it is essential that executives recognise the vital necessity of providing services which satisfy their customers' needs and expectations. The changes which must be made are so fundamental and far-reaching that they cannot be made simply by the adoption of new techniques or by working harder. Rather, it is necessary to create a new culture in each company or organisation. The board must take the lead and demonstrate total commitment to Cost-Effective Quality Management in which customers' needs and expectations will be fully satisfied and all jobs will be done right first time.

3

How Does Britain Rate on Quality?

'The more modern nations detest each other the more meekly they follow each other; for all competition is in its nature only a furious plagiarism.'

Charles Dickens
G.K. Chesterton

FRANK PRICE, Site Quality Control Manager, Mardon Illingworth Ltd.

Even a cursory glance at the following chapter reveals that what is contained is very different from what one normally encounters in textbooks aimed at managers. Not for Frank are the more typical forms of advice wrapped round with the rapidly expanding jargon of the management educationalist's trade. Instead you will find a hard-hitting and, some will argue, vituperative outburst at a British malaise concerning quality which, he maintains, has underpinned our relative economic decline. Confronted with such a manuscript there is little an editor can do that would not destroy the thrust of the writer's message; and as he had stuck to his assigned allocation of words I felt I owed it to someone with such a strongly held set of convictions to leave well alone.

As well as writing the best selling text *Right First Time* , Frank has written and appeared in videos produced for the Open University and is particularly keen to bridge the gap between the 'academic' and the 'practical', for the simple reason that he sees no fundamental difference between the two. He spent his whole working life applying a mixture of statistics and psychology to the quest for excellence and, as a consequence, is deeply concerned that as a nation we are losing somewhere between £2 billion and £20 billion through not getting things right first time. The message would appear to be as relevant to those in the service sector as to those in manufacturing.

★ ★ ★

The answer to the question 'how does Britain rate on quality?' depends, as answers so often do, on the viewer's standpoint.

Seen through the apathetic eyes of a Polish housewife with a purseful of useless zlotys, in a butcher's shop emptied of everything except a trio of surly assistants and a few scraps of unappetising offal, the bulging shelves of a British supermarket must take on the aspect of a fevered dream, a tantalising glimpse into a Gomorrah of gluttony supporting a quality of life so rich that it must be part of a different universe.

To the inhabitant of a West German city, walking to his place of work along avenues sparkling with Teutonic cleanliness after their overnight wash and brush-up by the squads of immigrant guest-workers, the sight of some of Britain's litter-strewn streets must indicate a shabby society in terminal decay enduring a swiftly declining quality of life.

Quality is relative, and to a large extent dependent on economics. Wherever there is an excess of money pursuing a shortage of goods and services to spend it on, quality is of secondary importance to sheer availability. In a free market economy such a famine of consumer goods is not long permitted to exist. Market forces, in the form of entrepreneurial capitalism, respond to the imbalance of too much money chasing too few goods. The balance is redressed. Soon there is an abundance of goods available to sop up the excess cash in the economy. The system overbalances in the other direction, and an excess of goods bloats the market, rival brands competing for the consumers' available spending power.

It is at this stage that the marketing and advertising specialists, whose task it is to move the goods which people do not need (but need to be convinced they want), inherit their kingdom. Now quality becomes a crucial factor in consumer selection. It becomes the most important non-price factor in purchasing once the consumer is able to discriminate between competitive purchasing options. It should prehaps be noted that 'quality' is not synonymous with 'grade'. The man buying a family saloon car is quite aware that it is of a lower grade than a Rolls-Royce, but he expects it to do its job and satisfy his needs. In a word, he expects 'quality'.

Quality is customer satisfaction. It is the fitness of the product or service for its intended purpose. Products which meet this criterion capture markets. Japanese motorcycle manufacturers appreciated this marketing truth and acted upon it to devastating effect. Their British competitors did not. The Japanese also grasped another vital aspect of what quality is: it is to do with the frugal use of manufacturing resources, of making the most out of the least. Quality control, or Total Quality Management, is a manufacturing discipline of thrift. It is about making a product which satisfies customers' expectations, and making it without wastage or rework, i.e. making things *Right First Time*.

We British are currently not very good at this. Indeed, the majority of us are appallingly bad at it. It has been estimated that our manufacturing industry wastes more than two billion pounds a year due to ineffective or even non-existent quality control (Lockyer, Oakland and Duprey 1982). American manufacturing industry also appears to waste a lot of dollars in this respect, though no collated figures have been published.

Why are we so wasteful? Who is betraying the stewardship of resources? Who is responsible for making these huge losses when Japanese competition scoops up huge profits from our domestic markets? Profits? Mr Matsushita, a Japanese, is on record as saying, 'Profit is the reward which society bestows upon a manufacturer for the way in which he has husbanded the scarce resources with which society has entrusted him'. He is also on record with another statement of non-British wisdom, 'First we make people, then we make things'. Herein lies part of the key to Japan's success and to Britain's failure as a manufacturing power. Ask a British captain of industry to define the purpose of his organisation and the chances are that he will tell you it is to make profits. Ask him about his attitude to his workers and the odds are that his evaluation will be nothing more than that they should voluntarily curtail their wage demands. Shallow thinkers, on the whole, we British.

We all know, to our cost, that the Japanese have wrought what is generally acknowledged to be an economic miracle. As recently as a generation ago they were an occupied island, impoverished members of the starvation league of the Third World. The prospect that Japan, imitator of everything and inventor of nothing, might ever aspire to become a manufacturing superpower was utterly unthinkable.

Unthinkable or not, somebody thought it. And when an American—W. Edwards Deming—took his concepts of Total Quality Management to Tokyo, because the industrialists of the USA chose to stay loyal to their traditional manufacturing practice of making things and inspecting them afterwards, he was welcomed with open Japanese arms and open Japanese minds. The Japanese 'adopted' the western philosophy and procedures of total quality management; then they 'adapted' them; thereafter they 'improved' them. This is their version of the classical and usually much maligned NIH syndrome (Not Invented Here). Even the fundamental philosophy of their marketing strategy is an adopted child of British original thinking. They use the Lanchester Strategy, a military concept of achieving victory by making an overwhelming attack with deep penetration by cascading into areas of perceived vulnerability. The only books available today dealing with this strategy of conquest are printed in Japanese.

What are we in Britain doing about all this? The truth is not much, so far. Until a year or two ago only one out of six of our manufacturing companies used quality control (Lockyer, Oakland and Duprey 1982). What did the remaining five out of six do? Rely on baffled optimism? On ignorant complacency? Inspect the product *after* the manufacturing event instead of using preventative quality control *during* the manufacturing cycle? One thing is certain: the management discipline of quality control is largely held in low esteem in the collective perception of British management. With the exception of those few British companies whose quality is renowned, in the majority of our industrial organisations the discipline is looked upon as a second-rate activity conducted by second-rate people.

This point of view has its origins in our manufacturing tradition of Scientific Management. Our work tends to be organised into fragmented and mutually-exclusive territories. Production people produce the goods. 'Quality' people inspect them. Personnel people lay claim to a monopoly of the understanding of human nature. Accountants sit in their counting houses shuffling money or balancing the books. Sales people commandeer sole rights to communicate with that inscrutable nuisance, 'the customer'. Purchasing officers beat suppliers down to the last penny following the principle of purchasing by price tag. Work study practitioners shred workers' time into hundredths of a minute. This is the ultimate in division of labour, where each labourer performs his ordained function and nobody comprehends the totality of the business in its environmental context.

How does this manufacturing strategy of work fragmentation usually operate in our British companies? Try the following for a typical description and see whether you recognise anything wearily familiar to your experience of Britain Ltd in action . . .

The factory machinery is churning out a steady stream of articles to be sold in a competitive market. The buyer has bought the cheapest raw materials which his ransacking of the market place has unearthed; he has done well, by his lights. Production staff, with output targets to be met, are flogging their machines at a pitiless rate and are praised by top management for doing so, as this is 'efficiency'. Inspection people, perhaps dignified by being falsely called 'quality controllers', are examining samples of the output against the specification. They decide that certain batches are not acceptable, so they stick dayglo red rejection labels onto the boxes of offending products. Production people vigorously resist this action.

The manufacturing director is called upon to arbitrate. He is under pressure to dispatch everything he can make and the marketing director continually emphasises the importance of meeting delivery deadlines. So he overrides quality, the red rejection stickers are peeled off and a 'commercial decision', or a 'customer's response' or a 'realistic decision' is taken. The euphemisms vary, but they all amount to the same thing — the factory is about to dishonour its contract with its customer by knowingly and unilaterally sending out a sub-standard product. Thereupon the finger of scorn is pointed at the boss, who is now privately accused of being a person who will accept and dispatch any low-quality rubbish. The quality people now lose heart: no point in working to the specification and rejecting inferior output if everybody else, including 'him' is going to pass it.

The rejectable output is sent to the customer. The customer sends it back. Now it is cluttering up the warehouse—it stands there gathering dust, a sagging monument to collective incompetence, to production without quality control. Now they are behind with deliveries: the pace of production is quickened, in an attempt to make up for lost output. The miserable cycle of make it, reject it, send it, get it back, is repeated. The heap of rejections grow higher. Morale sinks lower. This company is now well and truly ensnared in the British Trap. Sometimes the response is comic . . .

'How did this rubbish get out?', the boss demands of his quality department. This is a question of such stunning inanity that no coherent answer is possible. So, in the mad burlesque which typifies the style of much of British manufacturing industry, ritual games are embarked upon and ritual roles are adopted. The quality manager is obliged to don the mask of contrition, as if it really was his fault. Sometimes he is even ceremoniously conveyed, in the tumbril of repentance represented by the sales manager's red Ford Sierra, into the awesome presence of the customer, there to render personal account for his company's transgressions.

As a 'strategy' for curing its corporate quality problems, this outfit might just as well swing incense while chanting incantations, or sprinkle holy water onto the machines while murmuring benedictions, or rattle a witch doctor's necklace of crocodile teeth over the output to blind the evil eye which blights it. This company is in deep quality trouble and, for want of knowing anything more sensible than primitive magic to resolve its problems, it is sliding deeper into it. This is where the wasted two billion pounds comes from: it is a Danegeld extorted by ignorance and incompetence from Britain's economic body.

Companies such as the one described (and there must be many of them to generate such colossal sums of yearly wastage) are unaware of the true extent of their inexcusable ignorance of quality matters. Either they mistakenly believe that because they operate an inadequate inspection function they are 'doing quality control'; or, worse, they are convinced that for some reason their process is not suitable for the application of total quality management principles and procedures. Their justifications for not using this discipline of thrift are as naive as they are laughable. They say:

> 'It's the fault of the raw material.' (Is it? Sure it isn't sunspots? An adverse conjunction of astrological bodies? The malice of the gods?)

> 'Our process goes delinquent.' (A delinquent process? What manner of anthropomorphic projection is this which ascribes to an inanimate industrial process the attributes of a malevolent human being?)

> 'Ours is a unique process.' (They all are, so none of them is.)

> 'There is a touch of the Black Art about our process.' (Black Art, indeed. Then who and where are the Black Artists who are following their dark calling at such enormous cost in terms of process wastage and product rejections?)

> 'You cannot do quality control on our product, it shrinks as it gets colder.' (What doesn't?)

These are some of the more common 'reasons' advanced by ignorance to excuse incompetence. Only very, very rarely does anybody care to confess 'it must be *my* fault'. Only rarely is the truth acknowledged, and the truth is 'it is *our* fault'. Responsibility is collective. The industrial organisation is a collective, brought into being in order to achieve objectives which are beyond the scope of any one individual. Responsibility, no matter how much you may hear to the contrary, is collective. It does not reside within the confines of one group of people or one single person. If the buck stops, it stops for everyone. Consider the following example.

The company in question is a fairly large manufacturer, still a 'family' firm dominated by the descendants of the founding grandfathers. There is nothing wrong with that. The company brochures show a photograph of the group of seven directors posed on the steps of their imposing ancestral mansion-cum-office. Across the picture is streamed a banner headline bearing the self-congratulatory legend 'the buck stops here'. At the time when the magnificent seven were gazing nobly into the camera their company was laying-off over a hundred of its workers. Ask *them* where the buck stops. They truly and bitterly know. And there is plenty wrong with that.

However, a new enlightenment is spreading abroad in Britain today. Her Majesty's Government is now into the second year of its National Quality Campaign. Through its agencies companies can obtain professional help and guidance. Companies are offered financial inducement to install structured quality control systems and thereby become certificated under BS 5750. This standard is somewhat like a Christian Church without a Christ—all form and no content; but it has the merit of being better than nothing. To date, about 2,500 of the 60,000 or so eligible companies have taken it up; it's a start. 'New' ideas are beginning to influence organisational perception and, further, organisational behaviour.

Probably the most important of these ideas is the supply-chain concept. This begins as the initiative of a powerful customer organisation with a big purchasing budget which is therefore able to exert tremendous influence not only on its supplier, but on its supplier's suppliers as well, right back up the production/supply chain. The purpose of this approach is to maximise productivity and minimise wastage, through good quality management practice, at every stage in the chain, in the knowledge that the entire chain leads ultimately to one thing and to one thing only—the complete satisfaction of the ultimate customer.

Some outstanding companies have been using this system for decades and, indeed, have built their success upon it. One of our most illustrious high street merchandisers, for example, describes itself as 'a producer without factories', and its suppliers as 'shopkeepers without shops', in order to stress the commercial nature of manufacturing, lest manufacturers should lose sight of the fact that *they exist to service a market*.

One of our most dominant car companies, which really cares about quality and is a customer of hundreds of component manufacturers employing thousands of workers, goes further. It uses its immense buying power to insist that its suppliers improve their quality performance by sending a proportion of their employees to attend quality control training seminars. In this way it is enhancing the performance of its suppliers by broadening and deepening their knowledge. This is a very proper and laudable use of corporate power: it is truly the generation of industrial wealth for the common good by extending and using knowledge; by 'making people'. (First we make people, then we make things', said Mr Matsushita. Remember?) Such people then make things Right First Time by using *preventative* statistical process control instead of the creaking antiquated methods of inspection after the event. The debt owed by the whole of British industry to this automotive giant is incalculable. This company has stimulated an awareness of the prevailing ignorance of quality matters and has set out to provide an effective remedy. All this may be regarded, of course, as enlightened self-interest. But it is self-interest for *mutual benefit*.

Another of our leading companies has been using the *mutuality of benefit* philosophy for many years. It has used it for the benefit of its employees (whom it refers to, in absolutely unpatronising sincerity and honesty, as 'associates'), rewarding them with salary increases whenever their collective efforts have resulted in a measurably higher return on the assets employed to run the business. It has used it for the benefit of its suppliers by enhancing the quality and productivity performance and establishing long-term purchasing contracts based on mutuality. But most of all its customers, the consuming public, have benefited through being able to buy products of consistently high quality at very competitive prices, thanks to highly professional total quality management right back along the chain of production and supply. This is surely the acceptable face of capitalism.

Similarly, the world's largest perfume and toiletries house, with factories in Britain, has long used the precepts of total quality management to elevate the performance of its suppliers to its own high and successful level of market pre-eminence. So it *can* be done: success through quality is clearly attainable. How, then, does Britain rate? Evidence suggests that, apart from a handful of well-known all-British companies which have been applying T.Q.M. for many years, the 'British' companies which are now moving forward on the rising wave of interest in quality control are mainly those with American parents.

There seems to be a transatlantic willingness on the part of these organisations to look closely at themselves and their performance and to acknowledge that, whilst they are already operating effectively, there is still room for improvement; and that smarter quality control is the key to achieving it. They examine themselves and their affairs with a critical detachment and honesty. They search out their own defects, then actively strive to remedy them. This process of unembarrassed self-criticism, followed by enthusiastic self-improvement, seems to be beyond the scope of many of our all-British organisations. Why should this be so? Why is the motivation to do things better found more often in American-owned British subsidiaries than in the fully home-grown company? What factors are at work preventing us British from aspiring to do better through self-help? The reasons are probably many and varied and complex, but some might have to do with our history and our traditions.

As a nation of manufacturers, with a trading deficit in manufactured goods for the first time in more than two hundred years, we seem to prefer looking into the certainties of our past rather than facing our future. As we have grown too fond of warming our hands at yesterday's camp fires, nostalgia has become a growth business.

We seem to be developing an unhealthy obsession with the contemplation of the glories of our past. Our past, of course, though it had its many moments of grandiosity, could hardly be described with clinical accuracy as a chronicle of all that is glorious. Any economic system founded upon plantation slavery overseas and factory serfdom at home could hardly lay claim to a deal of glory. Opportunism, yes. Greed, for sure. Pagentry, of course. But glory?

Over the centuries we became adept at the tricky art of dipping our bread into other people's gravy; this phenomenon was called 'imperialism'. In those days we also happened to be one of the most inventive and self-confident nations in the world; inventive we still are, perhaps, though nowadays we allow others to exploit our inventions; self-confident we no longer seem to be. Once upon a time we were top dog; but, since we started the Industrial Revolution and grew into the world's pre-eminent manufacturing power, an insidious process of decay has been taking place. A canker has been gnawing at our roots.

This canker is called, for want of a better term, 'gentrification'. This spiritual affliction manifests itself as the overweening desire to be looked upon as a 'gentleman'. It has to do with that enduring structure of shadows and delusions which comprises the British Class System. We British, being British and therefore unconsciously and irredeemably steeped in the wormwood liquor of class, love to despise each other for it—so much so that an Irish playwright was prompted to observe 'no sooner does one Englishman open his mouth than another despises him'. This peculiarly English (no longer British—the Scots and the Welsh and the Irish are apparently impervious to this kind of mental aberration) disease shows itself as an irrational yearning to be thought of as being better than you secretly believe yourself to be. It is, of course, a delusion; a deeply-entrenched conviction of personal social inferiority which forever clamours for assurance that it is not really so. All in all, it is a strange state of mind; it has had profound international repercussions, including the capitulation of Singapore, and its sour fruits have affected some of our industrialists and hence much of our industry.

It is because of this hierarchical system of graded social insult that no sooner has a tycoon amassed a few million pounds than he becomes ashamed of having earned his money through the dirty business of manufacturing. So, lured by the seductive siren of social acceptance, he builds a mansion in a park and emulates a life-style appropriate to higher rank. He sends his offspring to expensive schools where they are taught to build themselves into monuments to their own superiority. This is all quite laughable, or it would be if it were not for the fact that money which might have been fruitfully re-invested in the growing business for the common good has been syphoned off in the trivial pursuit of social vanity. The British class system has a lot to answer for.

This phenomenon, this notion of upward social mobility, is still alive and well and with us. It flourishes like a rank weed throughout the land. It still commands the attention of industrial managers who should be deploying their efforts on more worthwhile objectives. Its industrial counterpart—a process of 'prissification'—exerts its own stultifying influence within our manufacturing organisations. Thus an organisation, British, ostensibly created for the purpose of collectively pursuing profit by servicing the needs of a market more effectively than its competitors are able to do, atrophies into something different. In losing its sense of its true founding purpose it becomes many strange things: it becomes a trading post for grievances. Managers fight each other in sly guerilla warfare and play 'office politics', instead of joining together to form invincible teams to overcome the competition. Paranoia and introspection prevail.

It becomes a forcing house for clones. People seeking promotion (and eventual gentrification through sustained prissification) consciously model themselves on whatever they perceive to be the approved conventional cardboard cutout. So they become less a real person and more an acceptance-seeking stereotype.

It becomes a given wisdom. Certain opinions about certain topics become enshrined as cornerstones of corporate faith. Thus the members of the organisation, in their endless search for social approval as a substitute for genuine achievement, embrace the received wisdom uncritically. In doing so they place themselves, without realising it, just one short moral step away from the dreadful gates of Auschwitz, whose executives also carried out the policies of an approving higher authority in unquestioning obedience.

It becomes a builder's yard for the construction of reputations. Mere frantic activity finds greater approval than quiet accomplishment, so that the socially ambitious try to metamorphose themselves and natural plodders strive to transform their serviceable legs into brilliant wings in order that they may pass themselves off as those organisational butterflies called 'high flyers'.

All these things, and more, and worse, might happen to an organisation once it has lost its sense of true purpose: perhaps because its purpose is so mundane; perhaps because making money in industry by being good at what you do is so boring, and problems are much more interesting than solutions. Maybe the business and the product are so commonplace that they are unable to satisfy an employee's desire to be 'somebody'. What could be more pedestrian, say, than doing nothing all day except converting tinplate into cans?

Yet what could be more exhilarating than doing it better than it has ever been done before and better than anybody else in the world?

How, then, does Britain rate on quality? Without the driving force of foreign parentage or foreign influence it seems to stand with one collective foot in a rosy past that never really was and with the other, private, foot on the rung of a social ladder that leads upwards to a cloud-cockoo-land whose only reward is disappointment because it exists nowhere except in the strangely deluded minds of its believers. The remedy to all this is a dose of hard realism. A most potent ingredient of this medicine is the philosophy of total quality management, because it is about much more than the application of statistical method to process and product problems. It has to do with bringing cultural change into the organisation. It is concerned with the restoration of wholeness to work shattered into fragments by the advent of Scientific Management. Its techniques are as holistic as they are analytical. It is a very strong medicine.

Britain is presently being administered such a dose. Some are gagging and choking on it. It is being offered from a spoon made in Japan. Some will find the draught too bitter to swallow, and will die for their outmoded dreams. Others will swallow it and survive, and prosper. Those surviving will be very different from those whose hidebound backward-looking captains let them fall in the face of the onslaught. A remedy there has to be. Without one we shall cease to be a manufacturing nation; instead, we shall be selling each other ice cream and wooden clogs. We shall then very likely find ourselves searching the near-barren shelves of emptied shops, looking as listless as a Polish housewife, for a few shoddy scraps of something to brighten our dreary post-industrial Britain—all this for the sake of renouncing the elegant and powerful techniques of the philosophy of Total Quality Management, which could have saved us. Surely this is not the path we wish Britain to tread?

4

Experience with Quality Circles and Quality Costs

'Nothing is costly to one who does not count the cost.'

Antonin G. Sertillanges

DR. BARRIE DALE, University of Manchester Institute of Science and Technology.

Some observers feel that Quality Circles are perhaps the latest management fad which will disappear from view as quickly as some of the earlier ones. In fact, there is a very real likelihood that what they offer is so fundamental that they could well be around for some little time. They clearly provide an opportunity for a very tangible form of job enrichment, while at the same time demonstrating a real commitment to quality management. They have gradually found favour in the service sector where they are likely to be labelled as 'Customer First' teams. To be effective the problems taken on board by a circle must be of prime concern, which suggests that the company knows where costs are being incurred through poor quality. Quality Costing is an approach aimed at identifying these contributory costs and, although not much practised in the services sector, it could readily be adopted there.

Barrie has been conducting research directed at discovering just how successful have been these two approaches, and in what follows he will be drawing heavily on that research. He himself is one of that rare breed of academics whose career started off with a craft engineering apprenticeship. Eventually, after a collection of production-management-related posts and various educational assignments, he wound up in the Management Sciences Department at UMIST where his current research energies are directed at quality-related issues. He is a member of the Institute of Production Engineers Quality Management activity group, the co-editor of the International Journal of Quality and Reliability Management, and is currently heavily involved with the training of suppliers to the Ford Motor Company in Statistical Process Control.

* * *

36

Barrie Dale wishes to thank the Science and Engineering Research Council for their financial support of the research project 'The Determination and Use of Quality-Related Costs in Manufacturing Industry' (GR/C33475) and the Manpower Services Commission for their financial support of 'Development Work on Quality Circles' (ST5/19/1984). He also wishes to thank Jayne Lees and Jim Plunkett for their comments and suggestions made during preparation of this chapter and for allowing their research findings to be used. He is grateful to American Express and North Warwickshire Health Authority for allowing their respective experiences with circles to be quoted.

The successful management of quality must be a company-wide effort. Quality is not just the responsibility of a quality department, as everyone in an organisation has a contribution to make to ensure a defect-free operation. It is also important that companies encourage their suppliers and customers to collaborate in attempting to eliminate defects in all links of the customer–supplier chain. There are a number of elements in a quality management system including, *inter alia*, failure mode and effect analysis (FMEA); quality circles; quality costing; and statistical process control. Organisations should become familiar with all these techniques and should not become preoccupied with only one.

Research carried out at UMIST has revealed that some quality managers all too readily fall into the trap of viewing individual quality techniques as the latest panacea, to be discarded as another becomes the latest 'flavour of the month'. The benefits of all quality techniques will be transient in nature unless they are underpinned by a total approach to quality, supported and driven from the top by a Chief Executive who has made quality his or her number one priority.

Quality techniques should be viewed as the tools adopted by an organisation in the development of a total approach to quality. They can also be helpful in providing the motivation to launch a quality improvement programme. This is particularly true when such a quality discipline is imposed by a major purchaser, as with the insistence by the Ford Motor Company that, as part of its quality system standard, suppliers use statistical process control.

In this chapter the specific techniques of *quality costing* and *quality circles* are examined. The reader might not unreasonably ask why these have been picked out for special attention. Certainly it is not because they are seen as more important than any of the others. It just so happens that at UMIST we have undertaken research on both these techniques and that on quality circles has encompassed companies from the service sector.

Quality Costing

Quality costing highlights where quality costs are incurred. There is a lack of information on the application of quality costing in the service sector and all our research relates to manufacturing organisations. That does not mean that this most fundamental approach is not relevant to the service sector but rather that it has not yet received the attention it deserves.

Quality-related costs are incurred by an organisation in the design, implementation, operation and maintenance of its quality management system. To these must be added those costs which are incurred due to failures of the product, the service or the system. Put simply, they are the costs associated with not getting the product or the service right first time. There is general agreement that costs can be conveniently divided into the following four core categories (BS 6143, 1981):

- *Prevention costs*—the costs of any action taken to investigate, prevent or reduce defects and failures.
- *Appraisal costs*—the costs of assessing the quality achieved.
- *Internal failure costs*—the costs arising from the failure to achieve the quality specified before transfer of ownership to the customer.
- *External failure costs*—the costs arising from a failure to achieve the quality specified after transfer of ownership to the customer.

Our research has shown that there are difficulties in deciding whether certain elements should be categorised as prevention or appraisal. Service organisations should also be alert to the fact that it is extremely difficult and even impractical to compile an all-embracing list of elements which would cover all eventualities. There will always be those which are specific to particular situations and organisations and each business must generate its own.

Quality costs in manufacturing are associated with inspection, scrap and rework, etc. Service organisations are more at the sharp end in terms of dealing with the customer or client, and more often than not they are responding to feedback. Quality costs are likely to be incurred in the following ways:

- loss of business
- lost opportunity
- legal claims
- penalties in terms of travel, freight, accommodation, cancellation, compensation
- liaison with consumer organisations
- setting-up systems
- auditing systems both in-house and at suppliers and sub-contractors

It is of interest to organisations in the service sector to know that those manufacturing companies which collected quality data costs had developed these systems as only one aspect of gathering quality-related information in attempting to discover what had gone wrong. Such companies based their individualised systems and methods on what they were doing rather than on any standard classification.

In most organisations quality costs are surprisingly high. The National Economic Development Council (1985) has estimated that quality costs in manufacturing organisations lie somewhere between 10 per cent and 20 per cent of sales turnover. Crosby (1985) claims that manufacturing companies incur costs amounting to 25–30 per cent of their sales by doing things over again, while in service companies it is estimated that 40–50 per cent of operating costs are wasted. Driving defects out of the system offers organisations the best chance of staying in business and the pursuit of this objective provides twin benefits. Improving the levels of performance leads to increased customer satisfaction, with a good possibility of improved market share, and cutting quality costs offers an attractive route to improved profits.

Despite the fact that quality costs are high and that a substantial proportion of them are avoidable, they are often not measured, and hence go uncontrolled. The principal advantages of quality cost data are:

- The measurement of costs allows quality-related activities to be expressed in the common language of cash. This allows quality to be treated as any other business parameter which, in turn, helps to emphasise the importance of quality in an organisation and influences attitudes towards quality. The determination of these costs helps to keep quality in the spotlight and their identification, measurement and publication can often achieve more than any well-orchestrated internal quality campaign.

- Quality costs help to establish the evidence of the need for quality improvement by assigning a price tag to chronic problems or waste. This focuses attention on areas of high expenditure and helps to shock people into action. Furthermore, the costs may also be used to set and measure progress towards cost-reduction targets.

- Companies are keen to know whether their quality performance in terms of quality related costs is good, bad or indifferent, but there is little information available for such comparisons. It is, however, dangerous to compare the quality cost data of different companies and industries unless the accounting practices and cost determination methods used are known. At present every company's calculation of quality-related costs is unique to that company.

- Knowledge of quality-related costs enables business decisions about quality to be made in an objective manner.

Some Pointers for the Collection of Quality Cost Data

Although our quality costing research covers only manufacturing companies, the following conclusions are undoubtedly of equal relevance to service organisations.

It is unlikely that management accounts will yield the required information. Hence it is essential to involve accountants from the outset. In those companies which boast quality costing systems the driving force behind their development has been the quality manager. Management accountants are under continual pressure to produce a variety of cost information and, if quality costing is to get off the ground, they have to be convinced that the exercise is worthwhile.

In view of difficulties with definitions, of knowing what should be included amongst quality-related costs, and the problems of gathering some of the costs, there is little point in pursuing the precise figures even where they can be obtained. On the other hand, the costs must be accurate enough to be credible even to those whose efficiency or performance is perhaps criticised in the resulting report. A cost report lacking credibility can be counter-productive as its value can readily be undermined by a skilled protagonist once a single weakness has been exposed. It is for this reason that only costs produced or endorsed by accounts departments should be used. Such figures are more likely to be compatible and consistent with other cost efficiency measures.

There is little virtue in collecting quality-related costs simply to see what they may reveal. Many managers have successfully resisted pressure to co-operate in the collection of costs on the grounds that they would not reveal any problems with which they were not already familiar. Clarifying the purposes of the exercise can go a long way towards avoiding such problems. If the prime purpose of the exercise is to identify high cost problems, coarse scale costs in known problem areas will probably suffice. If, on the other hand, the purpose is to set a percentage cost reduction target on the company's total quality-related costs, it will be necessary to identify and measure all the contributory cost elements in order to be sure that costs are genuinely reduced and not simply transferred elsewhere.

There is little or no point in gathering and presenting, on a routine basis, costs which do not change. Before instituting a cost determination system, it is, therefore, advisable to examine the potential for change of a cost element. The inclusion of fixed or immutable costs also has the effect of reducing the sensitivity of costs to changes in performance.

It will be necessary to decide how to deal with overheads, as many quality-related costs are normally included under this head, while others are treated as direct costs and attract a proportion of overheads. Failure to clarify this point can lead to a gross distortion of the picture derived from quality-related cost analyses.

Quality cost information needs to be produced from an organisation's existing system. It is easier to develop a quality costing system in a 'greenfield' situation than to attempt to break into an established system. A common fallacy is that larger organisations boast accounting systems from which it is relatively easy to extract quality-related costs. Such organisations typically have large immutable accounting systems and practices often imposed by head office with little flexibility to provide quality costs. On the other hand, smaller companies are less likely to have management accountants who are easier to convince of the worth of quality costs and are more likely to co-operate in their collection than are financial accountants.

In practice a large proportion of quality costs are incurred in failure activities. In the absence of a quality cost reporting system, start by looking at failure costs.

Once it has been decided which costs are relevant, it is important to collect and display all those cost figures which are available, and also to indicate the existence of relevant costs which cannot yet be quantified. Reporting only part of the costs can be very misleading and acknowledging the existence of unquantified costs keeps them in view and encourages attempts to measure them.

Price (1984) defines the following three rules for *systematic quality control*: no measurement without recording; no recording without analysis; and no analysis without action. These are just as apposite in the case of *quality costing*. Therefore, when cost information is available, analyse it. Attribute costs to department, defect type, product, cause, supplier, etc. Identify responsibility for costs by functions and people. Rank problems and cost reduction projects by size and importance. Integrate the collection, analysis and reporting of quality-related costs into the company accounting system—but keep paperwork to a minimum.

Quality Circles

A 'classical' quality circle is a group of between six to eight people from the same work area, meeting for around one hour each week in company time under the leadership of their supervisor, to solve quality and work-related problems in their section or department. Quality circles were launched in Japan in 1962, by which time the Japanese quality revolution was well under way. Circles were first introduced in America by Lockheed in 1974; and Rolls-Royce of Derby was the first British company to introduce them in 1978. In the United Kingdom there are currently 125 organisations registered with the National Society of Quality Circles (NSQC) which was formed in 1982. Eleven of these are from the service sector and, as elsewhere in the world, activities in this sector follow on from publicity given to successful experiences in manufacturing.

Since 1982 we have been undertaking surveys of the operation of UK quality circle programmes. These have established that some 500–700 manufacturing work sites have operational circles, along with some 50–70 locations in the service sector. Lees and Dale (1985) have recently reported on the findings of a survey of 27 UK service sector quality circle programmes and its main conclusions constitute the remainder of this chapter.

The Operation of Quality Circles in Service Organisations

Introduction of a Circle Programme

The five types of service organisation into which quality circles have been introduced are: public utility (five organisations); communications (4); hotels and catering (3); banking and finance (3); and business services (3).

Twenty-two of the 27 companies used the term 'quality circles', the five exceptions preferring these other labels: 'customer first teams', 'performance circles', 'improvement groups', 'participative management systems/work groups', and 'employee improvement groups'.

The top four motivators for the introduction of a quality circle programme were: to develop employees (21 organisations); to improve employee job satisfaction (19); to improve the quality of service provided (19); and to improve communications (19). Sixteen organisations felt they would help bring about cost-savings. These figures suggest that circles are being introduced by service organisations in order to involve and develop their employees. Manufacturing companies which have achieved a national reputation for the longevity of their circle programmes did not introduce circles for cost-saving reasons and have resisted the temptation to push their circles for quick results.

American Express serves as a typical example of why a service

organisation introduces quality circles. The initial objectives of the circle programme at American Express were:
- improved communication
- improved morale
- improved degree of involvement by all staff in the business
- improved commitment to quality

North Warwickshire Health Authority is another example. Here, circles were implemented subsequent to the 1982 restructuring of the NHS in an attempt to secure greater staff involvement and participation.

Attitudes to Circles

Management

Discussions had taken place with management in 23 of the 27 organisations and with supervisors in 22 organisations. Some managers objected to the introduction of quality circles, the three main objections being:

1. Scepticism that circles were just the latest in a succession of 'vogue' management techniques   11 organisations
2. A feeling that there would be some loss of control by management   10 organisations
3. A belief that priority must be given to other, more pressing, matters   8 organisations

Trade Unions

Prior to the introduction of quality circles, briefings took place in ten of the twenty unionised organisations with local full-time union officials, and briefings with shop stewards occurred in twelve cases. It almost goes without saying that, if the full cooperation of the trade unions is to be secured, it is vital that they be consulted and that the quality circle concept be explained to them before the introduction of a programme.

In five of the twenty organisations with union representation the trade unions had raised objections to the implementation of circles. The main objection was that quality circles would threaten existing union practices. Such fears are often founded in the belief that circles will interfere with the unions' channels of communication to the shop-floor which are often quite loose, rather than that they will affect negotiating procedures, which tend to be enshrined in documentation. Situations have been encountered where, prior to the introduction of circles, a departmental problem would have been left to the shop steward to take up with management. With the introduction of circles, such a problem would automatically be passed to a circle or, alternatively, a circle might actually be formed to resolve it.

Some Organisational Issues

The literature on quality circles stresses the need to establish a *steering committee* as part of the circle programme support structure. Such a committee comprises both management and union representatives, together with participants from the circle programme. The steering committee usually sets operational guidelines, objectives and goals for circles and provides continuity and structure to the programme. It also spreads the ownership of the programme, thereby ensuring that circles do not become too dependent upon the facilitator for their survival. Fifteen organisations had established a steering committee. However, Collard and Dale (1986) make the point that setting up a steering committee is very much dependent upon the culture and attitudes prevailing within an organisation and whether or not the opportunity exists for discussing the progress of circles between interested parties at other meetings.

It is now universally recognised that the appointment of a *facilitator* is a vital element if a quality circle programme is to succeed. The facilitator typically provides support for each circle in terms of training, advice, coaching and stimulation. Without guidance an immature circle will flounder. Only after a circle has achieved some degree of maturity can the facilitator reduce the level of support and allow it to achieve independence. It is important that circles develop a spontaneous life of their own, with the facilitator sustaining momentum. In spite of the agreed importance of the facilitator's role, three organisations had not identified such an individual. Nineteen organisations indicated that they had part-time facilitators for their quality circles, while in five it was a full-time appointment. There are conflicting views on the full-time versus part-time facilitator appointment. One view is that, once the circle programme is approaching 15 circles, the facilitator's job must be made full-time, whilst an alternative view is to increase the number of part-time facilitators in line with the growth in the number of circles.

A *pilot* circle programme prior to a full-scale launch enables an organisation to gather feedback from staff at all levels on the factors likely to affect circle success. Nine of the 27 organisations had not started off with a pilot programme and six of these featured only one or two circles in their programme. Programmes of this size, whether pilot or full-scale, are vulnerable in the event of one circle failing. It is, therefore, not too surprising that five of the eight service organisations whose programmes had been suspended since the first survey reported by Dale and Lees (1984) featured only one or two circles in their programme.

Choosing Circle Participants

Whilst the facilitator is usually nominated by management, circle philosophy dictates that leaders and members must be volunteers. However, in practice one finds few true volunteers. In general, a supervisor is asked by his or her superior and/or facilitator whether he or she wishes to lead a circle. If they have received some circle training, few supervisors turn down such an invitation. When the time comes for a circle leader to form a circle it is a normal procedure to select people with suitable experience and abilities rather than simply to ask for volunteers.

Twenty-three service organisations had first-line supervisors acting in a leadership role, while some 15 had some circles led by some other member of staff. When a circle is set up it is usually a supervisor from the same area who assumes the leadership role but, after a short period of operation, it is common practice for the circle members to choose someone from within their own ranks to be a deputy leader. There is no reason whatsoever why this person, once he or she has acquired experience and been trained in leadership skills, cannot assume the leader's role. Indeed, supervisors are often keen for this to happen. When persons below the level of supervisor lead the circle they come to the attention of management. This provides them with a boost in status and possibly improves their promotion prospects. It also provides an excellent learning environment.

Our research on UK circle programmes in both the service and manufacturing sectors suggests that the circle will have a better chance of success if the supervisor assumes the leadership role at the inception of a circle. Supervisors have experience of chairing and organising meetings, approaching people for data, etc. Generally, workers below the level of supervisor do not possess these skills and, if they are thrust into the leadership role from the outset, they could cause the premature demise of a circle. When a circle leader is not the supervisor from the area in which the circle operates, participants need to ask permission from their own supervisor to hold circle meetings, attend circle presentations, etc. However, in spite of these arguments, some circle members have resented the fact that their departmental supervisor was elected to be a circle leader, and have mentioned clashes between the 'natural' circle leader and elected leader. This is an area where clear communication is needed as to the reasons for the choice of leader.

Operating Characteristics of Quality Circles

Circles in the service organisations surveyed have undertaken a wide range of activities, as shown in Table 4.1. It is interesting that the top activity is quality of service. In recent years, quality has, of necessity, become established as the number one priority in many manufaturing companies, and there is an increasing awareness of the importance of quality in the service sector. Wages and bonuses, grievances, and individual personalities were quite rightly excluded for consideration in all the organisations.

Table 4.1   *Classification of Projects Undertaken by Quality Circles Operating in Service Organisations*

Project theme	Number of organisations
Quality of service	12
Administration	10
Productivity improvements	9
Communication	9
Service processes	8
Cost reduction	7
Wastage	5
Repairs/servicing	4
Energy savings	3
Catering	3
Purchasing	3
Training	2
Transport	2
Safety	1

Twenty organisations reported that, on average, their circles took four months or less to complete a project. The most popular circle meeting frequency is once a week; this pattern featured in eighteen of the organisations. At the other end of the spectrum, five organisations reported a meeting frequency of once a month. The vast majority of organisations (25) reported a circle meeting length of one hour held during company time.

Obstacles and Benefits

Seventeen obstacles were put forward by service organisations as hindering their circle programme, the three main ones being: the problem of maintaining initial impetus (14 organisations); a lack of management support (13); and labour turnover and company re-organisation (13). At some point most circle programmes encounter the problem of maintaining momentum. Hayward *et al.* (1985) found that adequate support from facilitators, periodic rests from circle activity, adequate recognition, publicity of circle activities, and further training where necessary were all measures likely to prevent atrophy.

Inspection of the obstacles reveals that most can be laid at management's door. All the experience with UK circle programmes points to the fact that top management rarely deliberately impedes circle activities. Its biggest mistake is rather in failing to be seen to support quality circle activity outside the circle presentation. It is middle management rather than top management which creates most of the barriers. Our research suggests that management resistance often arises because senior managers have not involved their middle managers early enough in the development of the quality circle programme and have failed to encourage them to take a more active role in circle activities.

The obstacle ranked third (labour turnover and company reorganisation), along with the problem of the multi-locational nature of the organisation, is perhaps more in evidence in service organisations than in manufacturing companies. This situation does not lend itself to the creation of a stable environment in which quality circles work best and militates against the circle programme fully taking root.

Twenty-one of the 27 organisations gave an unqualified 'yes' in answer to the question: 'Have quality circles been successful in your organisation?' The remainder thought it too early to say. The reasons proffered by respondents for the success of their quality circle programmes reinforce the points made earlier—namely, the need for an enthusiastic facilitator, along with full management commitment and thorough consultation at all levels about the philosophy and objectives of quality circles. The full list of benefits of circles mentioned by respondents is set out in Table 4.2.

The primary purpose of quality circles is to allow people closest to the job to utilise their skills and ideas to uncover and disentangle

Table 4.2   *Perceived Benefits of Quality Circles to Members in 27*
Service Organisations

Benefits to members	Number of organisations offering that benefit
Circles provide the opportunity to become involved in the organisation	19
Better team work within the department	19
Increased job satisfaction	16
Circles help relieve frustration by ensuring that something is done to remedy a bad situation	16
Better relationships with management	15
Increased feeling of 'belonging' to the organisation	15
Recognition for their own achievements	12
Increased pride in their work	9
Gives them a voice in their own future	8
Enables them to learn more about their jobs	5
Improved job security by helping the organisation to operate in a more cost-effective manner	3

problems which would otherwise not have been noticed, or at most
given a low priority, by management. Consequently, circle members
become more involved in the business and feel they have some real
influence over what goes on in their work area. Involvement in
problem solving provides circle members with considerable satisfaction and is certainly seen as a welcome diversion from what is often a
boring job for a short period each week. The benefits of circles all lead
to a more involved and interested work force.

Summary

UMIST research on quality circles has uncovered few major differences in the operating characteristics of manufacturing and service quality circles. The latter face additional difficulties, the most important being:

- Projects tackled by service circles are often intangible in nature which makes for difficulties in the evaluation of the benefits of the approach.

- Circle members are more likely to be dealing directly with a client. This can create problems in finding a time suitable for circle meetings and can result in poor attendance at circle meetings.

- Organisational changes and the movement of company personnel between different departments and functions tend to be a more frequent occurrence in service organisations. Some departments or sections are of a relatively small size in terms of the numbers of people employed and this has led to circles being formed of people from different functions and professions. Although offering obvious advantages, this non-classical circle structure creates difficulties in the selection of projects of common interest or concern to all circle members. To alleviate this problem, service sector circles often choose projects involving changes to systems and procedures. By their very nature such interface projects are complex. Consequently, in order to arrive at a solution, such circles require considerable assistance from outside circle specialists. It is not unknown for circles to encounter problems in obtaining assistance from support services. With projects of this type there is always the chance that elsewhere in the organisation system changes are being planned that may well negate any solutions the circle may propose. On the other hand, a circle formed from one small section can be insular and people from outside the section with direct interest in its work can widen its scope and interests.

- An additional difficulty is that quality circle programmes in the UK service sector are very much in their infancy. There are few models from which to learn and, consequently, there is little opportunity to discuss problems, training needs, etc. with people in a similar line of business.

One must, however, remain conscious of the fact that service organisations are, by nature, labour-intensive and as such have perhaps more potential for circles than do those operating in manufacturing environments.

5

Putting People First—
A Company-Wide
Approach to Good Service

'The courteous learns his courtesy from the discour-
teous.'

Turkish proverb

CHRIS LANE, Chief Executive, Scandinavian Service School
and Time Manager International.

Those who earn their remuneration in service industries are, by
definition, involved directly with customers. When their customers
have a choice it would seem almost self-evident that a considerable
effort needs to be directed towards ensuring that customer needs are
satisfied. Any reader can testify to the fact that the obviousness of this
was apparently lost on many such organisations.

Chris Lane recognised this and from that recognition sprang the very
successful 'Putting People First' programmes which his organisation
has mounted for a series of 'blue chip' companies including, amongst
others, American Express, Sheraton Hotels, Abbey Life Insurance and
British Airways, which alone had all 37,000 of its staff experience the
'Putting People First' message. This activity is but one of a range
offered by the two companies which Chris heads up. Time Manager
International has a turnover in excess of £5 million and employs
59 full-time people who provide short training programmes in Time
Management and Personal Planning, Managing Stress and Creativity.
The programmes are well established in over 20 countries and have so
far been mounted in 11 languages.

★ ★ ★

To claim that people have an important role to play in the process of giving service is both obvious and an understatement. It is perhaps surprising therefore that a closer investigation of many of our service industries reveals that much of their service training focuses more on the material and technical than on the personal aspects of service. To some extent this is understandable given the sheer complexity and volume of information which has to be understood in order to operate, for instance, the many different price structures within the hotel and airline industries, not to mention the ever-changing computer systems we are asked to operate.

The fact remains that in today's service world, where many companies offer what to the customer look like very similar products and services, a competitive edge can only be maintained if the personal aspects of the service are first-class. There is, however, a problem in defining exactly what first-class personal service is— many of us have tried and we feel we have made some progress but, by the nature of the subject, we are in the realm of feelings and qualitative measurements rather than hard facts and figures.

Scandinavian Service School does not carry out service quality research. Its role is to organise and manage companywide campaigns which go under a variety of titles including *Putting People First* or *Putting the Customer First*. A 'Putting People First' programme is a combination of events but would normally include the following:

- Identification of objectives for the campaign.
- Briefings of senior managers to secure commitment and to test the objectives.
- A series of *Putting People First* presentations covering everyone in the company. Between 50 and 250 people would typically be at each of these presentations which would normally last two full days.
- A series of follow-on activities which are vital to the longer-term success of the campaign. These could include 'Customer First' team meetings, features in company newspapers, video programmes, etc.

None of the components mentioned above are claimed to be original. What is different about 'Putting People First', compared with more traditional customer relations training activities, is that it focuses not so much on specific service skills but on the needs and potential of the individual service giver. In plain words, what this means is that on a 'Putting People First' programme, both the senior manager and the most junior member of the company will be sitting together considering their potential as human beings for giving service and obtaining satisfaction with a job well done. It sounds simple, but to be effective it requires a great deal of openness and honesty which is all too often missing from our hierarchical organisations.

'Putting People First' itself did not stem from any organised research—like many good ideas it happened almost by mistake. The first 'Putting People First' programmes were carried out for the Scandinavian Airline Systems in the early 1980s as an extension of management training which our sister company, Time Manager International, had been undertaking in the areas of time management and team motivation. SAS, under its new chief executive, Jan Carlsen, must be credited with having started the new wave of realisation that each individual in the company, irrespective of level or job function, has an important role to play in customer perception of service. Long before SAS introduced the material improvements in its service relating to uniforms and livery and before improvements in arriving on schedule were achieved, it focused its prime attention and resources on mobilising its staff to be more conscious of the effect each of them could have, not only on each other, but also on the ultimate customer.

Jan Carlsen's influence on SAS has been well documented elsewhere but what is perhaps not so well known is the wide range of other organisations which had been pursuing similar activities. The massive campaign which British Airways has mounted these last three years has involved 37,000 people and the background to it is featured elsewhere in this book. Other companies involved in similar 'Putting People First' campaigns include, *inter alia*, Sheraton Hotels, American Express, Abbey Life Insurance and Audi-Volkswagen, along with a host of other organisations representing a range of industries.

It has to be admitted that the effects of the 'Putting People First' initiative are extremely difficult to measure. Perhaps it might be more appropriate to say that the effects are extremely difficult to identify, as having resulted from the Putting People First campaign itself. Like many other qualitative service areas, it is a question of 'only knowing when you haven't had it'. One of the best approaches to judging the extent of awareness in a company about people aspects of service is to use a simple check list of day-to-day things such as the following:

• How do staff talk to each other? Do they use each other's names and do they talk to each other as friends, particularly those working in different departments?
• What kind of things do staff say to each other about their supervisors and management and how well do they feel management communicates with them?
• What kind of winner or loser statements are heard about the company? Is it a question of 'I don't know, but I'll find out for you', or is it rather 'That's not my department and I can tell you you'll never get that done around here'?

- How well do people acknowledge that they 'own the problem', whether or not it is their fault?
- To what extent is it acceptable to make mistakes and take risks?
- How much scope do people think they have for being creative and innovative? Equally, when ideas are suggested, to what extent are they really listened to and acknowledged?
- Does the company really welcome and value the views of its customers? Is a complaint really sought after and seen as a valuable means to improve service?
- What kinds of subject are covered by the company newsletter or newspaper? Does the newspaper report only the successes of the company in material terms or does it cover wider areas, including articles by people expressing their views?
- Is the company an 'us and them' organisation, often between head office and people in the front line?
- How bureaucratic is the organisation? Today's customers have a fine nose to smell out restrictions.
- What about training? To what extent is training aimed at examining people's personal skills as opposed to the functional skills they need to do their job? At Disneyland the roadsweepers have a 5-day training course—10 minutes on how to use a sweeper and the remainder on how to give information to guests!

This check list is by no means a scientific approach or an exhaustive list. There is no end to the questions one can ask to gain an impression of where a company is on the service spectrum. One might well ask how much value there is in collecting great masses of data when every company has an opportunity to improve its service level and, thereby, its competitive edge in the marketplace. 'Putting People First' is just one marketing weapon but it would seem, from recent activity in Europe and the USA, that 'Putting People First' is being acknowledged as a significant force both for maintaining a lead in the marketplace and also for mobilising and motivating the workforce.

TRAVEL

6

Customer Care in British Rail

'Looking after your customers is not merely good manners—it's good business too.'

Scottish proverb

DANIEL GIBLIN, British Railways Board.

Given the almost limitless number of jokes which comedians direct at British Rail, most readers will be pleasantly surprised to discover the flurry of activity which is now under way to bring about a change in both image and practice. In truth, any frequent traveller will have become conscious that something was afoot as evidenced by the obvious improvements in staff attitudes and decor. In what follows he will discover just how British Rail set about effecting those necessary improvements.

Daniel Giblin is well equipped to tell this story, having been involved in BR's first Customer Care campaign on the Bedford to St. Pancras line where he was the modernisation manager. The process of bringing a Victorian line up to the standards commensurate with the 21st century involved the electrification of the line, the introduction of the first driver-only trains and the training of 1,100 staff in customer care skills. From there he went to Scotland as Passenger Terminals Manager and was responsible for the multi-million pound improvement programme to ScotRail's stations. He actually joined British Rail's financial accountancy department in 1969, but switched to market research prior to completing a two-year advanced management training course in Operations Management.

★ ★ ★

Without doubt the customer thinks of front-line contact employees as the 'business'. Front-line people make or break the image of the industry by their performance when dealing directly with the customer. It is vital, therefore, that employees who interact with the customer possess the skills needed to deal in a professional, competent manner with the demands of the customer. The railway's most important asset is people, be they the people who work on the railways or the customers who travel by rail.

British Rail's *Customer Care* campaign is a high-profile programme which will continue to the end of the century. It is a continuing part of managerial strategy. The aim of the programme is to ensure that the highest possible standards of customer care are achieved. This takes in both the customer's physical experience of train travel at stations and on trains, and also his or her mental experience in terms of attitudes and feelings associated with rail travel.

British Rail has gone about getting its customer care right by first getting its management thinking right. Customer care is a committed policy from the Chairman on down and it cascades throughout the industry as a firm managerial objective for all managers. Thus engineers and operations managers as well as marketing managers share the common focus of putting customer care first. In raising commitment throughout their areas, managers develop the ethic in their supervisors, as well as their front line and backroom staff. Every employee now appreciates that wage packets are filled by revenue obtained from a customer. Employee commitment towards customer care is thus essential to its success.

However, if employees are important in 'getting it right' at the interface with the customer, there must also be a payoff for them. 'Staff care' must be given priority in tandem with 'Customer care' improvements. In every modernisation scheme associated with customer care, British Rail also effects improvements in staff facilities. In fact, in many respects staff care needs to come first to ensure commitment.

In order to make customer care work in a practical manner it must become a line management responsibility. In British Rail line management owns the resources and it is line management which creates the environment needed to ensure the success of the customer care impetus. Customer care objectives are now set in the annual appraisals of all managers and this is to be done with supervisors also. Objectives are personal objectives and are annually identified as priority items in management effort.

A clear understanding of each individual's role in customer care is achieved by allocating specific personal tasks which improve professionalism and performance. Each individual is encouraged to relate the functioning of the total job towards customer care. This requires employees to analyse and evaluate their personal effectiveness in dealing with customer needs. The key to this form of customer care development is team work and effective feedback processes. Supervisors and managers lead, facilitate and guide groups to ensure that customer care objectives are established, implemented and followed up. This managerial drive and determination must permeate the whole of the organisation so that at local level the impetus of the campaign is maintained, thus ensuring that customer care is a continuous process in the hearts, minds and actions of every employee. The application of customer care initiatives and objectives must ensure the maximum practical input with a minimum of philosophical argument. Objectives have to be explained clearly, simply and concisely in action terms in order that employees know exactly what is required of them.

By concentrating on behaviour and attiudes towards customer care it is possible to study and identify key problem areas and work on these. Comprehensive customer care research and surveys have been conducted to establish what the customer thinks needs to be done. The British Rail Public Awareness Study, for example, revealed that 81 per cent of the public have been to a station in the last two years. Thus British Rail has a highly visible nationwide profile, with an 'open day' virtually every day.

Travelling by train is seen by customers as an act of faith. They expect that the train will run; that it will be on time; that they will find the right train; that their ticket will be valid, and that there will be a seat available on the train. When things go wrong, stress occurs and this can result in a downward spiral which can culminate in upset and conflict.

Anxiety is a problem in all forms of travelling, but less so on trains than some other modes of transport. Nonetheless, our 1982 Station Survey revealed that 25 per cent of those joining trains said they felt harassed at stations. By 1985 this figure had fallen to 18 per cent. Most of the anxieties identified concerned coping with children or luggage, changing trains, being met and what to do if, by some unfortunate chance, the train were late.

Customers complain about many things: some of the main ones, in order of importance, are customer information, timekeeping, train service quality and conduct of staff. The Transport Users Consultative Committee has collected data on these complaints which, along with other data, have enabled British Rail to target and take action on priority items as part of the Customer Care Campaign. In Scotland, for example, there has been a substantial investment in train indicators at main stations, and Strathclyde PTE services, which is the largest outside London, has improved punctuality so that now 95 per cent of trains arrive at their destination within five minutes of the scheduled time of arrival. Station surveys have also revealed that 78 per cent of customers, excluding commuters, secure information from staff and most check twice to seek reassurance. Personal contact with staff is seen as a priority area by customers. Another key issue identified by research as needing some improvement concerns the conduct of staff. In the Public Awareness Study of 1982, 8 per cent of the public identified BR staff as helpful. Conflict, anxiety and stress among customers and employees when things go wrong have also been a key attention area for development.

Action has had to be taken to improve and develop performance, so carefully designed workshops (dubbed 'charm schools' by the media) produce joint management/staff action forums, as well as providing in-depth seminars on customer handling skills, including special skills for helping disabled people. These special attitudinal seminars are a launch pad for personal employee development at the work place, the underlying concept being that learning is continuous. The objective is to link thinking and practice acquired at the Customer Care Seminars with the live situation at the front line work place. New learning must be applied, monitored and reviewed, with the emphasis being on practicality and improvement.

Apart from debate and discussion the seminars include action learning situations based on real customer conflict cases. These are role played and everyone is subsequently provided with feedback and advice on their adjudged personal strengths and weaknesses. 'Before and after' surveys are used to measure effectiveness and changes in attitudes. In one region a recent survey identified a 40 per cent improvement in attitudes towards customers over an 18-month period. Public complaints about staff attitudes dropped by 70 per cent over this same period. These seminars are seen as an investment in customer care, with the payoff being a better deal for customers and improved job satisfaction and reward for employees. Improvements resulted in a more objective approach to handling customers, often by knowing how to defuse situations under severe provocation. The obnoxious customer exists. Drunks, excited football supporters and some sneering city clerks can cause difficulties, but attacks are usually directed at the system rather than at individuals. However, customers are the lifeblood of the business and it is a continuous part of the job to aim to provide quality customer care in all circumstances.

Over half of British Rail customers make use of station facilities and the need for investment in station infrastructure, to provide a 21st century environment in 19th century buildings, was clearly identified in the station surveys. A modern, welcoming and pleasant environment is a vital element in station operation, as any rail journey starts when the customer steps into a station and finishes when he leaves the station at the other end of the journey. Stations have, therefore, to be seen as an important part of the package of train travel. They need to meet the expectations and demands of customers who are used to standards set in the High Street by Marks and Spencers, building societies and banks, and by competitors such as airlines, bus companies and the admitted luxury and convenience of the private car.

In order to develop a total customer care environment, station improvements have taken place at a furious pace, often making stations into tourist attractions in themselves. These improvements have included the refurbishment of older stations by blending the romance and charm of their original architecture with modern top-quality interior and design. These stations are often in prime selling locations in the centre of towns and cities, and are very much BR's 'shop window'. Travel centres, waiting areas and bar or restaurant facilities have been improved to match, and even go beyond, the best offered by the competition.

New travel centres are air-conditioned, carpeted, light and attractive—a long way from the decaying and dismal images portrayed in some old Will Hay films. Bars and restaurants are modern and convenient. They attract not only rail travellers but non-rail customers who choose them for their good quality. They include 'Free House' pubs and fast food outlets branded 'Casey Jones'. These activities make a major contribution not only to British Rail's customer care but also to its revenue. Developments are now underway which will attract High Street shoppers and major stations will boast exciting shopping piazzas incorporating everything from flower kiosks to major branches of international retail outlets. Station concourses are being modernised with white tiling and 'sun' lighting which provides a bright attractive environment. This, linked to good concourse seating facilities, music, and clear information and announcement systems using the most up-to-date technology pro- duces the ambience our customers should expect.

Many stations now operate the 'Open Station' system so that customers no longer have to queue to have their tickets checked at barriers. Instead, tickets are inspected on trains. This reduces total journey times marginally but it also serves to provide greater personal customer care on trains. A recent audit on ScotRail showed, incidentally, that the number of customers travelling without tickets is less than 0.2 per cent of travellers. With the introduction of new computerised ticket issuing systems, the speed of ticket transactions between customers and staff will be further improved. These systems will also be used in a portable form by train staff, thus enabling tickets to be issued during the course of the journey.

Cleanliness of stations is another vital ingredient in the presentation of the product to the customer. Specialist 'heavy cleaning gangs' have been formed at many locations to clean up to 180 stations per group intensively on a three-monthly cycle. Recent public awareness studies in Scotland showed a 20 per cent improvement in the travelling public's perception of station standards.

Train Care is the core part of the 'total package' concept of BR's Customer Care Campaign. Trains are the frontline hard sell point of contact. The ultimate aim is to provide excellence in quality; a multi-million major refurbishment and renewal scheme is well underway to ensure that on-train customer care targets are met. This includes up-market decor, faster speeds and improved comfort on all new trains and the refurbishment of older vehicles to bring them up to modern standards. In the next few years, for example, local train services will have an injection of 856 new 'Sprinter' or 'Pacer' vehicles replacing much of the stock on provincial diesel unit trains. The InterCity business is beginning to boom as customers flock back to new improved services. 250 InterCity coaches are now being modernised each year, thereby providing greater customer comfort linked to improved on-train catering. New simplified seat reservation systems make it easy for customers to reserve seats and this, combined with videos and telephones on trains along with better car parking at stations, all adds up to an improved quality package of service for the customer. A good deal of investment is going into future customer care now, with the introduction of brand-new coaches and new 140 mph 'Electra' locomotives. These will speed InterCity into profitability through its campaign for customer care.

It is accepted that defects are not free and that shoddy work costs money. Attention to detail is a major theme in ensuring that standards are maintained. There is ongoing management attention, audited through customer care strategies, to check that increased maintenance schedules ensure minimal failures in locomotives and coaches. Punctuality, reliability and cleanliness are key attention areas which emphasise pride in the product.

Creative marketing to match customer expectations has resulted in new express services and named trains, all of which are welded to flexible operational and maintenance processes to ensure the application of customer care on a continuous basis. Customer care is therefore the cornerstone of train care developments, never forgetting that maintenance and operating depots also need to have the tools to turn out trains which match customer expectations.

Customer care panels have been instituted which enable a panel of customers to talk at regular intervals with the manager responsible for their services. These panels provide a two-way communication channel from which many new customer care initiatives are launched. These are linked to regular communication with Transport Users Consultative Committees, local councils, MPs and a number of other influential groups. Views and recommendations are all taken into account in building up customer care plans. A broad range of opinions can be secured, but the best is undoubtedly direct communication from customers themselves. Regular *Customer Care Audits* are undertaken of specific services and all letters of complaint and commendation are examined to identify pluses, minuses and areas for remedial action. Feedback to customers on the development of these initiatives is important in maintaining customer involvement and support. Our best advertisement has to be satisfied customers.

Customer Service Managers have been appointed in virtually every area of British Rail to ensure frontline management of the organisation's customer care campaign. Getting closer to the customer is a key part of that campaign. Thus high quality presentations incorporating videos and slides are made by managers in public forums, institutes and to many groups wishing further information on British Rail. These presentations are supplemented by major events to which the public is invited. They include, *inter alia*, Open Days, locomotive-naming events and the opening of new stations and facilities where celebrities often do the honours. Quality advertising is used for customer care and on television actual staff are shown dealing with customers. This TV advertising is linked to popular themes which help personalise rail travel as an attractive, effective and economic mode of transport.

The industry has progressed from being production-orientated to being business-led, with the accent now on putting the customer first. New marketing strategies concentrate action on customer needs which are clearly identified in research. The business has been divided into specific identifiable sectors, each with 'bottom line' accountability and responsibilities. This has resulted in simplified management structures with a reduction in the number of tiers of management between policy makers and frontline management. Responsibility and authority in dealing with customer care initiatives have thereby been largely devolved to local level resulting in the ability to respond more quickly to customer needs. This is nowhere better reflected than in the Area Business Groups set up throughout the country. Here managers meet across functional barriers and formally plan their own area strategies and budgets within well-structured accountabilities and responsibilities. Entrepreneurial spirit is encouraged to ensure that the business is operated for the benefit of the customer at all times.

It is important that the core of the industry apply customer care policies and that structures routinely reflect the importance of the customer care dimension in much the same way as 'Safety of the Line' has always been and will continue to be of paramount importance. The internal face must be right but, equally importantly, so too must be the external face of the industry in order that the customer gets what he feels he is buying.

Uniforms on British Rail have been redesigned and modernised, after taking into account what employees say their needs are. All employees in customer care jobs in all regions have now been provided with new uniforms and buffer stocks are kept at key locations so as to ensure that everyone is spick and span at all times. Novel features are encouraged in uniform design. *Travel Centre* staff in Scotland, for example, felt it would improve the image of the business if they wore tartan uniforms and, as a result, tartans, varying from Black Watch to McLeod, can be seen throughout 'ScotRail'.

Simplified timetables and posters have been produced for at-a-glance information, and these have been streamlined further to eliminate the amendments and alterations which have often baffled and bemused customers in the past. In a similar vein, a major campaign aimed at eliminating jargon has meant that, instead of customers hearing 'shorthand' technical terms known only to British Rail staff, they now encounter far more plain English.

Customer care starts with people and British Rail has reinforced its Equal Opportunities Policy to ensure that the right people, capable of the correct performance, are appointed and developed. Good customer care must not be an accident of just who happens to be on duty—frontline staff can make or break the business. The intention is to develop each and every employee as an ambassador for the industry. The format of employee participation includes key, on-going strategies which create maximum participation and commitment to customer care and to this end a major Employee Development activity is underway. Customer care is injected into education and training programmes and into communication strategies. Specific specialist customer care coaching has been a key part of BR's strategy. Over 60,000 employees have attended seminars on customer care linked to personal action plans, employee suggestion schemes and self-development packs which provide an on-going practicality to training at work. Supervisors act as mentors to staff with specific remits on counselling and targeting among the employees for whom they are responsible. Feedback processes keep the customer care information flowing through the organisation with all teams being kept well informed of improvements, problems and actions.

A network of designated *Key Communicators* is subjected to an intensive education and development programme on key concepts which need to be communicated. This takes the form of a *Customer Care Kit* which includes videos, slides, worksheets and a personal action plan for each participating employee. The kit promotes, in simple practical terms, the acquisition of personal skills. Every employee can achieve progress through applying the skills constructively. The tasks in the kit can be completed individually, in small and large groups, in written replies, or on a timed work basis. Flexibility and responsiveness are important ingredients in applying the Customer Care Kit. Thus the tasks which reflect real cases and research are presented in an uncomplicated, easy-to-understand manner. Each task in the kit is designed as a 'tool in the kit bag' of customer care so that new learning can be easily applied to the job situation. The 'Key Communicators' encourage practice in acquiring skills and develop confidence among employees. In order to achieve a high degree of awareness and performance when meeting customers, individuals are coached at the workplace in key skills. Supervisors perform this role on a rotational basis as part of their normal duties.

The Customer Care Programme is versatile and it can, therefore, be incorporated into other programmes such as Management Supervisory and Induction Courses. Key tasks can also be used to preview management and supervisory meetings. Targeting is a key part of the action planning. Each person undertakes a Personal Plan covering specific action points which are monitored through counselling and employee meetings. Much of the impetus in Customer Care skill development has been geared towards personal development, i.e. individuals are encouraged to take personal responsibility for deciding how far they should go and which skills they should concentrate on. A Personal Development Pack consisting of '39 Steps to Good Customer Care' has been developed for supervisors. There are solid guidelines to follow in achieving good standards in customer care, but ultimately it is the effort which each individual makes which guarantees the success of the programme.

Certain features of some jobs are carried out routinely time after time. From a personal examination of the items in the routine, and by meticulously reviewing, improving and redesigning individual routines in the light of new experience and learning, the skills of customer care can be refined to a high standard and individuals can obtain a real sense of achievement. The Customer Care Campaign has engendered a stimulating environment for developing people's skills in the areas of caring and listening, with target and action planning being key elements of the success of the campaign.

The customer care ethic has opened up new vistas for the industry in the fierce, highly competitive transport market. The Customer Care Campaign has provided a new beginning, an enlightened new era where the customer comes first. Customer care has become an obsession within the industry and it is infectious. The industry's image and its practices have changed as a consequence of a corporate renaissance aimed at getting British Rail close to its customers. This business-led, innovative approach to customer care has resulted in new standards of performance and motivation. Sound leadership has promoted improvement at an unrelenting pace and has focused all parts of the business on the common goal of satisfying the customer by the provision of higher standards of service than were ever experienced before.

Creating the right climate and corporate frame of mind has resulted in more direct communication with the work force. Close communication and the sharing of objectives have brought a new realism to the hearts and minds of all employees. It has created the attitude of mind that, to survive and grow, the business needs new thinking and understanding about customer care. The Customer Care Campaign in British Rail has produced a swift evolution in how railways are run in the UK. It has started to shape tomorrow's railway and it has developed an approach which will aim to ensure that the customer is on the receiving end of a service which is consistently excellent.

7

Airline Performance as Rated by Frequent Passengers

'For my part, I travel not to go anywhere, but to go. I travel for travel's sake. The great affair is to move.'
Travels with a Donkey
Robert Louis Stevenson

CAROLYN EVANS, Operations Manager, International Airline Passengers Association.

Most readers will be aware of having seen airlines advertise themselves as having received an award for the best airline of such and such a year. Some may well have reflected on the fact that the number of awards seems to exceed what one might have expected: the disparity is due to the number of organisations or journals claiming the authority to act as judge. The editor was therefore confronted with something of a dilemma as to which agency to approach for a contribution. As IAPA bases its ratings on the assessments of those who find themselves travelling extensively, it seemed entirely reasonable to draw on that experience, for this particular group has long since lost interest in the 'excitement' of flying and concentrates its evaluations on the quality of service provided. Its assessments are secured annually and, because the IAPA membership is worldwide, in what follows results are tabulated separately for the British respondents.

Prior to joining IAPA, Carolyn Evans spent six years with the Aircraft Owners and Pilots Association where she was involved on consultative and technical committees covering airspace legislation in connection with the production and operation of light aircraft worldwide. This experience, coupled with another six years in the travel and tour operating industry, has equipped her for work with international travellers. Her limited leisure time is also directed skywards. She holds a private pilot's licence and competes regularly, sometimes successfully, in British and European air races and is currently attempting to master the art of aerobatics.

* * *

IAPA—History and Background

IAPA—the International Airline Passengers Association—was the first body set up to represent and protect the interests of frequent travellers throughout the world. The association has grown dramatically since its first office opened in New York in 1960. By 1970 membership exceeded 15,000 and by 1975 had grown to 25,000. Today it boasts more than 100,000 members in over 175 countries. For an annual fee members receive flight insurance, protection against loss of luggage, discounts while travelling and the appeal of belonging to an association whose interests coincide with those of other frequent airline passengers. IAPA's goals have consistently been to provide air travellers with safety, convenience, comfort and economy in their travels. A London office was opened in 1977 to help European travellers and those visiting the continent. This was followed by the opening of offices in Hong Kong in 1982 and Panama City, Rotterdam and Berlin in 1983.

The current direct benefits provided for members include:

- Preferential rates and services from top quality hotels and car rental companies worldwide.

- Representation of members' interests to airlines, aviation organisations and governments on matters concerning the safety, comfort and financial fair treatment of the airline passenger.

- Highly specialised insurance programmes.

- A lost luggage and property retrieval system which involves members' luggage being identified by a numbered luggage label. In the event of loss, a search and retrieval programme is initiated by trained IAPA personnel. This device also helps eliminate those burglaries which originate with a reading of addresses on normal luggage labels of departing holiday-makers.

- Regular information in the form of a bi-monthly newsletter and colour magazine.

- As a result of surveys conducted among members, airlines will, hopefully, strive to improve their standing and put right the deficiencies identified by travellers.

IAPA's policies reflect the views of its membership—these views themselves being established through membership surveys, from regular correspondence and from a number of regional advisory bodies composed of industrialists, politicians, aviation experts and other distinguished individuals, all of whom themselves are IAPA members. The Association is totally independent and has no ties with any airline, airport or any other organisation within the airline industry. It is funded entirely from income generated by its marketing services and membership subscription. The IAPA membership is drawn from a wide range of occupations. Membership surveys indicate that the majority of members are married men between the ages of 35 and 54. Typical IAPA members take an average of 42.5 flights per year, of which 35.6 are for business purposes.

IAPA's Areas of Consumer Involvement

IAPA increasingly finds itself involved in and consulted on a wide range of issues relating to air passenger safety and quality. Those with which IAPA has been actively involved during the past year include:

- EEC proposals to increase the flexibility of the European air transport system and its pricing policies. IAPA has met with EEC staff to discuss those aspects of direct relevance to consumers. While the association favours a gradual approach towards a competitive and fair air transport market in Europe, it is keen that free competition, as set out in the Treaty of Rome, is implemented within a realistic but specified time limit.

- The formation of a new passenger safety unit within the Canadian Civil Aviation Authority. IAPA has helped formulate the framework of this.

- The increase in US Federal Aviation Agency inspection staff to pre-1981 levels. IAPA has told the aviation sub-committee of the US Congress that the large number of new regional airlines combined with the cost economies made by all carriers requires increased vigilance over maintenance procedures.

- New Federal Aviation Agency regulations on the quality of life jackets carried on aircraft follow pressure by IAPA and the National Transportation Safety Board.

- Regular discussions with the newly instituted International Air Transport Association (IATA). IAPA is a founder member of this consumer contact group and IAPA's intention is to press consistently for increased passenger safety and comfort as well as the introduction of pricing systems which are fairer to frequent travellers.

- IAPA has joined the International Federation of Airline Pilots Associations in opposing the early introduction of twin-engine passenger aircraft over large areas of water or desert. IAPA believes that the safety and technical aspects of such operations have not yet been fully explored.

IAPA Survey Results

Once every two years the whole IAPA membership is sent a questionnaire in which its evaluation of airlines is solicited.

19,000 members returned the survey questionnaire in 1985. Of the 9,072 replies from members outside North America, 2,003 respondents were British. In what follows, some of the more interesting results from this 1985 survey are tabulated. Unless an indication to the contrary is shown alongside the table, the results presented are based on the total responses.

Table 7.1   *Reactions to a Ban on Cigarette Smoking in Aircraft*

	On flight of less than two hours %	On flights of two hours or more %
Strongly in favour	45.4	33.5
Somewhat in favour	12.5	17.9
Makes no difference	21.1	17.9
Somewhat opposed	6.9	7.5
Strongly opposed	14.0	23.3

Table 7.2   *The Ten Airlines Most Frequently Flown by UK Members over the Previous Two Years (%)*

1.	British Airways	95.7
2.	British Caledonian Airways	56.9
3.	Air France	53.7
4.	KLM—Royal Dutch Airlines	49.8
5.	Lufthansa	48.6
6.	Swissair	42.0
7.	Pan Am	40.3
8.	TWA	33.6
9.	British Midland Airways	32.6
10.	SAS—Scandinavian Airlines	31.2

Table 7.3   *The Ten Airlines Most Frequently Flown by International Members over the Previous Two Years (%)*

1.	British Airways	73.9
2.	Lufthansa	53.4
3.	Air France	51.8
4.	Swissair	51.6
5.	KLM—Royal Dutch Airlines	47.7
6.	Pan Am	45.1
7.	Eastern	37.6
8.	Alitalia	32.9
9.	TWA	32.2
10.	SAS—Scandinavian Airlines	32.0

Table 7.4   *The Six Airlines Most Preferred by IAPA Members**

International Members (%)		UK Members (%)	
1. Swissair	40.1	British Airways	48.2
2. Lufthansa	27.5	Swissair	29.0
3. Singapore Airlines	26.4	British Caledonian Airways	26.0
4. British Airways	21.8	Singapore Airlines	20.7
5. KLM—Royal Dutch		KLM—Royal Dutch	
Airlines	20.4	Airlines	18.8
6. Cathay Pacific Airways	16.2	Lufthansa	17.7

*Members could nominate up to four airlines.

Table 7.5   *Airlines Judged to Provide Best In-Flight Service**

International Members(%) Top 10		UK Members (%) Top 5	
1. Swissair	37.9	British Airways	38.4
2. Lufthansa	25.0	Swissair	28.3
3. Singapore Airlines	25.0	British Caledonian Airways	26.4
4. British Airways	18.9	Singapore Airlines	20.2
5. KLM—Royal Dutch		Cathay Pacific Airways	17.3
Airlines	17.2		
6. Cathay Pacific Airways	16.1		
7. SAS—Scandinavian			
Airlines	15.4		
8. Air France	10.6		
9. Thai Airways			
International	10.6		
10. British Caledonian			
Airways	10.5		

*Members were allowed to nominate up to four airlines.

Table 7.6   *Airlines Judged to Provide the Best Ground Service**

International Members (%) Top 10		UK Members (%) Top 5	
1. Swissair	32.7	British Airways	37.7
2. Lufthansa	25.3	Swissair	21.0
3. KLM—Royal Dutch		British Caledonian Airways	20.3
Airlines	19.5		
4. British Airways	18.2	KLM—Royal Dutch	
		Airlines	19.3
5. Singapore Airlines	17.0	Lufthansa	16.2
6. SAS—Scandinavian			
Airlines	13.4		
7. Cathay Pacific Airways	9.4		
8. British Caledonian			
Airways	8.0		
9. TWA	7.9		
10. Pan Am	7.2		

*Members were allowed to nominate up to four airlines.

Table 7.7   *Factors Judged to be Most Important when Choosing an Airline**

	Length of flight					
	Under 2 hours		2-5 hours		Over 5 hours	
	%	Rank	%	Rank	%	Rank
Convenient schedule	67.8	1	59.9	1	44.2	1
Frequency of flights	33.8	2	13.3	11	6.5	11
On-time performance	30.7	3	22.0	4	16.1	10
Past experience	27.8	4	28.4	3	29.5	3
Low fares	18.0	5	19.1	6	22.0	6
Safety record	17.1	6	18.7	7	22.3	5
Attitude of personnel	16.8	7	21.4	5	23.6	4
Quality of in-flight service	15.7	8	29.5	2	38.5	2
Aircraft type	10.4	9	14.2	9	21.1	7
Availability of Business Class	7.8	10	14.1	10	16.2	9
Quality of ground service	6.8	11	5.8	12	4.8	13
National flag carrier	6.6	12	4.9	13	5.3	12
Quality of food and drinks	6.5	13	15.1	8	20.5	8
Frequent Flyers Programme	3.2	14	3.8	14	4.3	14
Others	1.0	15	0.9	15	1.1	15

*Members could nominate up to three factors.

Table 7.8 *Class Flown Most Often by International Members*

	Today (%)	Two years ago (%)
First Class	12.6	15.1
Business Class	40.9	24.8
Economy (full fare)	30.8	45.1
Discount	15.1	14.1
Holiday Charter	0.5	0.8

Table 7.9 *Airports Flown Into in Past Two Years by IAPA Members*

International Members (%)		UK Members (%)	
1. London (Heathrow)	77.9	London (Heathrow)	96.7
2. Amsterdam	53.0	London (Gatwick)	76.5
3. New York (Kennedy)	52.5	Amsterdam	60.8
4. Paris (De Gaulle)	52.2	Paris (De Gaulle)	58.2
5. Frankfurt	51.6	Frankfurt	44.3

Table 7.10 *Airports Liked Most by IAPA Members**

International Members (%)		UK Members (%)	
1. Amsterdam	20.6	Amsterdam	25.7
2. Singapore	14.5	London (Heathrow)	17.0
3. Zurich	9.5	Singapore	11.6
4. Frankfurt	7.8	London (Gatwick)	10.5
5. London (Heathrow)	7.8	Zurich	4.7
6. Paris (De Gaulle)	5.6	Frankfurt	3.8

*Members could nominate only one airport.

Table 7.11 *Airport Services and Facilities Deemed to be Most Important by International Members' Evaluations of Airports**

Feature	Percentage of times that feature was mentioned
Quick baggage claim	63.1
Quick and easy check-in	44.1
Rapid customs clearance	40.6
Ease of changing planes	31.1
Short walking distance	27.6
Comfortable waiting areas/lounges	20.5
Jetways (loading bridges)	14.1
Good security	11.6
Cleanliness	11.3
Moving walkways	10.9
International signs/directions/information	6.2
Duty-free shops	5.9
Availability of ground transportation	5.2
Frequent transportation between terminals	3.2
Good restaurants	2.8
Close-in parking	2.6
Frequently placed schedule monitors	2.6
News-stands	0.6
Other	0.9

*Members could nominate up to three factors.

Table 7.12 *The Factors That Members Feel are Important in Choosing a Hotel (%)*

Location	89.5
Past experience	71.5
IAPA Discount	33.1
Low price	23.4
Special services/amenities	22.3
Airport shuttle availability	15.2
Corporate rate	14.6
Executive floor/suites available	5.2
Choice of smoking/non-smoking accommodation	4.1
Frequent Flyer Programme tie-in	2.6
Meeting/convention facilities	2.6
Other	8.0

*Members were invited to nominate up to three factors.

Table 7.13 *Favourite Hotel Chains of International Members (%)**

Inter-Continental	16.7
Hyatt/Hyatt Regency	12.8
Hilton	12.2
Sheraton	10.5
Holiday Inns	10.4
Others	37.4

*Only one hotel chain could be nominated.

Table 7.14 *The Factors Judged to be Most Important in Choosing a Car Rental Company*

On-airport location	65.8
Low price	44.2
Condition of cars	39.9
IAPA discount	38.4
Fast pick-up and delivery service	29.4
Types of cars available	21.8
Express check-in/check-out	20.5
Guaranteed reservations	12.9
Courteous service	11.5
Corporate rate availability	9.0
Off-airport location	2.9
Frequent Renter Programmes	1.2
Other	1.6

*Members were invited to nominate three factors.

Table 7.15 *Car Rental Agencies Judged to Provide the Best Overall Service (%)**

Avis	42.4
Hertz	31.3
Budget	7.9
Europcar	7.5
National	5.0
Others	5.9

*Only a single car rental agency could be nominated.

Table 7.16   *Aircraft Manufacturer Judged to Produce the Best Commercial*
Aircraft (%)*

	International members	UK members	French members	German members
Airbus Industries	16.6	15.4	45.5	47.8
Boeing	68.4	67.9	47.2	44.9
British Aerospace	2.3	6.0	0.4	0.4
Lockheed	4.4	6.0	0.9	1.8
McDonnell Douglas	7.9	4.3	4.3	4.8
Other	0.5	0.3	1.7	0.4

*Only one aircraft manufacturer could be nominated.

8

Quality in British Airways

'The habit of courtesy, when once acquired, is almost impossible to get rid of.'

Solomon in All His Glory
Robert Lynd

BRIAN HAMILL, Quality Assurance Manager and **ROGER DAVIES,** Manager, Operational Performance, British Airways.

In the run-up to the privatisation of the airline, BA has achieved a quite remarkable increase in productivity which has brought about a dramatic turnaround in the profit and loss picture. Running in parallel with this has been an equally substantial effort aimed at bringing about just as big a revolution in customer service. A major element of this has been the 'Putting the Customer First' campaign and the programme labelled 'A Day in the Life' which is attended by all BA staff and which is intended to improve their awareness and understanding of the business. While 'Fly the Flag' might well be a message appealing to British travellers, it is apparent that no airline is going to succeed commercially with just that domestic market. With so many flights available on most routes, what determines whether a passenger elects to book with a particular airline must to a large extent depend upon how he or she was treated on previous occasions or how he or she expects to be treated on the basis of perceptions or recommendations.

Brian Hamill joined BA's management training programme in 1977, and a variety of operation attachments overseas were followed by a planning role in the Far East network. After two years co-ordinating the company's marketing activities in Australasia he was appointed Quality Assurance Manager in 1985. In that role he interfaces with all customer contact areas throughout the organisation working with their management teams to review and improve service standards constantly.

Roger Davies joined BA in 1979 after experience in consulting. He has supervised many projects aimed at bringing about greater airline efficiency and many of these have involved staff participation to develop better procedures and improved levels of service. He was instrumental in launching the 'Putting the Customer First' campaign. Only recently appointed to his present post, he is actively involved in sponsoring quality control processes across the airline and ensuring that the associated reporting mechanisms are effective.

★ ★ ★

Putting the customer first has become a way of life for all of us in British Airways. If we do not clearly and regularly establish the needs of our current and potential customers we will not be providing a compctitive seivice. If we do succeed in meeting their expectations, they will stay with us, come back for more and encourage their friends and colleagues to fly with us.

The cornerstone of the *Customer First* campaign which the Chief Executive, Colin Marshall, launched in 1983, was detailed research into what our customers expect in terms of personal service. We then established monitoring mechanisms which continue to tell us what the customers expect, and how well we are doing against these expectations. Our research identified the vital contribution made by customer contact staff in developing goodwill with our customers. It also revealed just how difficult it is to recover from a bad reputation. In order to generate the former rather than the latter, each employee needs to understand what his or her contribution can be.

In what follows we explain the background thinking by which we have drawn up guidelines for personal service and how we relate these guidelines to activities across the whole passenger handling process. From booking to disembarkation and beyond it the flight generates either a compliment or a complaint.

Background Research for the 'Customer First' Campaign

Colin Marshall's arrival as Chief Executive in 1983 triggered off a series of initiatives which led to the total transformation of British Airways' attitude to the quality of the service it delivers. Greater awareness of customer needs was required and to respond we needed staff on our side.

Market research covering both customers and staff formed the starting point for a fully integrated campaign to improve standards of service. An extensive survey amongst air travellers covered those flying on both British Airways and other airlines. This survey provided feedback on customer expectations, both on the ground and in the air. The research focused on areas where customers' goodwill, and hence their business, could be generated. It was addressed to the quality of our services.

How, though, do you set about measuring quality? The term can obviously be applied more readily to a tangible product than to a service. Defining quality as conformance to requirements, we must then specify whose requirements are to be met. In research terms, for example, respondents can be asked to rate the 'overall quality' of a meal, but the same phrase is not appropriate to cabin service for which an assessment of 'overall satisfaction' is needed.

A number of dimensions can be identified which contribute to customer satisfaction. Whereas a meal might be described in terms of texture, flavour and presentation, cabin service is more readily rated by staff attitudes such as courtesy, smiles and friendly attention. Passengers were asked about their typical experiences with all airlines and the best and worst incidents they could recall. The research showed that interpersonal staff factors were twice as important in determining satisfaction as operational aspects of the flight.

Gaining positive goodwill can spring from many circumstances. Turning difficulties to advantage, showing special concern and other anxiety-reducing actions were highlighted. Attitude research amongst our employees revealed the need for a campaign to transform their appreciation of the part they could play individually in contributing to customer satisfaction by more empathetic service. Quality in this context relates to the personalising of the service to meet the needs of each particular customer. The 'Customer First' campaign was designed to enhance the quality of the services we offered while at the same time restoring staff morale recognising, of course, the inter-relationship between the two.

The campaign was aimed at refocusing the airline's attention on the marketplace. It was to encourage staff to act with spontaneity and strengthen management's resolve to involve the staff in implementing customer service improvements. The four main features of the campaign were an Integrated Briefing and Training Programme, the introduction of Customer First Teams, a series of Management Workshops and Regular Monitoring and Feedback.

Integrated Briefing and Training Programmes

The launch incorporated a variety of integrated activities including a 2-day seminar entitled *Putting People First*—a personal development course looking at such aspects as handling feelings, understanding and coping with stress, and being assertive. This programme continued throughout 1984, initially covering our 21,000 customer contact staff. From the autumn, it was extended to embrace all non-customer contact staff. Great emphasis has been placed on teamwork and on an appreciation of the contribution that each individual and each role make towards the success of the airline as a whole.

Run by Time Manager International, the programme has been conducted both in London and overseas. Staff were brought together from the various disciplines within the airline for what proved to be an effective training technique. Staff particularly enjoyed and greatly benefited from talking through the problems of other areas, between working sessions, with colleagues who were previously only a name at the end of the telephone.

In parallel with these sessions for staff, a further programme was undertaken to reinforce the corporate objectives through improvements in management style. The airline has a long history of effective participation and this programme, which was built on this past experience, was intended to develop the areas of visible management presence on the shop floor. It included effective communications training to improve performance and the use of task forces to implement practical solutions. This style change was supported by a series of week-long small group management training courses, attended by all managers selected from differing locations and disciplines.

The process of identifying opportunities for further progress is continuous. The phase which commenced in November 1985 introduced a new corporate programme named *A Day in the Life*. This programme, which will be undertaken by all airline staff, examines the various ways in which British Airways goes about its business. For each event, staff attend a series of theme presentations to learn about many different parts of the company. Our philosophy is that staff who have a greater awareness and understanding of the business should be able to provide high professional standards of customer service and also be in a strong position to act as ambassadors for the airline. Messages delivered at the original 'Putting People First' courses are reinforced and the concept of teamwork at British Airways is encouraged. The programme also provides a powerful communication vehicle for the company during a very important period in its development. By the end of 1986, it is hoped that every staff member will have attended 'A Day in the Life'.

Customer First Teams as the Mainspring for Customer Service Improvement

Customer First teams constitute another major plank of the campaign. The early teams were formed in November 1983, with the help and guidance of PA Management Consultants. The teams consist of staff volunteers charged with improving customer service within their own work areas. Team leaders receive formal training. Each team consists of around ten members. Customer First teams provide a forum for staff creativity. Teams active in the UK and overseas meet together to investigate and recommend customer service improvements. Progress has been rapid, and many excellent suggestions have been fully researched and presented to management for consideration and subsequent implementation. The benefits are twofold. Customers perceive service improvements, both on the ground and in the air, which are tailor-made to suit their requirements. Staff enjoy participating in the improvement process. Not only do staff see gains for British Airways and its customers but they also experience personal development from their working sessions.

With no specific physical product, a service industry needs to modify the grist of its *Quality Circle* mill. We have done this by providing a substantial programme of customer surveys which feed back to the service producers detailed measures of customer perception and consistency with which our services are delivered. The Customer First teams show how adaptable quality circles can be. The latter were introduced as a deliberate instrument of managerial policy, both to stimulate the rebirth of the airline as a commercial organisation, and as an antidote to low staff morale after the setbacks of recent years. They are a central part of the campaign and, despite initial scepticism, quality circles found ready support among staff when they were invited to form Customer First teams.

There was careful preparation. Volunteer team leaders receive training in the skills of running a meeting and helping the team to identify, analyse and propose solutions to problems. Membership of the teams is voluntary, and anyone can leave or apply to join at any time. Team membership tends to rotate, with new people coming in as projects change. Indeed, there are waiting lists in many areas. Some teams have now been in existence for two years. There is no forcing, and a team will be set up only where a joint commitment of staff and local management seems likely to ensure success. Initially, Customer First teams were set up in areas of direct customer contact, but they are now spreading into areas such as engineering, catering and ramp services. There are now approximately 145 teams in existence in the UK and overseas. Ideas cover all those parts of our business where we are in contact with customers. Two examples which illustrate the range of improvements are:

- An enhanced *Young Flyers* service that takes care of unaccompanied children in improved facilities, providing greater choice of meals and generally tailoring the service to meet their specific needs.
- More interesting and informative inflight announcements.

Whereas a quality circle chooses its own subjects of investigation in its own work area, excepting only pay, terms of employment and personalities, a Customer First team is charged with the objective of improving service to the customer. In practice, however, the difference is often more apparent than real, since what affects the work area can also affect the customer, directly or indirectly, and the Customer First team can select its own priorities and avenues of approach to a subject. The difference is of orientation and priority, rather than of kind.

Role of Management Workshops

Another difference between a more traditional quality circle and a Customer First team approach is the way in which the findings of Customer First teams are fed to management workshops. These have been set up in all major customer contact departments of British Airways. In most companies quality circles report to their management only when they have a solution, but at British Airways leaders of the team are invited to sit in on regular management workshops to ensure that there is a genuine two-way flow of information. On occasion, the whole of a management workshop session is given over to presentations by Customer First teams. The structure is designed to convince everyone of the commitment of the organisation as a whole. That commitment begins, as always, at the top. Putting the customer first has Colin Marshall's continued, constant and enthusiastic backing. It is one mechanism for achieving the corporate goal of becoming the world's best airline.

Management workshops are the local driving force of the campaign. Their role is important in communicating what is happening at the centre to each of the teams in that area of the company. They are also involved in ascertaining local standards and writing them up. Various initiatives have been pursued which have involved the interpretation of data against these standards, as for example: sampling individual performance within the reservations function and encouraging supervisors to assess the 'warmth' of service provided by check-in staff.

Measures of both technical performance and personal warmth are needed. We refer below to some of the ways in which such data are collected. It may have been adequate in the past to understand technical standards alone, but in today's competitive environment, an understanding of how to influence each staff member's relationship with the customer is crucial. Because the credibility of the management workshop in progressing ideas initiated by Customer First teams is so vitally important, we insist that:

- all staff must feel that the management means business
- the teams must feel involved in defining and meeting customer needs
- their performance must be measured against standards
- their complaints and suggestions must be followed up

Team members feel that their work is 'for real'. Staff enjoy being involved in the decision-making process and being given the opportunity for personal development. There is a danger of creating cynicism, though, if the enthusiasm of the team is not reflected by management's actions. Team members must be convinced that implementation will follow their recommendations. With each team likely to produce around six ideas for customer service improvements annually, the management workshops have an important and demanding role to fulfill. Many may not come to fruition, but already around 1,000 improvement ideas have been implemented as a result of the work of the Customer First teams.

Outreach to Our Customers

In order to gauge more 'accurately' customer perceptions of the service British Airways provides, extensive monitoring is now a fundamental part of quality assurance. Each quarter, 1,100 customer interviews are carried out with passengers arriving and departing at our main Heathrow base. Further interviews are carried out at Gatwick, Manchester, Glasgow and Birmingham, all the results being fed back into the management workshops for action. An important characteristic of these surveys is that they relate to both 'hard' and 'soft' data. We have made use of the initial research on which the campaign was founded to classify the type of data and to reflect the actual words which passengers used to describe aspects of the service quality. The quarterly survey covers each aspect of the airline's contact with passengers. We monitor particularly the perceived attitudes of the staff they encountered, whether they were addressed by name, and their overall satisfaction with the service received.

We also ask what aspects of the service are likely to influence passengers' future decisions to fly with us and how they were assisted if they had special requests or experienced difficult circumstances. Such surveys are backed up with more qualitative enquiries, often involving group discussions, in which we can test out service innovations which have yet to be introduced. The discipline of subjecting products and services to this regular scrutiny is essential in our striving for excellence. It provides a basis for a range of data from quantitative measures about travel habits to much softer indications of how happy we make our customers. The data form an immediate feedback to the Customer First workshops. Each workshop has now spent some time writing a service specification for distribution to staff based on customer research feedback. This specification is divided into customer expectations, and how staff can satisfy those expectations.

These specifications form an integral part of staff training programmes and performance appraisal. For the first time, staff have their
own copy of service standards based on customer input. Training
programmes have been amended to reflect these criteria, and staff
assessments will be based on their effectiveness to fulfil expectations.
The onus is on local management and supervision to have effective
quality control mechanisms in place in each area.

Market research will continue to play an essential part in the
campaign. For example, customers interviewed on arrival and
departure in London are questioned about their satisfaction with
service standards both on the ground and in the air. These remarks
are passed on to workshops and Customer First teams each quarter in
order that strengths and weaknesses can be identified and new
service improvement initiatives introduced. This information is
invaluable for training departments which can incorporate into their
courses the information on service elicited from our customers. In
addition, a 'quick-fire' report system allows British Airways to pick
up extremes of customer service and take any necessary action
quickly. It is essential that messages from all parts of the campaign
are carried through with consistency to other training activities. All
training programmes are being reviewed in terms of method and
content, and in particular the balance between classroom and on-site
coaching by supervisors is likely to be modified.

Monitoring Within the Organisation

A key function in the new organisation established by Colin Marshall
was Marketplace Performance, which was deemed sufficiently
important to warrant its own director. It provides a 'conscience' to the
airline, ensuring that it adheres to its mission. A major preoccupation
of this department is the level of performance of the services British
Airways delivers matched against its customers' expectations. Performance data are routinely monitored against agreed standards.

Recently, the activities of our Quality Assurance unit have been
increasingly focused on defining detailed customer service standards
and developing quality control mechanisms by which we can
measure our local performance against customer expectation. The
work started in the big UK customer contact areas. However, it is just
as vital to set standards and measure performance away from home
base as this forms an important ingredient in the total customer
experience. A service Quality Audit has been developed to meet the
needs of overseas stations. This recognises local differences and
difficulties but, despite local variations, it does not compromise on

the key areas of customer service on which all activities must deliver consistently well. Responsibility for auditing quality clearly lies in the hands of those with local marketing responsibility—namely, the Area or Country Manager. Similarly, the management teams at the airport, in sales outlets and in reservations units, must assure themselves that they provide an effective contribution to the corporate quality effort. Achievement of quality can only be a line management responsibility.

It would be inappropriate to demand instant responses to the Quality Audit on the basis of impossible corporate standards. Local managers are asked to define local standards, but these must be challenging and must reflect customer expectations and competitor performance. This process also enables managers to decide appropriate monitoring mechanisms, sampling approach and data collection methods. Corporate staff, where appropriate, will provide whatever help is needed to review current approaches and set up new processes. We will soon be able to assess results. From these we will generate robust quality reporting mechanisms which can then feed data and views into the central monitoring data provided by Marketplace Performance. This is not a search for massive amounts of data—rather, we need just sufficient to have a continuously revealing dipstick into the quality of our worldwide service.

Many features of how adequately the quality of our services meets customer expectations can be measured more or less precisely by setting targets for performance. These are validated through direct contact with samples of passengers, cargo agents, tour operators, etc. Our ongoing activities can be and are assessed against these standards. In each area of activity there are relevant measures, many of them traditionally monitored by all airlines. The quality improvement drive takes discrepancies between target and achievement as indicators of malaise. Repeated shortfalls require perceptive action.

The range of measures for which hard data may be collected is illustrated by the following points:

(a) On first contact with passengers at a sales shop—
   • acceptable maximum waiting times
   • evidence of out-of-date sales material
   • comfort of the environment
(b) When telephoning to make a reservation—
   • speed of answer
   • additional facilities offered
(c) At airport check-in—
   • number of counters open
   • queuing times
   • use of passenger's name

(d) During the flight—
  • availability of offered amenities
  • speed with which calls are answered
  • cleanliness
(e) On arrival at destination—
  • adequacy of announcements
  • transfer arrangements from aircraft to terminal
  • delay in retrieving baggage

Clearly, these measures need to be supplemented by softer data which relate to the adequacy of the relationship established between staff and passenger. Supervisors have a key role to play here in the sampling of transactions. They look for warmth, eye contact, readiness to provide unprompted assistance, and so on. It is, however, through the communication to staff of what standards are expected that the quality of service can be enhanced. The whole Customer First programme is designed to establish the basic recognition amongst our employees as a whole that their individual commitment to the integrity of requirements is what makes the airline prosper.

The Opportunities Provided by Complaints

Customers complain to us for a variety of reasons. Regaining their goodwill must be our ultimate aim. Our reply needs to be a sympathetic response which adequately covers the points of criticism and contains a sincere apology. Similarly, our contractual obligations must be observed within a friendly response. We know the importance of staff dealing well with extreme situations. Each complaint offers an opportunity to retrieve that customer's loyalty. Although the passengers who take the trouble to write in may be biased in their view of our services, we ignore their pointers to service deficiencies at our peril. Customers expect action to redress the problems they have experienced and to put things right for the future. It is now recognised that these complaints are a crucial source of information. At British Airways, systematic analysis of the letters received is undertaken to highlight areas requiring attention. We record both complaints and compliments and an automated filing system is available to provide descriptions which will elaborate some of these 'hot spots' to task forces set up to rectify such weaknesses.

One of the conundrums of quality measurement in service industries is that customers' expectations rise with the improvements made in services. In some cases the level of complaint can be deceptive. Some improvements may generate greater numbers of complaint letters because the airline has shown itself to be reacting and thus 'worth' complaining to! Our advertising also contributes to this somewhat paradoxical situation. The *Supercare* campaign, for example, encourages raised expectations by reflecting externally what has been happening within the organisation. Even the publication of this chapter is bound to add to the pool of prospective correspondents!

Benefits of a Quality-Based Approach

Our experience demonstrates that showing the organisation cares about its customers is worthwhile. In fact, without this concern, the airline would miss out on major opportunities and eventually fail. In our marketplace, we need to be able to react quickly to developments and to changing customer requirements. If trends in taste are not properly identified, we cannot improve our services to match customer needs. The approach we have developed helps create a climate in which the individual's contribution is sought and recognised. Greater motivation results and there is more job satisfaction and a greater understanding of the rationale for change. But this is not simple to achieve. We not only have a need to inform staff but we also have to seek their involvement. Only if our employees use a caring, human approach can they hope to defuse a difficult confrontation, for example. The corporate skill lies in maintaining motivation through a proactive association with the company's success.

Overriding all the activities has been a highly effective communication programme, pursued locally through special management bulletins and centrally through in-house magazines. Four times a year, the Quality Assurance unit produces a newsletter which highlights the work of Customer First teams and affords recognition of valuable contributions to improve our service quality. The message of 'Customer First' has been consistently conveyed to staff, and our current 'Day in the Life' sessions continue the theme of initial understanding and support through teamwork. Management backing and commitment to action, which are essential ingredients for the success of this quality initiative, have been consistently strong from the Chief Executive downwards. The process of identifying opportunities for further progress is continuous.

The campaign now embraces both customer contact and non-customer contact staff. Our aim is that all staff within the company will become actively involved and committed to help us realise the corporate objective of improving customer service. To quote our campaign slogan: 'Putting our Customers First—if we don't, someone else will'.

HEALTH

9

What the Patient Thinks

'I think it frets the saints in heaven to see how many
desolate creatures on the earth have learnt the simple
dues of fellowship and social comfort in a hospital.'

Aurora Leigh,
Elizabeth Barrett Browning

DR. ANDY THOMPSON, University of Wales Institute of
Science and Technology.

This study is the one alluded to in the Introduction which was
originally conceived out of the editor's own experience as an outpatient. The idea of determining just what were the concerns of NHS
customers was taken up by two army officers who were pursuing a
postgraduate course. Their opening foray did indeed reveal what were
considered to be the important issues and Andy then proceeded to
develop that effort along more rigorous lines. The end product is a
detailed 32-page questionnaire which most observers inherently feel
might be too long. In fact, the response rate is typically around 50 per
cent and this is undoubtedly attributable to the considerable effort which
went into ensuring that respondents would find both the content and
style user-friendly. Hospital administrators can now discover just how
their patients respond as against an expanding national sample.

Since first working on this project for three years after graduating from
UMIST in 1974, Andy has held a number of research posts which have
involved him in studying regional employment patterns with the North
West Industry Research Unit at Manchester University's geography
department and, latterly, the effects of cuts in public expenditure on
London's health services with the Greater London Association of
Community Health Councils. Since 1985 he has held a lectureship at
UWIST, where he continues to develop the methodology described
below.

★ ★ ★

What Does the NHS Think Patients Think?

The commonly held view among administrators and practitioners in the NHS seems to be that their patients are well satisfied with the services they receive. This is not to say that they believe the quality of care is as high as they would like, or that improvements are not possible. How is it that this view prevails in a system which, until recently, lacked any mechanism for determining patients' views?

Since 1948 the NHS has provided people in Britain with a system of health services which is dependent on needs rather than the ability to pay. Until recently, alternatives in the form of private insurance schemes were extremely limited, effectively making NHS services the only source of health care for the vast majority of people. It would be fallacious, therefore, to argue that satisfaction with hospital services has been shown by the willingness of people to continue to use the NHS.

The yardsticks have been of two types. First, there is the informal measure of opinion, which operates through feedback from patients in the form of letters of thanks, gifts, and deference to medical status. It would be difficult to quantify this form of opinion, but it obviously creates a climate of belief that the system is generally working to people's satisfaction. The second indicator of patients' views is the formal complaints system which enables someone to register an official complaint about his or her treatment in hospital. However, as a measure of opinion it is of dubious merit. Sufficient evidence exists to demonstrate that formal complaints procedures are more effectively used by certain population groups. More importantly, poor quality with some particular aspects of care does not exist in some absolute sense, but is likely to vary in degree. A formal complaint would probably indicate that a point has been reached where the level of quality is quite unacceptable to that individual, but this threshold will vary from person to person. An organisation should not wait for the system to deteriorate to that point. Rather, it should be concerned with identifying all potential causes for complaint before they happen, taking into account the variability of human tolerance.

1983 witnessed a radical change at the formal level in NHS thinking about the views of patients. An inquiry into the management of the service, chaired by the Chief Executive of Sainsbury PLC, recommended in its Report (DHSS 1983) that the NHS should become more aware of its reception by its users. What had previously been considered to be a rather tangential concern of the NHS was subsequently raised in status through the widespread appointment of Directors of Patient Services or Quality Assurance.

It is instructive to look at what had been happening in this regard prior to 1983. The seminal work is that of Abdellah and Levine (1957) in the USA, who wished to determine to what extent good nursing practice was being carried out. By asking patients some very specific questions about their current episode of care, they felt they would provide a clear and unbiased picture of mismatch between theory and practice. Almost 9,000 patients in 60 hospitals across six states were sampled on a single day and a parallel study of nearly 10,000 hospital staff identified differences in perception.

Early British attempts at evaluating patient satisfaction were those of McGhee (1961) and Cartwright (1964) whose studies covered 490 and 739 patients respectively, but the major thrust was that of Raphael (1967). Using unstructured interview schedules, she compared the responses from patients in different acute specialties in four similar, non-teaching general hospitals. Her study formed the precursor to the widely used King's Fund questionnaire (Raphael 1969). This was a written schedule covering 100 aspects of hospital care, to which a patient simply had to tick a response of 'YES' or 'NO'. This survey tool was taken up by several hospital authorities but, as Raphael (1974) tellingly noted, very few actually claimed to have introduced any fundamental changes as a result of the findings.

Many small-scale surveys were conducted at hospital level on particular aspects of the service, such as the food, the size and design of wards, communication between doctors and patients, etc. However, the next major reported study which recognised Raphael's exhortation to cover the whole period from pre-admission to post-discharge was that undertaken on behalf of the Royal Commission on the NHS (Gregory 1978).

Thus, although work on users' views of services has existed for several years, it is not until recently that the NHS has recognised the importance of routinely building this feature into its planning and analysis of services. Part of the problem was that the existing tools had failed to provide a standardised method of comparing hospitals, wards or specialties. Furthermore, the problem of actually dealing with the plethora of detail resulting from such studies has probably discouraged management from taking it on board. What is required, therefore, is a means whereby patients' opinions can be routinely collected and analysed. This should provide a broad view of their satisfaction with the major dimensions of care, supplemented by the detail necessary to enable action to be taken on identified deficiencies on specific issues.

How Can We Find Out What Patients Think?

At the outset it was decided that a questionnaire-based approach
would be pursued. The production of such a tool by the author
spanned a period of nearly three years, encompassing seven discrete
but cumulative phases of development. Each phase represented a
parallel attempt to produce questions that go to the heart of the issues
from the patient's perspective, and to evaluate the efficacy of the
method of sampling. The following brief discussion provides some
insight into the process of development, but the interested reader is
referred to Thompson (1983) for a fuller exposition.

To begin with it was necessary to discover what issues are of
concern to patients. It is important not to impose preconceived
notions based on professional values, since these may not accord
with the user's perspective. The most effective way of doing this is
through in-depth, unstructured interviews with people who are, or
have been, hospital inpatients. The first phase was undertaken by
Hayman and Spurrell (1975) who adopted this approach with 100
patients discharged within the previous two years. The contacts were
made by the 'cold-call' technique of knocking on doors and talking to
willing respondents, loosely divided into those from working class
and middle class areas. Through the non-directive approach of asking
people to talk generally about their stay in hospital, an idea is gained
about the important and unimportant aspects of care.

In the second phase the author went over the same ground again,
using the same cold-call sampling technique with a further 42
discharged patients, but this time the interviews were a little more
structured. People were encouraged to talk about the issues they
wanted to discuss. They were prompted on those aspects which they
had not touched on and probed further on those which required
deeper analysis. At the conclusion of this phase it had become clear
what were the aspects which concerned people and those which
appeared to be irrelevant.

The third phase was concerned with translating the interview
schedules and responses into their equivalent written form
endeavouring always to reduce the acknowledged drawbacks of
questionnaires. These are relatively low response rates, inability to
probe or explain further, and difficulties for those who have problems
in reading and comprehending written English.

Having produced an initial draft of a written questionnaire which
was structured into a chronological sequence of hospital experience,
the author next tested it on a large sample of discharged patients.
Some 10,000 households around Britain were contacted through
leaflets, to produce a sample of patients who would participate in this

exercise. This provided a valuable group of 334 self-selected individuals, who had been discharged from hospital within the previous two years, on whom the wording and structure of the questions could be tested.

The essence of the approach was to make the questions colloquial and as specific as possible in order that they would evoke a response. Questions which produced a high proportion of replies of the 'Don't know' variety were deemed to be poor, since they clearly failed to generate an identification with the particular topic. An important methodological concern relates to the distribution of the responses to each question. Should the responses to a particular question bunch up at one end of the range of possible answers it is indicative of a poorly discriminating test. The technique employed to rectify this problem was to stretch the bunched set of responses until the point was found where roughly half the respondents lay on either side. An example may help to clarify this.

Suppose that patients were simply asked whether they considered the nurses responded quickly to their need for help at night. It could be almost guaranteed that the overwhelming majority of people would strongly agree with this. By shifting the balance of the response set to include an extreme statement, to the effect that every single nurse responded immediately to their need for help at night on every single occasion, some patients would now respond negatively. This does not mean that the respondents have been manipulated in their views; simply that the response sets have been manipulated to produce a more balanced pattern of replies. The three versions of the question on boredom illustrate this 'massaging' process:

Boredom	%
(a) I was thoroughly bored throughout most of my stay	13
I normally found something to occupy my time	66
There was never a dull moment in such a busy ward	21
(b) I was thoroughly bored throughout most of my stay	2
Occasionally I found things to do to relieve my boredom in the ward	11
Although I didn't have much to do in the ward, I wasn't particularly bored	31
I normally found something interesting to occupy my time	37
There was never a dull moment in such a lively ward	20
(c) I was quite bored during my stay in hospital	18
Although I didn't have much to do in the ward, I wasn't particularly bored	36
I normally found something interesting to occupy my time	31
There was never a dull moment in such a lively ward	14

The need to reshape the response sets to each question in line with this philosophy of response patterns demands considerable piloting with different samples. In phase five the sample was generated by the 'snowball' techniques from the respondents in the previous phase. They were asked to supply further names of recently discharged patients, including themselves if they wished. A further 160 people agreed to participate at this stage, and question revisions were tested out.

It now became increasingly important to test the emerging questionnaire on a more randomly selected sample, while at the same time continuing the question refinement. This penultimate stage also involved making a personal approach to patients who were awaiting discharge from a hospital bed. As it turned out, the problems associated with gaining access to such patients rendered it unworkable as a routine method. However, 64 patients from one hospital co-operated in developing the questionnaire one stage further, allowing added insights to be gained into the wording of the questions. A final revision of wording and structure resulted in a questionnaire which could be properly tested on a random sample of discharged patients. This final version was professionally printed as a 32-page document in A5 format; a one-page extract is shown opposite.

What Do Patients Think?

The power of the questionnaire is represented by its ability to discriminate between hospitals or groups of patients within a hospital so that real differences are highlighted. The following selection of questions is drawn from the original set of seven hospitals around England which participated in the seventh phase of development. The sample of discharged patients was randomly selected to produce equal numbers of female and male patients and equal proportions of general medical, general surgical, and traumatic and orthopaedic patients. There were also equal numbers of people in each of the four periods of time since discharge: 0–2 weeks, 3 months, 6 months and 1 year. All the tabulated figures are percentages for each of seven hospitals, along with that for the total of 1,357 individuals.

Information from a patient's own general practitioners or a hospital doctor prior to admission can help to make a patient feel that he or she is properly involved in the process of care. Table 9.1 reveals that, while two thirds of the sample felt well informed, wide variations occurred between hospitals. Emergency admissions have been excluded.

The way in which a person is admitted to a hospital can precondition their perceptions of the residential stage. Arriving at

18. FOOD

(a) Location

(i) Once up and about I had to eat either on the bed, or
immediately next to it ☐
Once out of bed, I had to eat at a communal table ☐
When I was fit enough to be out of bed, there were no
restrictions on where I could eat at mealtimes ☐

(ii) *I thought that these eating-place arrangements were too
restrictive.*

AGREE ☐
DISAGREE ☐

(b) Diet

(i) Were you asked by the staff when you arrived in the ward,
or beforehand, whether you were on any type of diet?

YES ☐
NO ☐

(ii) To the best of my knowledge, I was not meant to be on any
type of diet in hospital (Go to question 18c) ☐
My diet was very strictly controlled ☐
Occasionally I was given the wrong meal for my diet ☐
Rarely did I receive the correct meal for my diet ☐

(iii) What type of diet were you meant to be having?
Slimming diet ☐
Diabetic diet ☐
Religious or cultural diet ☐
Any other special medical diet ☐
(Tick more than one if applicable)

(iv) If the staff didn't ask you whether you were on a diet, did
you tell them?

YES ☐
NO ☐

(c) Menu

(i) The menu gave us a good choice from a wide selection of
dishes ☐
There was a reasonable choice of food on the menu ☐
On the whole there was little choice on the menu ☐
We were not given menus to choose from (Go to question
18d) ☐

(ii) We always received what we ordered from the menu ☐
It was very unusual not to receive what we ordered from the
menu ☐
In spite of the menu, what we actually received was sometimes
not what was ordered ☐
The menu was a waste of time, as we rarely, if ever, received
what we asked for ☐

(d) Variety

We tended to get the same sort of food day after day ☐
Although the food was fairly predictable it was reasonably
varied ☐
The food was always different and interesting ☐

Table 9.1

Prior to my admission to the hospital, the information I was given about the reason I was being admitted:	Hospital							Total
	A	B	C	D	E	F	G	
Left me very much in the dark	0	2	5	3	1	6	1	3
Was rather sketchy on many details	17	13	8	10	8	17	14	11
Gave a very full picture, although I would have appreciated a little more	8	20	21	16	18	23	23	20
Left no shadow of a doubt in my mind	75	66	67	71	73	55	62	67

hospital, which can often be a bewildering and frightening experience, can be made much smoother if someone is there to welcome you. Although half the patients rated this aspect highly, as can be seen from Table 9.2, there is clearly a wide difference between the situation in Hospital A and Hospital F.

Table 9.2

My first reaction to the hospital was a feeling of:	Hospital							Total
	A	B	C	D	E	F	G	
Being part of the furniture	2	2	2	2	2	3	1	2
Being just another patient	26	45	39	43	50	60	56	47
Being made very welcome	72	54	59	56	49	37	43	51

Once inside the ward, the patients' environment includes not only the physical conditions and facilities, but also personal relationships with staff and fellow patients. The decor of the ward (Table 9.3) would be expected to vary considerably between hospitals, particularly between the relatively new establishments, C and D, and the others. The actual differences, however, are quite startling.

Table 9.3 *Decor*

	Hospital							Total
	A	B	C	D	E	F	G	
Very pleasant and well decorated	40	34	66	76	41	22	25	46
In quite reasonable condition	51	50	32	22	53	66	55	46
Drab paintwork in need of redecoration	9	16	3	2	7	12	20	9

It is entirely reasonable for patients to be concerned with the hygiene in hospital, particularly in the bathroom and toilets, and it is disconcerting to reflect that this aspect of the service (Table 9.4) is *not* rated as highly satisfactory by one in three patients, overall. The figures for Hospital F speak for themselves, with one in five being extremely critical of the standards prevailing there.

Table 9.4 *Hygiene*

The level of cleanliness in the bathroom and the toilets:	Hospital							Total
	A	B	C	D	E	F	G	Total
Was such that they were very pleasant to use	66	58	89	84	55	34	65	65
Was quite good, although not of a particularly high standard	33	33	11	14	39	46	33	29
Was barely adequate, leaving considerable room for improvement	2	9	0	2	6	20	2	6

One of the aspects of hospital care that receives a lot of attention, and one about which people are usually unequivocal, is food. A more detailed discussion can be found in Moores and Thompson (1985). but the data in Table 9.5, which relate to the variety of food, offer a taste (sic) of the views of patients. The high satisfaction of patients in Hospital C contrasts sharply with that in A and F.

Table 9.5 *Variety of Food*

	Hospital							Total
	A	B	C	D	E	F	G	Total
We tended to get the same sort of food day after day	23	16	4	5	13	25	17	13
Although the food was fairly predictable it was reasonably varied	57	63	46	57	66	59	66	59
The food was always different and interesting	20	21	50	38	21	16	17	28

Although patients come into contact with a range of professional and ancillary staff, the strongest relationships are undoubtedly likely to be established with the nursing staff, given that they provide the continuous care for patients. The importance of having time to chat with patients is often in conflict with the pressures of work faced by nurses. Nonetheless, patients are sensitive to the importance placed on such activity by nurses, as revealed in Table 9.6. Similar responses are found in each hospital, with only slightly lower levels being experienced in Hospitals *A* and *F*.

Table 9.6 *Relationship With Nurses*

	Hospital							Total
	A	B	C	D	E	F	G	
The nurses seemed to go out of their way to chat with us whenever they could	24	33	33	29	30	19	31	29
The nurses seemed to find time for a chat with us at some time during the day	52	43	50	48	43	53	42	47
The nurses seemed too busy to spend much time with us, other than when they were actually doing something for us	21	19	10	18	25	23	23	20
For one reason or another the nurses spent little of their time on the ward talking to us	3	5	7	5	2	5	4	4

A more detailed discussion of the nursing aspects of care is to be found in Moores and Thompson (1986) and Thompson (1986).

With regard to the quality of medical care, an important consideration is the degree of confidence of patients in the ability of their doctors. As would be expected this is generally quite high (Table 9.7) but, even so, two out of every five patients were less than absolute in their confidence, with more than one in ten expressing some concern.

Table 9.7 *Confidence in Medical Staff*

	Hospital							Total
	A	B	C	D	E	F	G	
I had absolute confidence in everything the doctors did for me	57	63	61	61	60	53	59	59
Overall, my confidence in the doctors was quite high	37	27	27	29	29	33	32	30
My confidence in the doctors was not as high as I felt it should have been	3	8	10	10	9	11	9	9
I had no confidence in the doctors who treated me	3	3	2	1	2	4	1	2

A number of researchers have pointed to the importance of the communications processes between patients and staff (Ley and Spelman 1967; Byrne and Long 1977). In fact, Kinston (1983) believes that the role of communicating, which is a necessary precondition for patient-centred care, is increasingly being divorced from the skills, interest and time made available by doctors. Doctor-centred communication, where information is seen by the patient as a one-way process, was seen to exist for nearly two out of every five patients, with Hospital C exhibiting particularly poor standards, as shown in Table 9.8.

Table 9.8

Whenever the doctors had any instructions or information for me:	Hospital							Total
	A	B	C	D	E	F	G	
They always discussed it *with* me	74	61	55	68	65	63	65	63
They always talked *at* me about it	18	25	34	21	25	22	27	25
Someone else had the job of passing it on to me	8	13	11	11	11	15	8	11

Skeet (1971), in her revealing study of discharge from hospital, emphasised the lack of communication between patients and staff, as well as the poor links between hospital and community services. Lack of consideration of the notice required by patients to return home has been pointed out by Daniel (1975) as a common failing of hospitals. From Table 9.9 we see that one in four patients was dissatisfied with this aspect, but there were wide variations between the seven hospitals.

Table 9.9

When it was time for me to leave hospital I was given:	Hospital							Total
	A	B	C	D	E	F	G	
Much less warning than I would have liked	6	20	9	8	16	15	14	13
Hardly enough warning to inform friends or relatives	11	13	16	10	11	15	10	13
Plenty of advance warning	84	67	75	82	74	70	76	75

These few examples, which have been selected from nearly 300 tests of different aspects of hospital care, have served to demonstrate the high degree of specificity in the wording of questions and the power of the questions to discriminate between or within hospitals. In a sense the acid test of patient satisfaction is the attractiveness of the hospital for future possible treatment. On this global measure, Table 9.10 perhaps comes as no surprise, even from the brief insight gained from the above selection of questions.

Table 9.10

If for any reason I had to return to hospital, given the choice I would:	Hospital							Total
	A	B	C	D	E	F	G	
Be very happy to return to the same one	56	58	75	69	66	39	61	61
Not mind going back to the same one	34	33	23	28	30	41	37	32
Prefer to go somewhere else	10	9	2	3	4	21	3	7

There is, though, a danger of concluding that in some overall sense Hospital C is good and Hospital F is bad. Certainly, a look back at the components of care would indicate that on many aspects these hospitals do indeed represent extremes. However, as we saw in the question on communication (Table 9.8), Hospital C is not always highly rated *vis-à-vis* the other institutions. The problem arises when a single dimension is assumed to exist on which patients view quality of care. In fact, through the statistical technique of factor analysis, it was found that six independent dimensions are used by patients in determining their satisfaction. These are:

- Medical care and information
- Physical aspects and food
- Non-tangible environment
- Nursing care
- Quantity of food
- Visiting arrangements

Hospitals may receive a high rating on certain dimensions but be poorly rated on others. A single statement that Hospital X is perceived by patients to be good or bad is, therefore, meaningless, unless it applies to each and every index of satisfaction. In the case of Hospital C, it turned out that it was the highest rated of the seven participating institutions on the indices relating to physical aspects and the non-tangible environment, but was, in fact, accorded the lowest rating on medical care and information. Conversely, Hospital F was the lowest rated on physical aspects, non-tangible environment, and nursing care, but it secured the highest rating on visiting arrangements.

Conclusions

The importance of asking patients their views on the delivery of care is now recognised as being an essential part of the feedback for a hospital. Not only does it provide management with a measure of the quality of the process and output of the services for which it is responsible, but numerous research studies have identified the link between patient compliance and medical therapies. It is no longer acceptable to many people that their views are discounted on the grounds of being ill-informed. The Government has now formally recognised the importance of seeking the views of NHS users, and the need is for a measurement tool that will inform rather than submerge managers under a pile of data.

It has been demonstrated that it is possible to produce a tool that can effectively tease out the real concerns of patients in a meaningful and reliable way, thereby enabling comparisons to be made in a variety of settings. Not only does this allow inter-hospital comparisons to be made, but it also provides a monitoring tool to test the effect of a policy change on the same institution over time. Health Authorities increasingly commission surveys using the questionnaire and, at the time of writing, the data base of patients' views, against which the responses from a particular hospital can be compared, numbers well in excess of 3,000.

10

Medical Quality Assurance in Brighton Health Authority—Can American Translate into English?

'Physicians are like kings—They brook no contradictions.'

The Duchess of Malfi
John Webster

DAVID BOWDEN, District General Manager; **DR. GLEN WILLIAMS,** Director of Quality Assurance and District Medical Officer; and **GEOFF STEVENS,** CASPE Research Coordinator, Brighton Health Authority.

It is a fact of life that there has been far more activity directed towards assessing the quality of medical care in the United States than here in the United Kingdom. The reasons for this disparity are many and varied. The fact that the health care delivery systems in the two countries are so fundamentally different is one contributory factor, as is the associated difference in attitudes of the medical professionals involved. Brighton Health Authority has been to the fore in exploring the extent to which the best of American practice in this field can be translocated across the Atlantic.

David Bowden's commitment to Quality Assurance is well known and his appointment as the district's general manager, following the implementation of the proposals of the Griffiths enquiry, provided the opportunity to set up mechanisms for bringing over appropriate elements. In this he has been assisted by Dr. Williams who spent several years in Australia prior to two years in California where he worked in health planning and standard setting. Geoff Stevens joined the CASPE Research project in 1985 after six years lecturing in information systems and computing at Warwick University's Business School and, before that, nine years in computing, information services and planning in the NHS.

* * *

In one sense, Quality Assurance in medical care (QA) is well established in the NHS. All doctors have quality of patient care at heart, and over the years they have evolved informal systems of improving the standard of medical care by attending meetings, reviewing literature and simply attending to quality in carrying out their work. There has been some degree of national concern through confidential enquiries, training accreditation and other formalising initiatives by the professional colleges. The idea of widely formalising concern with quality is, however, a recent one. Why is this?

The present Government has made specific changes affecting the NHS in the last couple of years. The Griffiths Report (DHSS 1983) was associated with the replacement of a consensus team management in the NHS by a system in which increased devolution to the local level was matched by the appointment of District General Managers, some of whom have been recruited from outside the health service. Management budgeting is now being introduced by health authorities. These dramatic and potentially far-reaching management innovations by the Government have been coupled with more specific actions aimed at achieving greater value for money in the NHS. These initiatives have included, *inter alia*, publication of a centrally approved list of prescribed drugs, the Rayner 'value for money' audits, and the requirement that health authorities subject the 'hotel' aspects of their ancillary services to competition with the private sector through competitive tendering.

Patients are now being encouraged to behave more like consumers, and health authorities have set up senior posts to ensure that the public voice is more effective than had been found possible through Community Health Councils in the pre-1982 management structure. To a large extent this builds on broader changes in the way the public views the NHS and its professionals, notably doctors. The growth of private medicine is now clearly evident after many years of the NHS during which the impact had been marginal, and the public appears to be ever more demanding. From the media and in other ways, people are better informed about the capabilities of medical science, and more critical of the quality of the services they receive.

In this new climate, a belief has grown up that the NHS has something to learn from other industries, and from health systems in which the commercial element is stronger. Brighton Health Authority was determined to be at the forefront of the practical development of QA and, as part of an exchange scheme set up between Brighton and the George Washington University Medical Center in Washington D.C., two of us (G.W. & D.B.) visited GWUMC in May 1985 to study the QA programme there in depth. In this chapter, we report on the way in which this study affected the Quality Assurance strategy document which was accepted by the Brighton Health Authority in February 1986 as a blueprint for QA development.

Why QA? The Two Health Systems Compared

It is clear that QA in Britain must differ, to an extent, from that practised in the USA. Health facilities in the USA are trying to 'pull customers in' and waiting lists for treatment are uncommon in most sectors. Those in the UK find themselves keeping patients out as an inevitable consequence of resource limitations and the reduction of waiting time is a likely objective of QA in this country. The USA is widely regarded as being over-provided with doctors, in marked contrast with the UK; and so on. It has been observed, for instance by Nicholls (1985), that current concerns in the two countries have much in common:

- cost containment
- what to do about the modern epidemics, e.g. AIDS
- ensuring quality as well as efficiency
- ethical issues in both resource allocation and medical practice
- the rise of informed consumerism which demands high-technology medicine while challenging the exclusively medical model of health care
- increasing numbers of elderly people in the population

The starting points, though, are very different. Health services in the USA consume a much higher proportion of the Gross National Product than in the UK, although American activity has been directed in the main at hospital inpatient services only. It is only compara- tively recently that ambulatory patient care services have been involved. This contrasts with the wider range of services provided in Britain's socialised system. Even more striking is the way the services are financed. Here in the United Kingdom it is mainly funded centrally by the Government, whereas in the USA private insurance (third-party payers) dominates the picture. The federally funded MEDICARE programme provides cover for the population aged 65 and over, and the joint federal and state MEDICAID programme gives cover to certain indigent groups. In the USA, Health Care Maintenance Organisations have evolved. Under this arrangement prepaid group practices deliver ambulatory and hospital care to an enrolled population—but their main concern is to minimise hospital admissions and develop health screening and prevention program- mes. Ironically, this emphasis on positive health care may well have had a greater impact in practice than that achieved in the UK.

There is no doubt that the motives of American hospitals in setting up mechanisms for QA are related to the risk of malpractice litigation and fear of failure to convince third-party payers to pay the hospital. Doctors have been prepared to accept a high level of management control for the same sort of reason—loss of income.

In the United Kingdom, there is as yet very little tradition of legal action against doctors and hospitals, although recent settlements would suggest that the situation is undergoing a transformation. To date, the apparently high levels of training and professionalism have encouraged both professional and public faith in the 'clinical freedom' of doctors to practice as they see fit, within the available resources but with little explicit consideration of the financial constraints in relation to individual cases. Now, the inevitability of clinical management budgeting is being accepted, slowly and often with great reluctance, by some doctors and other health professionals in this country. Some of them are convinced of the ethical imperative of so doing, some are not. Some already see QA as a vital antidote to an over-concentration on economy and efficiency, or a way of arguing against cuts in funding.

Only limited progress has so far been made, however, in setting up structures for QA in the present absence of motives for participation that are as clear as those prevailing in the USA. The periodic reviews that now go on between the DHSS and the Regional Health Authorities and between the region and the districts are likely to be expanded to include QA matters. The Brighton Health Authority views this as a framework within which district initiatives can be accommodated.

Quality Assurance in the USA

To understand the considerable extent of QA work in the USA, it will first be necessary to give some historical details. For our purposes, QA activity in the USA began in 1952 with the creation of the Joint Commission of Accreditation of Hospitals (JCAH), the function of which was to allow professionals to monitor themselves without outside interference. Accreditation was voluntary. The incentives for accreditation were, and still are, prestige and automatic certification for the reimbursement of services by third-party payers, most notably of late the federal government. Accreditation of a hospital depended on meeting structural criteria and minimum personnel standards, and on a QA programme known as Performance Evaluation Procedures (PEP) for Auditing and Improving Patient Care—Medical Audit. Depending on size, hospitals were required to carry out from 4 to 22 PEPs annually by using a set methodology. Topics were selected locally by each hospital and criteria and standards were established for a selected disease or process against which care was audited. In the case of confirmed deficiencies, efforts were made to solve the problem, which was then re-audited and the result reported to the JCAH.

In 1972 legislation created 203 Professional Standards Review Organisations (PSROs) designed to involve doctors and other health professionals in diagnosis-specific Medical Care Evaluations (MCEs). When compared with PEPs, these new agencies were very much physician-centred rather than patient-centred in their approach.

More recently (1983), the Social Security Act Amendments of 1983 replaced PSROs with Peer Review Organisations (PROs). Acute care hospitals seeking MEDICARE reimbursement were obliged to enter into contracts with PROs by October 1984 to perform the following functions:

- Review of the necessity and appropriateness of hospital admissions
- Reviews of the quality of care provided
- Validation of the diagnosis and procedure information that determine MEDICARE reimbursement

The purpose of the new American system is to change hospital behaviour through financial incentives and to encourage more efficient medical management of health and medical care. The PRO, under its QA objectives, must achieve significant outcome-orientated improvements and/or resolve problems in patient care quality—for instance reduction in at least one of the following:

- Unnecessary admissions caused by poor care during a previous admission
- Avoidable deaths
- Unnecessary surgery
- Avoidable post-operative complications

Clearly, these are examples of areas of great interest to UK health authorities, but what can be learned from the US experience?

Whilst it is too early to judge the PRO contribution to QA, there is a considerable consensus on the achievements of the previous QA programmes; but before studying in detail what can be learned from one hospital's experiences, there are some general points to be made that can be seen as warnings against too hasty an attempt to translate US structures to the UK:

- QA was introduced too quickly. Initially, there was no clearly defined concept of QA, and no standard techniques or models by which to develop QA programmes.
- There was too much concentration on audit. The effort needed to produce large numbers of audits hindered other QA initiatives and, despite the guidelines, medical audit topics were chosen to reflect high compliance

with existing standards. There was no focus on real problems.

- The two objectives of the PSROs—cost containment and QA—were uneasy bedfellows and, inevitably, the main effort has been directed at cost containment. As will be seen again later in this chapter, this is a particularly topical issue for the UK.
- There was a lack of decision making following QA, with little evidence of change in medical behaviour. In the hospitals, it was felt that the organisation of QA did not support change and did not improve patient care.

Faced with these and other criticisms, there seems to have been a re-orientation of approach to QA, which in part reflects the difficulty of positively defining quality and how it should be measured. The dictionary definition is 'degree of excellence', which does not help much, save to confirm that it is a relative concept. What has been found is that it is easier to agree on what is POOR quality performance. The emphasis now is to introduce QA structures and processes aimed at problem solving, the major conceptual and organisational challenges being to design systems to identify problems, and to set up mechanisms for peer reviews on a regular basis. These methods try to embody the following characteristics:

- using a comprehensive approach which addresses medical care irrespective of setting (inpatient or outpatient) or provider (physician, nurse, other professionals);
- cutting across professional and departmental lines;
- adopting a closed-loop process incorporating problem identification, problem assessment against standards, implementation of solutions, and reassessment.

The individual hospital may build on the basic elements depending on the resources the hospital wishes to invest. The George Washington University Medical Center set itself comprehensive objectives, and here in Brighton we have learned much from the experience gained at that particular institution.

Quality Assurance and Problem Solving in the George Washington University Medical Center

Organisation

The objectives of the GWUMC QA programme are to monitor, coordinate and integrate QA activities and to focus accountability for such activities. Primary responsibility for this lies with a multi-disciplinary Quality Assurance Committee. The Committee, whose membership is shown in Table 10.1, delegates responsibility for review of clinical practices to clinical department chairmen and the medical staff through their own committees.

Table 10.1 *Membership of the GWUMC Quality Assurance Committee*

Dean for Clinical Affairs
Director for Professional Services
Director of the Office of Quality Assurance
Chairman of Utilization Review/Quality Assurance Committee
Chairman of the Patient Safety Committee
Chairman of the Surgical Case Review Committee
Chairman of the Infection Control Committee
Medical Center Administrator
Assistant Administrator responsible for Risk Management
Director of Nursing
Chairman of the Hospital Space Committee
Chairman of the Hospital Capital Equipment Committee
Director of Management Information
Director of Financial Services
Director of the Quality Assurance Department

In the NHS it is difficult to make QA truly multi-disciplinary. Essentially, resources are committed by the treatment decisions of doctors under conditions of minimal interference with those decisions at the level of the individual patient. In Brighton, a Quality Assurance Committee was set up in June 1984, consisting of consultants from the major service and clinical departments—14 in all. This has achieved a great deal in securing commitment to the idea of formal QA, but although formal QA is now being adopted by senior officers of paramedical/community services, there are only small signs that doctors are prepared to involve other professions on a regular basis. Quality assurance in nursing is being developed separately through the support of a Director of Consumer Affairs/ Chief Nursing Officer.

Administrative Support

The GWUMC QA department has a staff of thirteen, including a medical director, eight professional staff assistants (all nurses of various sub-specialities) and four administrative support employees. The QA department provides staff support to the Quality Assurance

Committee and to medical staff and other committees engaged in QA work. The QA staff are also responsible for utilisation review, and the dual responsibility is seen as advantageous because of the impact of one on the other.

It would be very hard or even impossible to justify such a large department in a UK hospital or even a health authority, but it does reveal that, if the QA process is to happen, it must be supported. The modest resources commanded by even such an enlightened authority as Brighton must be used to the best effect in relation to a clear philosophy of QA. That philosophy is briefly described below, and is implicit in Figure 10.1 which is extracted from Brighton's QA strategy document.

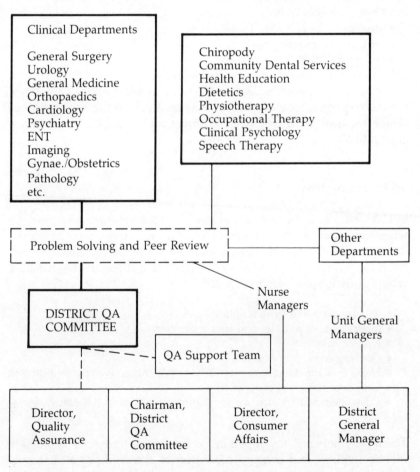

Figure 10.1 *District QA Group: Organisation for Quality Assurance in Brighton HA.*

Problem Solving

In the GWUMC system, multiple data sources are used to identify problems in order to ensure objectivity in topic selection. Minutes and reports, drug profiles, case conferences, questionnaires, etc. are all used, but the main source of data is the patient's medical record.

Problem assessment verifies the extent and cause of an identified problem using objective criteria. The setting of standards for the judgement of quality is the responsibility of 'peer groups', standards being set in relation to previously identified problems.

In Brighton, the problem solving model has been taken as a central principle of the QA strategy for the next three to five years. It is seen as fundamental that mechanisms should be set up, and responsibilities clearly assigned, for:

• Monitoring and problem identification
• Problem assessment
• Follow-up action
• Evaluation of that action

The Brighton experience to date leads us to believe that support of voluntary peer review is the best way to mobilise the motivation of senior medical staff. But what information should be provided to enable this?

Information Systems

In GWUMC, a sophisticated computerised information system exists which has enabled the accumulation of a substantial data base over the period of the JCAH, PSROs and PROs QA programmes. It will provide, by speciality, ward or doctor, for individual diagnosis or group of diagnosis information on:

• Patients admitted by unit of time
• Inpatient days prior to, and after, operation
• Operation details
• Occurrence of complications
• Number of inpatient days on which the patient received no medical care
• Length of stay
• Cost—itemised for surgical procedures, investigating, therapy, drugs, etc.

The facility is being developed in a collection of computer systems to identify, collect and collate by occurrence screening of all patients' medical records, case notes, all instances of adverse patient occurrences, or potentially compensatable events. This permits problems to be identified retrospectively and currently, the events attributed to diagnostic groups, wards, investigations, etc.

It is clear that some degree of computer assistance will also be necessary for QA in this country. Although some of the above data items are collected by Hospital Activity Analysis in the UK, and soon will be in systems following the recommendations contained in the various Körner reports, this will not be enough. Sophisticated as the GWUMC computer systems are, there is a singular absence of indices relating purely to quality of care, and this makes us even more aware of the difficulty of agreeing on measures of quality of care.

A Simple Beginning in Brighton HA

In Brighton Health Authority, we are trying to adopt parts of the GWUMC method, but in a more modest and inductive way. We accept that methods and the pace of change will vary from department to department into the foreseeable future. The Brighton QA strategy involves the setting up of a small number of computer-assisted trials beginning this year. Clinical departments can experiment with the collection of new data and the analysis and presentation of indicators based on the data. A key innovatory feature will be that senior clinicians will be in control of the microcomputer-based systems and may use them for other purposes, such as research and some word processing. The objective is to make QA an integral part of the management by senior clinicians of their own departments. It is accepted that the demand on medical staff time must be minimised, but in this way we hope to concentrate the use of limited support staff on a few departments and to find out what is useful before proposing widespread implementation. Meanwhile, the inadequacy of existing medical records for assessing quality of care is a problem for which we do not have an easy solution, save to make it a continuing and major issue for the District Quality Assurance Committee. A review of what information is required to be included in the medical and nursing notes of a patient, and by whom such information should be recorded, is being undertaken but it is too early to report on its impact.

Risk Management and Budgeting

In the USA, risk management is normally the responsibility of an administrator directing a twofold programme whose goals are loss prevention (protecting patients, visitors and staff from injury) and loss control (safeguarding the hospital's assets from losses from professional liability claims). Risk management, then, is concerned with minimising fiscal loss. In contrast, QA does not have financial concerns other than to identify inappropriate and unnecessary care. That said, a recent review of American health care observed that 'little happens in the US unless it is cost effective, however much of the innovations may appear patient oriented' (Halpern 1986).

As noted at the start of this chapter, all UK health authorities have been encouraged to develop arrangements for management budgeting. In Brighton and elsewhere this includes 'clinical budgeting', whereby consultants are given some control over the resources they command. The price of this is that the consultants will in future be more explicitly accountable for the use of those resources in providing care. In relation to budgeting, some consultants see assessment of quality of care as a necessary counterweight, whereas others see it as yet another burden. The Brighton strategy is to keep the two activities separate in these early formative stages. The desirability of their relation and eventual integration is kept very much in mind, as evidenced by the appointment of the CASPE Research Coordinator, but the first step is to see whether QA proves its worth.

Once More—Can American Really Translate Into English?

The Brighton QA strategy has certainly been influenced by developments in the USA, but it would have been foolish to attempt wholesale transfer. For instance, hopsital accreditation is a fundamental building block in the American QA structure. With the growth in private medicine in the UK, the concept might prove influential in the future NHS, but for the time being it is by no means clear how accreditation could be used in practice.

The directly commercial nature of most American hospitals makes them inherently consumer-orientated, but there is no clear parallel with the recent wave in the UK of NHS interest and senior appointments in the field of 'consumer affairs'. Brighton HA has taken a particular lead in relating QA and consumer affairs with two directorial posts, but the two fields are seen as distinct, though complementary.

Several lessons have already been learned, among them the importance of not running with QA until it has been seen to walk. Brighton is walking, but it is walking with commitment— commitment from the doctors, commitment from the managers and commitment from the authority.

11

The Approach of the NHS Health Advisory Service in England and Wales

'Extremely foolish advice is likely to be uttered by those who are looking at a labouring vessel from the land.'

Friends in Council
Arthur Helps

DR. PETER HORROCKS, Director, NHS Health Advisory Service.

The Health Advisory Service emerged out of the well-publicised reports which exposed the poor quality of care being delivered in a number of long-stay institutions. These various committees of enquiry were often set up as a result of complaints from staff which in several cases led to criminal charges being brought against their colleagues. Research in this field had identified wide disparities in practice and expectations and it was felt that there would be considerable benefits to be derived from the setting up of an agency charged with observing and commenting on current practice in these long-stay institutions which governments of all political persuasions are committed to closing. The mode of operation has changed little over the years. It still involves a multi-disciplinary team spending several weeks at a particular location after which a report is submitted to the appropriate authorities. Since 1976 the brief of the service has been extended to include community services but the members of a visiting team are still drawn from a range of professionals who are seconded to the service.

The current director was appointed as a consultant in geriatric medicine in 1969 at Hull. His unit has become well known as one of the 'high turnover' geriatric units, the increased throughput being reflective of new approaches to the medical treatment and rehabilitation of elderly patients. Indeed, the department is a national demonstration centre in medical rehabilitation of the elderly patient. He is a former advisor in geriatric medicine to the Government's chief medical officer and in 1983 was appointed on a four-year secondment to the directorship of the NHS Health Advisory Service.

* * *

Background

The National Health Service Health Advisory Service (HAS) was created in 1969 as an independent Hospital Advisory Service by the then Secretary of State for Health and Social Services. At that time there was increasing anxiety and embarrassment about conditions in long-stay hospitals for the elderly, mentally ill and mentally handicapped people. A series of public enquiries had revealed many examples of callousness and even brutality towards patients, conducted against a background of appalling environments and the comprehensive failure of lay and professional managements.

The Ely Hospital Enquiry findings published in March 1969 led the Secretary of State to announce *a new system of visiting and inspection* of such hospitals, to be responsible personally to himself so as to ensure independence from the previous arrangements for monitoring and control which had so signally failed. In November 1969 the Hospital Advisory Service was set up and the first visit took place in February 1970.

HAS was specifically not required, nor empowered, to investigate individual complaints or allegations, but to provide general supervision and review. Hospitals were to be visited by multi-disciplinary teams made up of professional people seconded from work in similar fields for the duration of the visit, returning to their own work once the visit was over. HAS directors were similarly seconded for periods of about four years. Following each visit a report was made personally to the Secretary of State containing the team's findings and advice. Copies of the report were widely circulated to the health authorities concerned.

In 1976 the work of the HAS was reformulated. Mental handicap services in England were now to be the responsibility of the newly created National Development Team, though similar services in Wales remained with HAS. The HAS remit was now to include community health services as well as those provided in hospital; this was reflected in a change of title to Health Advisory Service. Visits would henceforth be conducted jointly with the DHSS's Social Work Service (later renamed Social Services Inspectorate) allowing review of complementary social services for the client group being visited and the ways in which health and social services inter-related. Most importantly, the role of HAS in disseminating good practice was given much greater prominence. Transition had been achieved from a service which was 'advisory' to the Secretary of State to one which was now primarily 'advisory' to the authorities and professional groups under review.

The last milestone in the evolution of HAS was the decision by ministers that, with effect from 1985, all HAS reports would be public documents. Hitherto, reports on individual services had been confidential in status though widely circulated, and not infrequently leaked in sensational ways. A lucid analysis of the various public inquiries and a detailed account of the origins and developments of the Health Advisory Service is to be found in Martin and Evans (1984).

Extent of Current HAS Activity

Each year HAS conducts 35–40 major visits to health districts in England and Wales, each visit lasting from three to five weeks depending on the size and geographical spread of the service under review. A similar number of shorter follow-up visits are paid two years after a major visit. A number of unplanned visits also take place each year, often in response to an urgent request for guidance. About one third of all districts receive advice from HAS in any particular year.

Some districts are visited as their turn comes up in the continuing national round. Others invite ad hoc visits, having perceived a need for assessment and advice. Yet other visits occur through the director's own knowledge of impending or actual difficulties. Some visits are arranged partly because available performance indicators give rise to concern. HAS visits do not have to be 'by invitation'. Arrangements for a main visit begin about a year in advance. A visit programme is negotiated which covers all hospital and community health facilities for the client group concerned (elderly or mentally ill). Services for elderly people with mental illness are included in both types of visit. A selection of social services and voluntary provision is included in the programme. Statistical information, management arrangements, plans and personal evaluations of the service by professional leaders are sought for the information of the team. By the time the visit begins each team member's briefing papers can weigh several pounds!

The Teams

All teams include a medical consultant, a senior health administrator or manager, a senior nursing manager, a senior member of one of the remedial professions and a social services manager. Some teams also feature a clinical psychologist, a clinical or community psychiatric nurse, or a financial manager of health services. Teams usually

number not more than six people. The majority of members, as in the
original concept of the HAS, are seconded from working situations
for the purpose of the visit. Most team members meet each other for
the first time at the start of the visit. All are chosen because of their
wide experience and most will have particularly distinguished
themselves in services for the client group concerned and be familiar
with multi-disciplinary work. No one person is in charge of the team,
though a natural leader often emerges.

Recruitment from some disciplines is assisted by national bodies
who submit 'likely' candidates. Nominees then have the opportunity
to visit HAS and discuss the process and intentions of visits.
Following secondment, team members are invited back to discuss
visit arrangements and to air general topics of concern. All agree that
participation in HAS work is a powerful learning experience, over
and above the help and advice they are able to convey in the district
under review.

The Visit

Visits begin and end with a formal meeting between the team, lay
members, senior officers and professional staff of the authorities
whose services are being visited. The initial meeting is intended to
enable local people to voice their own views of the service and their
current intentions; the final meeting is for the visitors to state their
findings and the advice which they intend to offer.

Further formal meetings are held with general practitioners,
community health councils and local voluntary organisations to gain
impressions of the service from people working outside it. Original
HAS procedure also included writing to former patients for their
views, but this was discontinued because replies were invariably
bland and uncritical.

The fact of the visit is itself therapeutic—plans are dusted off and
staff join together in a useful way in the face of impending outside
scrutiny. Visits often provide the opportunity for problems which are
normally submerged by local convention or conspiracy to surface. It
is, of course, frequently the case that solutions to local problems have
already been sought and identified by local people but need the fresh
air of outside evaluation to be voiced. More often than not the
eventual advice given by the team is locally developed but has
hitherto been suppressed by over-rigid 'pyramidal' management and
planning systems.

During the course of the visit, team members spend much of their
time listening and looking, moving as individuals in the company of

their 'opposite numbers', sharing ideas and impressions on the basis of common experience. The complexities of service provision are consistently related back to the treatment and care accorded to the individual patient. Every opportunity is taken to contact patients in the various settings. Hospitals are routinely visited at night as well as by day. The team will comment on all services that affect quality of care and their report will cover laundry, clothing, catering and hotel services as well as the work of the care professions themselves. At the end of each day, team members meet to share their impressions. Gradually, a clear picture of the pluses and minuses of the service begins to emerge. The impediments to change and the best and most locally appropriate methods of securing progress are identified.

The Report

At the end of their stay in the district, team members return to HAS headquarters where they spend a week constructing their report. Each report is jointly edited, integrating the contributions of each team member in turn. Reports are currently about 35 pages long. They incorporate commendations of good practice but their main content is a description of the extent and quality of current provision interleaved with advice on how improvements can be brought about.

The reports are sent in draft form to the authorities concerned, affording a final opportunity for factual errors to be eliminated. Publication is the joint responsiblity of the health authority and local authorities concerned. Procedures allow a period of one month for authorities to prepare their response prior to publication. The whole process takes four to six months. Further copies of each report go to ministers, to regional health authorities and to the various divisions of the Department of Health and Social Security responsible for policy development, regional liaison and social services monitoring. An annual report is also produced, copies of which are available on request from the Health Advisory Service.

Follow-Up

Six months after a report is issued, the health authority concerned is asked to provide a progress report on the advice contained in it. A detailed response is obtained showing where action has been taken or what action is planned. Authorities are asked to state specifically why any item of advice is being disregarded and, if this is the case, what alternative steps are being taken to correct the identified problem.

Two years after the issue of each report, the authority is visited again by a smaller team for a short period to assess progress. A concise follow-up report is produced, circulated and published as before.

Additional Functions of HAS

The HAS inevitably gains a unique national overview of services for mentally ill and elderly people. The Director's Annual Report provides the opportunity to highlight issues which are recurrent and which deserve national attention. Recent examples of such wider themes have been:

- the rapid growth of private institutional care of old people;
- the redeployment of mental illness services from the traditional base in large mental illness hospitals to 'care in the community';
- the widespread absence of effective joint planning arrangements to coordinate the activities of health and local authorities;
- the effect of new NHS management arrangements on provision of services to elderly and mentally ill people; and
- the lack of evaluation of quality or effectiveness in almost every service listed.

Annual reports also permit a short statement of the work of the HAS in the previous year and acknowledgements to the 150–200 people who have constituted its teams.

Some issues have been given further attention by making them the subject of a special HAS project. 1983 saw the publication of *The Rising Tide*, a manual of guidance on the provision of services for elderly people with mental illness (HAS 1983). The manual received wide publicity and remains a highly regarded planning tool. Its publication was linked by ministers to a special allocation of funds to promote better services in this area. The HAS is currently completing a similar exercise, this time on the needs of disturbed adolescents, and further special projects are planned.

In the course of visits it has become clear that authorities in individual districts have surprisingly little knowledge of developments in the same field in other, even adjacent, districts. A normal HAS visit provides an ideal opportunity for principles of good practice to be disseminated, but main visits occur too infrequently for this to be sufficient. Accordingly, annual reports now highlight examples of good practice seen on visits, and individuals and authorities are invited to make use of the HAS's Index of Good Practice when considering service developments. Through the index, HAS is able to put interested parties in touch with each other and accelerate the diffusion of good practice and standards.

The HAS Philosophy

In essence, the HAS visit provides an objective, external assessment of services by professional people who have current direct experience in the same field. Their assessment is accompanied by advice generated from the experience of the visitors, blended with the ideas received in the course of the visit from local staff. Advice is tested and agreed as far as possible locally before the visit is concluded.

There is no 'ideal service' concept which underlies a HAS visit, though some methods of working and care will be common goals of all teams. The importance and success of genuine multi-disciplinary participation in the planning and provision of good quality care is beyond dispute. Similarly, all teams will wish to promote individualised patterns of care and the avoidance of institutionalisation. But most advice stems from the individual experience and knowledge of team members.

What is recommended as the best policy for a particular district may be at variance with existing departmental advice. Further, two teams presented with an identical set of problems may generate widely differing solutions in their respective reports. Accusations of inconsistency therefore bedevil the life of the Director.

Although national or regional norms and guidelines exist and can be useful reference points, numerical or data-based evaluations are not a main feature of HAS visits. There is no HAS check list to underwrite an inspectorial approach. Adherence to norms can provide an unreliable guide to quality and effectiveness of services. Much good, sensitive and effective care is provided by 'wrong' numbers and grades of staff in 'wrong' places! In contrast, the 'feel' of a particular service to an informed team member can be a very powerful measurement indeed.

Comparative performance indicators and measurements of service provision, though rarely of service outcomes, are an increasingly prominent feature of present-day statutory services. Ostensibly they are provided to allow managers to compare their own services with those of others and to prompt self-examination. It seems possible that such measurements may also come to influence the allocation of resources.

In such a climate, the subjective, impression-based techniques followed by HAS can come to be seen as 'soft' compared to assessment based on 'hard' data. The experience of sixteen years' HAS visiting suggests that its reports match any evaluation based exclusively on data and do far more to assess quality and appropriateness of provision. In particular, they offer unique sensitivity to the infinite variations in local conditions, expectations and personalities.

Implementation of HAS Advice

HAS does not possess 'teeth' to ensure that its advice is adopted. It is open to authorities receiving reports to disregard them completely, as was sadly the case at Normansfield Hospital and St. Augustine's Hospital, both the subject of subsequent public enquiries. In practice, follow-up enquiries and follow-up visits show that the vast majority of visits result in widespread positive action for the better. The process of follow-up itself is a useful prompt to authorities to continue to address themselves to the contents of reports. The fact that HAS findings are regularly used in the top-down annual regional and district HAS management reviews gives further emphasis to their importance.

Routine publication of the findings of each visit, and a public record of the advice rendered, also make it less likely that any report can be buried and forgotten. Community health councils, voluntary organisations and other interested parties can make full use of HAS reports as they pursue their advocacy on behalf of elderly and mentally ill people.

Most power behind HAS advice, however, stems from the good standing and credibility of the service, itself due to the ability and professionalism of team members over the years. The detailed attention and response given to HAS reports basically reflects the belief that they contain an honest, objective and locally sensitive appraisal of the service under review.

Financial Consequences of HAS Advice

Many items of advice in HAS reports relating, for instance, to planning procedures, communication and collaboration do not carry any significant financial consequences. In other instances, reports clearly indicate where economies can be achieved by discounting outmoded, unnecessary or wasteful practices. Nevertheless, most reports inevitably include advice which has implications for revenue and capital spending to achieve better services.

In situations where resources are already severely constrained, advice to spend more can easily be seen as unrealistic. It is firmly held by HAS that serious financial consequences should never inhibit clear statements of need. It is only when the need is demonstrated and publicised that spending priorities are re-examined at both the national and local level.

Flexibility and Adaptability

The independence from government which is integral to the constitution of HAS has been a major factor in preserving the adaptability to changing circumstances. The customary replacement of directors at regular intervals and reliance on seconded members of staff for the bulk of its work has ensured that the activities of HAS have not become fossilised in standardised procedures and inflexible practice.

A look back at HAS reports of the early 1970s reveals the essential concentration at that time on the basic needs of patients for personal self-esteem, decent food, privacy and accurate assessment of their medical needs. There was widespread acceptance of poor standards of staffing and care and poor management of hospitals. A general failure to appreciate the importance of multi-disciplinary contributions to patient care, and pessimism about the potential of elderly and mentally ill people to respond to treatment that was anything more than custodial were all-pervasive. Teams were unable to look outside the hospital at the wider world where the majority of people are treated.

Conditions for patients and attitudes towards them which were the norm in the hospitals 15 years ago are today highly unusual, though sadly not wholly eradicated. Most teams conducting visits now, though still conscious of the need to ensure proper inpatient treatment of all sorts, have the latitude to consider primary care teams, social services, specialised housing and voluntary activities for the elderly or mentally ill people concerned. A particular concern now is to ensure that services are planned effectively, with appropriate contributions from the professional staff and 'consumers'.

Current visits reveal a wide spectrum of standards, some of which are very high indeed. For each visiting team the challenge is to help those responsible for a particular service to lift their aspirations a couple of rungs up the ladder from their present position. Receptiveness to advice and openness to constructive criticism are characteristics of the more advanced services. Far greater efforts are needed to convince those lower down the ladder: for such services advice has to be geared to feasible goals; to offer visions of perfection is invariably self-defeating.

The ways in which HAS has chosen to operate and the changing membership of its visiting teams have equipped it to adapt to changing needs over the years in a smooth, almost imperceptible way. It may be presumptious to claim sole responsibility for the changes which have occurred, but it seems inescapable that HAS has contributed significantly.

Future Developments

It is possible to envisage a number of ways in which HAS can continue to develop its role of promoting change, development and improvement in services for its particular client groups. One major task must be to promote much more local, 'internal' evaluation of services by the providing authorities. Roles for HAS will be to stimulate the creation of mechanisms for evaluation and to suggest standards by which authorities should judge themselves. Closely allied would be the further refinement and development of 'good practice' activities by HAS.

The applicability of HAS techniques to other health service problem areas would be worth testing. It is tempting to think, for instance, that the organisation of orthopaedic service delivery across the country could benefit from peer review and better systems for disseminating good practice.

The effectiveness of HAS activities is partly measurable in the precise follow-up techniques which are adopted, each authority showing to what extent advice has been followed, and to what effect. Nevertheless, it is entirely right to ask whether an organisation in the business of providing external evaluation for 16 years should not itself be subjected to a similar study.

12

Measuring the Quality of Nursing Care— The Monitor Experience

'Count what is countable, measure what is measurable, and what is not measurable make measurable.'
Galileo

LEN GOLDSTONE and VERONICA ILLSLEY, School of Health Studies, Newcastle-upon-Tyne Polytechnic.

The editor can claim some responsibility for having instituted the work which led to this particular project. Back in 1979 the North Western Regional Health Authority was anxious to implement some mechanism for determining just how many nurses were needed on hospital wards. Several schemes had been suggested since the war but none had taken root and it would be fair to say that staffing levels were determined by the classic decibel law. Asked for my advice, I had no compunction in recommending that the Authority secure the services of Len who at that time was a colleague at UMIST. Recognising that his brief was not to produce yet another approach which would forever be buried in a library, he set about ascertaining just what was available and usable. That search led him to a recognition that one could not examine nurse staffing levels without some reference to the level of quality associated with those manpower figures. It also took him to the United States where considerably more progress had been made in both these complementary areas. The project did indeed lead to a workable system for determining nurse staffing levels but, in truth, the element of that system which has found wider acceptability nationwide is the anglicised version of the Rush Medicus system for measuring the quality of nursing care. This is now routinely used by numerous British health authorities.

Len himself is not a nurse, having trained originally as a statistician in government service. He has, however, been extensively involved in health care projects over the years and this activity eventually culminated in the post of Head of the School of Health Studies at Newcastle Polytechnic. Veronica joined him there in January 1985 to assist in the development of quality indicators in district nursing. She is a nurse, having qualified as an SRN in 1979. She then put that qualification to good use in a variety of temporary and part-time jobs while securing a degree in psychology from Birmingham University.

★ ★ ★
125

We frequently hear pronouncements such as 'standards of nursing care are falling', or 'British nursing is the best in the world'. Those who make statements of this kind are presumably looking at some clear indicators of the quality of care. Are these indicators comprehensive, valid and reliable? Further enquiry usually reveals that the statements have been made from conviction or personal belief rather than being founded on a systematic examination of the facts. Sometimes we are told that 'the quality of nursing care cannot be measured'. Somewhat surprisingly, it is often the same people who have informed us that standards are falling or that British nursing is best who preach this impossibility of measurement gospel.

Those who make judgements on the quality of nursing must rely on some implicit criteria. Can we elicit these, expand them, and increase their objectivity and comprehensiveness? Those who say that quality cannot be measured may nonetheless agree that there are some identifiable aspects of quality whose presence or absence can be observed objectively, and which can act as pointers to a more general view of quality. The *Monitor* technique seeks to make explicit those criteria which are implicit in the quality statements of many nurses, and relies on aspects of nursing that are observable as having occurred (or not).

Monitor is based on research which has demonstrated that there are aspects of nursing care which can be readily and objectively observed, and which are valid and reliable indicators of quality. The methodology is based on the care of individual patients and so, by using it for all the patients on the ward (or a representative sample) an index of the quality of nursing care provided on a ward can be made available. The quality of nursing is assessed in relation to:

- the *planning and assessment* of care
- the *physical* and *non-physical* care actually delivered
- the *evaluation* of that care

A further index, contained within Monitor, assesses the quality of practice, procedures and management of the ward. This 'Ward Monitor' is independent of the 'Patient Monitor'.

The complete system is available in a single publication (Goldstone *et al.* 1983). Health authorities use it without external help or consultation—even the calculations are done simply so that a computer is not necessary, although at least one company has produced an associated software package for performing the calculations.

Overview of the History and Development

Monitor is an adaptation for the United Kingdom of the Rush Medicus Nursing Process Methodology. In the USA this is one of the most widely tested and most thoroughly analysed methodologies for indicating the quality of nursing care. The first step of the extensive research underpinning this methodology was an in-depth examination of a large number of studies and instruments each concerned with the measurement of the quality of nursing care. From an initial list of approximately 900 quality-related items of nursing care, a final set of 257 evaluative criteria was developed by the Rush Medicus researchers. Pilot testing covered 115 patient units in 21 different hospitals (Jelinek et al. 1974 and 1977).

Research was subsequently carried out on Monitor in the United Kingdom on 32 acute medical and surgical wards within the North Western Regional Health Authority. Although it was developed against a 'scenario' of the nursing process, it has been successfully used in wards where 'task allocation' is the mode of operation.

Overview of the Structure of Monitor

Monitor consists of checklists relating to the presence or absence of quality-related observable phenomena. Not all questions can be answered with an unqualified 'yes'. Accordingly, there are several alternative versions, e.g. 'yes, incomplete', 'yes, sometimes', 'yes, partially'. Such responses receive a half mark compared with one for an unqualified 'yes'. The scoring system focuses on the applicable questions and on the percentage of those to which a 'yes' response is obtained. The closer to 100 per cent, the better the care being delivered.

Monitor does *not* embrace all aspects and dimensions of quality in nursing care. A total approach to quality assurance and assessment requires a consideration of the structure, process and outcome of nursing. *Structure* relates to the prerequisites for good nursing care, such as buildings, heating, technical facilities, staffing levels and mix and other factors which are essential, but not amenable to change on a day-to-day basis. Monitor does not 'measure' structural aspects of the quality of nursing. However, the 'Ward Profile' contained within the Monitor document does provide a description of structural factors and, in itself, is a useful audit of relevant factors in the provision of care.

Outcome covers such factors as patient satisfaction, reductions in morbidity, mortality, accidents to patients, complaints, wound infections, pressure sores and other undesirable events. The absence of pressure sores in itself does not 'prove' good quality nursing, just as their presence may not necessarily indicate poor nursing. However, if pressure sores outcomes are considered in a 'package' of indicators as listed above, together they may collectively indicate a generally desirable result of the nursing process.

Any quality assurance programme should properly record and study outcomes. Monitor, though, is focused on *process* rather than structure or outcome. Nevertheless, within the confines of its coverage, it provides valuable information for nurses and demonstrates inequalities and the need for training and education. Monitor can provide arguments for changing structural factors such as staffing levels. Monitor should also positively influence outcomes through helping to ensure 'good' nursing.

Content of Monitor

The items in Monitor are based on a master list of over 200 criteria. These are split into four sub-lists, each appropriate to patients of different dependency levels. Thus there are 81 items for those patients requiring minimal care (Category I), 107 items for patients requiring average care (Category II), 148 items for patients requiring above average care (Category III) and 118 items for patients requiring maximum or intensive care (Category IV). In addition, there is a list of 43 quality-related items for the ward as a whole.

The criteria for measuring quality hinge on the extent to which nurses realise and use their comprehensive roles to meet patients' needs. The process of nursing is, of course, a continuum of 'caring', but a useful starting point is an examination of the assessment of the patient's needs and problems upon which the plan of care ought to be based. The care should refer to whatever physical needs the patient has, as for example, hygiene, mobility, treatments, diet, fluids, bowel care and others. The non-physical needs are equally important and typically encompass 'information', 'education', emotional support, privacy, etc. Monitor checks that all the appropriate care, from the stage of assessment and planning through to implementation and evaluation, has been completed.

Each of the four sections includes a series of pertinent questions under the major heads set out in Table 12.1. Each of the subheadings comprises three to seven specific questions. In Table 12.2 we can see how the number of questions varies according to the dependency of the patient.

Table 12.1 *Subjects covered in Monitor*

SECTION A. Planning and Assessment	SECTION C. Non-Physical Care
Assessing the patient on admission Information collected on admission Assessment of patient's current condition Co-ordination of nursing care with medical care plan	Orientation to hospital facilities on admission Nursing staff courtesy Patient's privacy and civil rights Consideration of patient's emotional and psychological wellbeing Measures of health maintenance and ill-prevention are taught Involvement of patient's family and/or carers
SECTION B. Physical Care	
Protecting the patient from accident and injury Provision of physical comfort and rest Needs for hygiene are met Needs for nutrition and fluid balance are met Needs for elimination are met	SECTION D. Evaluation of Care Appropriateness and evaluation of objectives Patient's response to treatment is evaluated

Table 12.2 *The Number of Monitor Questions per Section for the Four Categories of Patients*

Number of questions in Monitor	Category of Patient			
	I	II	III	IV
A. Planning Care	23	24	28	25
B. Physical Needs	16	34	73	62
C. Non-Physical Needs	29	34	32	17
D. Evaluating Care	13	15	15	14

Table 12.3 shows two typical pages of Monitor, with the layout having the following distinctive features:

• The care given to all patients in a particular category is recorded in one document. For any particular question the responses for all patients are immediately visible.

Table 12.3 *Two Typical Pages from Monitor*

Source of information		Patient's Code or Initials	

Ask Patient	b IS THE PATIENT HELPED WITH ACTIVITIES OF DAILY LIVING WHEN NEEDED? To Patient: In the past 2 days, when you needed some help in your daily activities, such as bathing, did someone come to help you within a reasonable length of time?	No Yes, always Yes, sometimes Not applicable/ Not available 82 SCORE	☐☐☐☐☐☐
Records	c ARE RANGE OF MOTION EXERCISES, EITHER ACTIVE OR PASSIVE, PERFORMED AT SPECIFIED TIMES? Check if indicated to be done. Does not apply to routine turning or leg exercises as in the immediate postoperative period	No Yes—off schedule Yes—on schedule Not applicable 83 SCORE	☐☐☐☐☐☐
Ask Patient	d DO THE NURSING STAFF TELL THE PATIENT TO DO LEG EXERCISES IN BED (OR HELP HIM TO DO THEM?) If contra-indicated code 'Not applicable'. To Patient: Do you do any leg exercises or move your legs very much while you are in bed? For both yes and no responses ask: 'Did one of the nurses tell you to do them or help you to do them?' Code 'Yes' or 'No' Applies to knee flexing and ankle rotation e.g. for patient in immediate postoperative period, bedfast patient etc. Does not apply to turning or range of motion exercises.	No Yes Not applicable/ Not available 84 SCORE	☐☐☐☐☐☐
Observe Patient	7. *The Patient's Need for Skin Care is Met* a ARE OSTOMY BAGS PROPERLY IN PLACE? Check proper care of skin round ostomy, and application of	No Yes Not applicable	☐☐☐☐☐☐

Source of Information

Patient's Code or Initials

Source of Information	Question	Responses
Records	b IS THERE A WRITTEN STATEMENT OF THE CARE GIVEN TO PRESSURE AREAS ON THE SKIN? Refers to direct care of skin, assessment of risk, care provided to prevent skin breakdown	No / Yes / 86 / SCORE
Records	c IS THE CONDITION OF THE SKIN AROUND THE IV SITE RECORDED? e.g. reddened, swollen, complaint of itching or pain, infiltration, etc.	No / Yes / Not applicable / 87 / SCORE
Records	d IS CARE GIVEN TO AREAS OF SKIN BREAKDOWN AS OFTEN AS REQUIRED? Applicable to any areas of skin breakdown, such as decubitus or laceration. Check to see if special care is needed, and whether plan indicates schedule for giving such care. If care should be given and is not, record 'No'. If care is scheduled note whether records indicate care is given as often as scheduled. If not, record 'Incomplete'.	No / Yes, incomplete / Yes, complete / Not applicable / 88 / SCORE
Observe Environment	e IS THE PATIENT'S BED CLEAN AND DRY? Not applicable for use of high humidity.	No / Yes / Not applicable / 89 / SCORE

- The most likely source of the information sought is given in the left margin.
- The questions for response are in upper case. Notes to help the assessor are in lower case.
- Individual patients can be followed by reading down a particular column.

History and Development

The original Rush Medicus methodology was intensively tested for validity and reliability in the USA, and our own work confirms its acceptability. After being carefully 'anglicised' it was scrutinised by over 100 active nurses in the acute medical and surgical areas, and then systematically tested within the North Western Region. Initial trials of Monitor in the North Western Region were aimed at discovering whether the questions generated for use in the USA were applicable to the NHS.

The first Monitor trials were conducted in two surgical and three medical wards. Each had between two and four consultants, around 25 beds and was using task allocation. Medical students and student nurses were present in all wards, but pupil nurses were present in only three. Ward clerks and domestic assistants were available in all wards, and physiotherapy services were provided both on and off the ward in most cases. Occupational therapy was a regular service in only three of the wards but a CSSD service was available in all five. In three wards 'plated meals' were provided, while the other two featured 'trayed meals'. There was only one case where the meals were not exclusively served by the nurses. The ward design in four of the wards was typically Nightingale-style but the fifth, Ward E, consisted of six open bays. Monitor was applied to a randomly selected sample of three patients in each of the four dependency categories on all five wards.

The results are presented in Table 12.4, wherein is shown the mean percentage of 'yes' responses obtained for the patients on each ward. With the exception of Ward E, the uniformity of figures within each ward is striking. These trials revealed that no major revisions to the Rush Medicus questions were needed, but considerable further attention to language was required. It was also felt important to check on the reliability of the results from one assessor to another. A sample of four wards in two teaching hospitals was chosen for the reliability trial. On each of these wards two qualified and experienced nurses independently carried out the full Monitor evaluation on the same patients and they also completed the ward-Monitor questionnaire.

Table 12.4 *Monitor Results from Initial Trial on Five Wards*

			WARDS		
	A	B	C	D	E
Category I	80.9	—	68.0	59.2	50.4
Category II	81.2	74.3	66.3	55.8	54.4
Category III	82.5	72.1	67.4	62.5	38.9
Category IV	—	66.0	65.3	58.2	42.0
Ward Mean	81.6	72.5	66.4	60.0	48.5

The percentage agreement between the two observers averaged 94.8 per cent.

A sample of approximately 10 per cent of acute medical and surgical wards in the North Western Region was chosen on the basis of willingness to try out Monitor. Scores were obtained for each of the wards using a random sample of three patients per category in each ward. Table 12.5 shows the Monitor scores, along with some of the other management information collected. The *nurse satisfaction score* is a percentage obtained from a simple questionnaire in which the nurses were asked to rate their own satisfaction with the care they were able to provide. Perhaps the most interesting feature of Table 12.5 is the lack of correlation between the columns! The only two columns exhibiting any degree of association are the Monitor scores for the ward and the patients, between which there is a simple correlation of 0.62. Wards 1 and 2 both devote more minutes to Category I patients than average, but considerably less to the more ill patients in Categories III and IV, and a lesser percentage of nursing time in general to direct care, resulting in a very low level of service as measured by both Monitors. In contrast, on Ward 13, with the highest Monitor score for patients and a similarly high score for the ward, nurses devote the highest minutes of direct care to patients, especially to those who are most ill. The table also contains some interesting contrasts: in Wards 5 and 12 a very high score for the ward—suggesting a well organised, tidy ward—is not matched by a high patient score. It would appear that, while the ward receives a good deal of attention, patients' needs are not always met.

Finally, it is noticeable that the range of scores, i.e. from 49 to 82 per cent, is almost identical to that obtained in the 5 pilot wards, confirming Monitor's ability to discriminate. In all the work to date a mean Monitor score of 66 per cent has emerged.

Table 12.5   North Western Region Nurse Staffing Levels System: Information Matrix (Pilot Study)

Ward	Nursing activity per 24 hours:						Monitor Scores		Nurse Satis- faction scores (%)	Ward type and number of beds	
	% of nursing activity which is classified as direct patient care	Average minutes of direct care dependency category					Ward	Patients			
		I	II	III	IV						
1	50	71	107	206	206		48	53	77	FS	19
2	47	54	92	104	270		51	49	—	M	35
3	69	47	108	174	315		65	61	61	FS	29
4	74	53	95	207	313		67	60	—	FM	28
5	61	51	92	194	311		87	72	70	FM	27
6	40	45	77	203	—		69	78	—	MM	31
7	51	37	141	170	418		66	61	—	FM	30
8	50	75	135	218	218		68	73	59	FM	24
9	56	29	99	165	267		66	72	54	FS	22
10	55	29	58	171	316		76	66	72	MM	28
11	57	37	74	130	215		79	73	78	FS	27
12	46	52	99	177	276		88	65	57	FS	32
13	53	85	102	204	544		80	82	71	FS	26
14	54	86	138	267	430		76	60	—	MS	22
All wards mean score	54.5	54	101	185	315		70.4	66.1	—	FS Female Surgical MM Male Medical	

Source: Ball *et al.* (1984).

The Good, the Bad and the Average

The variations in the Monitor index between wards, found in the development work, have been mirrored closely by those subsequently found between health authorities. Monitor is the first tool which makes such comparisons possible. In Table 12.6 the average Monitor score for patients in 20 wards in three British health authorities is set out. There were usually 4 patients in each of the four patient categories per ward. The average *ward* scores in three authorities were 63, 81 and 89 respectively.

Table 12.6 *Mean Monitor Score for Wards in Three Different Health Authorities*

Authority W		Authority Y		Authority X	
A	38	R	69	L	87
B	41	S	67	M	84
C	42	T	64	N	83
D	44	U	59	P	82
E	55	V	66	Q	70
F	60	W	70		
		X	71	Mean	82
Mean	47	Y	59		
		Z	65		
		Mean	66		

Perhaps the most striking feature of the table is that patients in a medical ward in Authority W score on average 38 per cent on Monitor, while their counterparts in Authority X on Ward L score 87 per cent on average. Another striking feature is that the 'best' ward in Authority W scores approximately the same as the worst ward in Authority Y and, in turn, the best ward in Y scores approximately the same as the 'worst' ward in Authority X. The most common pattern of scores is that found in Authority Y, which indicates that there is a considerable potential for 'better' nursing in many health authorities.

It is possible to be much more specific in reporting back from a Monitor study. Table 12.7 shows the level of detail suited to use by a unit manager or nursing officer for a particular ward, in this case Ward F. The Monitor scores for each aspect of care for each category of patient are presented, along with the average score for the dependency groups (bottom row), the aspects of care (last column) and the overall score for the ward (i.e. 60 per cent). Managers would probably read the information in this table in reverse order, starting at the bottom right-hand corner.

Table 12.7   *Monitor Results for Ward F*

Aspect of Care	CATEGORY OF PATIENT				
	I	*II*	*III*	*IV*	*All Patients*
A Planning	26	48	29	54	41
B Physical	90	81	84	65	76
C Non-physical	61	83	83	63	72
D Evaluation	59	47	63	46	51
Overall Care	53	66	61	58	60

The overall score of 60 per cent is achieved by the averaging of relatively low scores of 41 per cent on planning and 51 per cent on evaluation with high scores on physical care (76 per cent) and non-physical care (72 per cent). However, even the high score of 76 per cent is unevenly distributed over the patients, being 90 per cent for Category I patients, 81 per cent and 84 per cent for those in the middle two categories, and only 65 per cent for those in Category IV. The most dependent patients obtain the lowest physical care score, and the least dependent obtain the highest. This would indicate a need for a serious review and changes in the pattern of nursing of the most ill patients. The low planning score is also surprisingly erratic.

A 'prescription' for this ward could include detailed attention to the use of records and the improved planning of care so as to tailor it to the needs of patients. Some attention to the physical and non-physical needs of the most ill patients in Category IV and to the non-physical needs of Category I patients is also called for. Obviously, the non-physical needs of these two groups of patients are quite different, and the factors involved must be made explicit. The nursing officer and ward sister would, hopefully, examine the actual Monitor document in detail (question by question and patient by patient). This would enable them to develop a strategy for improvement which would most certainly involve a greater attention to the evaluation of care. The time scale for improvements will vary and it is important to set realistic and objective goals. Only in this way can managers demonstrate and impel the principles of the process of nursing.

We have found that, despite considerable academic debate on what Monitor actually 'measures' and what it excludes, the differences observed can be so dramatic that enormous improvements can be clearly signposted. The reality of using Monitor is that change can be demonstrated to be required, and the nature of the change clearly identified. Many health authorities using Monitor have produced a catalogue of undeniable improvements in care resulting from its use, while others have identified a single fundamental change for which Monitor was the catalyst.

The Consequences of Monitor

Monitor has been widely used in the UK and abroad since its publication in 1984, and many positive and appreciative observations have been communicated to the authors by its users. In several cases extensive teaching programmes have been instituted as a result of the Monitor exercise; the nursing process has been both introduced and re-introduced; patient information has noticeably improved and patient care has undoubtedly benefited because nurses widely report subsequently adopting practices which Monitor included but for which they had scored 'no'. Nurses frequently report improved confidence in their work after being 'Monitored'; and the concept and practice of practical quality assurance has undoubtedly received a major impetus through the medium of Monitor. We believe Monitor to be only the first step. Because that first step has been taken successfully, many health authorities now routinely use Monitor and have moved on to explore other new tools.

New developments currently in progress are a version of Monitor for use in geriatric wards, a version for psychiatric wards, and a cousin of Monitor for use in district nursing, all of which should come 'on stream' in the near future. A recent article in the *Nursing Times* perhaps indicates best the current position on Monitor: 'Monitor is proving popular with the ward sisters and nurses because it shows exactly where care is failing and where improvements should be focused. It is popular with managers because it indicates which wards may be failing and why.' (Slack 1985)

RETAILING

13

The Development of a Quality Measurement System for a UK Bank

'George goes to sleep at a bank from ten to four each day except Saturdays, when they wake him up and put him outside at two.'

Three Men in a Boat
Jerome K. Jerome

DAVID BUSWELL, Business Decisions Ltd.

Only rarely does a piece of research conducted in part fulfilment of the requirements for a higher degree find its way into practice. The work described in what follows is one such exception. The Yorkshire Bank was persuaded of the good sense of sponsoring a postgraduate student on the Master's Marketing programme at UMIST and, after consulting with the staff of both the university and the bank, it was agreed that an examination of how one might set about assessing the level of customer satisfaction with the service being provided would be a particularly useful exercise. Such a study would be one element in a wider recognition by banks that marketing concepts are just as relevant in their environment as in any other sphere of business.

To say that the exercise was successful would be something of an understatement. Not only was the approach implemented throughout the bank but David himself was taken on as the bank's Advertising and Market Research Manager, and one of his duties was to refine and develop the approach and put it on a routinised basis. He actually stayed in that post for eight years before moving on to be the Marketing Manager of AGB Financial Market Research which is a wholly-owned subsidiary of Europe's largest market research company, AGB Research Plc. He was recently appointed a Director of Business Decisions Ltd, where he has special responsibility for consultancy and research in the financial and services industries. It is, perhaps, of some interest to record that David presented a paper at the health service symposium at which this text was originally conceived. Far from believing that his banking experience was irrelevant, those present were of the opinion that what he had to say about measuring quality in one service industry was indeed of considerable import to those in another. Indeed, the strength of that feeling is attested to by the fact that he has since provided a consulting resource to several health authorities.

★ ★ ★

Over the past ten years there have been a number of fundamental and accelerating social changes which have given rise to a concern for quality. People have become more individualistic: a phenomenon which manifests itself in terms of a need for greater self-expression and for the outlet of creative abilities, and in a distrust of stereotypes and role playing. There has been a negative reaction to cold, distant, anonymous and formal relationships, both at work and socially. The Protestant work ethic has been in decline and has been replaced by a growing desire for meaningful work, job satisfaction and self-fulfilment.

These trends have been accompanied by a greater number of increasingly potent and vocal consumer pressure groups which, dissatisfied with the shortcomings of mass-produced goods, have induced within consumers a heightened awareness of the benefits of quality. But the cry for quality has not been confined solely to manufactured goods. The quality-conscious consumer seeks quality, value for money and high levels of service in all areas of life. In order to ensure quality, the provider of goods and services needs to measure that quality; he needs to know what 'quality of quality' is being delivered and, thereafter, to measure it so that performance is not only maintained but also, where necessary, improved.

Whilst quality control has for long been a feature of manufacturing industry, it is a concept which has only recently gained a wider currency in the financial services industry. One of the first banks to undertake work in this field was Yorkshire Bank Plc, a regional bank established in 1859 by Colonel Edward Akroyd of Halifax and known, for the greater part of its existence, as the Yorkshire Penny Bank. Today it is owned jointly by four of the major clearing banks. It boasts a network of over 220 branches, extending from Newcastle in the north of England to Coventry and Luton in the Midlands.

In 1979, the Bank sought to develop a simple, quantified and objective monitor of the quality of service received by customers in their own branch of the Bank. The purpose was to provide the head office management of the Bank with a continuous measure of service so that individual branch performance could be evaluated and improvements implemented. Publication of the techniques employed has resulted in its imitation by a number of other British and foreign banks.

What is to be Measured?

As a preliminary, it is necessary to be clear about what is to be measured. Banking, like most service industries, is labour-intensive and a high proportion of the work force, particularly its more junior members, interacts with customers either continuously or from time to time. For this reason, it is mostly the performance of people that is to be measured.

This performance can be divided into two parts. The first is *technical* performance which is concerned with the effectiveness with which the operational aspects of banking are carried out, with the knowledge of banking procedures and with the effective utilisation of technology and equipment. For example, a satisfactory technical performance is achieved when a customer has been granted a loan or when, in response to a customer's instructions, money has been transferred from one account to another.

The second dimension on which it is possible to evaluate service quality is that of *expressive* performance. This is abstract and non-technical and evaluation takes place at a psychological level. It is concerned with the attitudes of staff, with their relationships and interactions with customers and with the manner in which staff deliver the banking services. It is essentially people-based.

While the technical and expressive aspects of performance are interrelated (indeed, they are inseparable), it is argued by Swan and Coombs (1976) that expressive performance is the more significant because it is this that determines the total satisfaction experienced by the consumer. The bank customer may well be pleased with the technical outcome of having arranged a loan but may have taken exception to the manner in which it was granted. This will not only reduce his level of satisfaction with the technical performance but will diminish his perception of the overall quality of service being offered in that particular branch. The management of the quality of service in any service organisation is therefore more likely to be biased toward an evaluation of the expressive performance of the staff than toward the assessment of technical skills. Moreover, customers will hold a set of expectations about the quality of service they should receive. These will be the product of a number of factors: past experience, advertising, the price being paid, media comment, hearsay, cultural tradition, etc. Whatever the source, the customer will expect a certain level of service which may or may not be equal to that which he actually receives. The measurement system needs to take into account this gap between expectations and the reality.

The quality of service will also change over time. In banking, one of the more powerful agents of change is likely to be a new branch manager or assistant manager whose style of leadership, supervision and motivation will inevitably differ to some extent from that of his predecessor. When measuring quality, the dynamic nature of that which is being measured should be recognised. Finally, measures of

performance need to be compared with a common standard or
benchmark if they are to have any substance or value.

The Research Problem

The problem, as suggested earlier, is fourfold:

- to measure in a quantified form the abstract and nebulous dimensions of
  service performance;
- to take account of the gap which will exist between customers' expectations and their perceptions of the reality;
- to devise a system which will allow for both static and dynamic measures
  of performance, which will permit comparisons between individual units
  (e.g. branches) and which will identify trends;
- to provide a benchmark against which the results of individual units can
  be evaluated.

The Methodology

The development of a quality measurement technique for Yorkshire
Bank proceeded in a stepwise progression. This is described briefly
here but a detailed exposition is to be found in Buswell (1983). The
steps were:

- to define service and its key components;
- to ask customers to isolate those components which they themselves
  use to distinguish between 'good' and 'bad' service;
- to incorporate the isolated components into a postal questionnaire in
  which the customers of a branch are asked to rate the performance of their
  branch on these particular components;
- to establish a benchmark.

Definition of Service

The definition of service was based upon a survey of the literature
and, especially, on earlier research undertaken by the Bank. It was
concluded that 'service is an offering to customers of benefits and
satisfactions beyond the product itself, which is controllable and
which may incur costs'. Service is not concerned with the actual
financial products but with the way in which those products are
delivered to the consumer and with the manner, attitude and
knowledge of the people who deliver them and with the environment
in which they are delivered. Service activities are controllable,

although the responsibility for control may rest upon different people. For example, the smile of a counter clerk cannot be controlled by policy decisions made at head office; conversely, decisions on the exterior and interior design of branches can only be made centrally and not by individual cashiers.

Finally, some service activities such as staff training or the provision of regular bank statements incur costs while others incur no financial cost at all: as, for example, tact, politeness, cheerfulness and helpfulness.

Key Service Areas and Their Components

Based on earlier research commissioned by the Bank, a list of five key service areas and their components was compiled. From qualitative research, 131 verbal statements made by customers of the Bank were collected and these formed the basis of the components of service. The five key service areas were:

- **Knowledge:** this is fundamentally relevant to all members of branch staff and 14 components of service included in this key service area covered knowledge of the range of products, banking practice and branch methods and routines. Generally, customers tend to feel guilty about their own lack of knowledge—for example, they may not know of a product's existence or they may not understand technical jargon—and the knowledge of the staff should aim to help, support and reassure customers.
- **Communication:** 60 service components fell into this cluster which is an indication of its importance to customers. Distinctions were made between different types of communication: oral (either face-to-face or on the telephone); written (with standards of grammar, spelling and typing being as important as the content), or a visual and sensory communication in which much is conveyed by movement, stance, facial expression, dress, cleanliness, neatness, etc. Non-personal communications such as advertising, leaflets, displays in the banking hall or in branch windows and public relations were also components of this area.
- **Expertise:** this key service area is the one which comes closest to technical performance, being concerned with such things as accuracy, speed, efficiency and honesty. Among the 27 components were a number which covered the willingness of the Bank to create products where special circumstances dictate and to deliver all products in an uncomplicated and trouble-free manner.
- **Willingness to lend:** although there were only 8 components identified, this key service area concentrated on the ease of obtaining credit.

- **Branch design:** the wide range of components in this cluster covered attributes related to the physical environment and its amenities: car parking, the number of writing desks, the degree of formality, the quality of the decor, lighting and furniture.

Isolating the Significant Components of Service

In order to identify those aspects most commonly used by customers when evaluating service, it was necessary to isolate those which customers felt to be of greatest significance. Personal interviews were conducted with a sample of 1,300 bank account holders.

During the interview, respondents were asked to filter the 131 service components so that those which were important to the respondent in his evaluation of service were selected. Respondents were given a pack of 131 cards, each card having one component expressed in the form of a positive statement printed upon it. Informants sorted the cards into two piles: those which were (1) necessary or (2) not necessary to good service. They then sorted the 'necessary' cards into two further piles: those which (1) mattered strongly or (2) mattered slightly to good service. Finally, interviewees selected from their 'matter strongly' pile the 10 components which they felt were most important to good service. From this process, 24 statements emerged as being of real importance to customers, and it is on these dimensions that branches are now routinely evaluated.

Developing a Questionnaire

Having collected 24 important measures of service, it was then required to develop and test a postal questionnaire. This medium was chosen on the grounds of cost. The questionnaire went through several drafts and various versions were completed by nearly 7,000 people before it was finalised. Respondents were asked to score their own branch of the bank on each of the 24 attributes. A further question asked for an overall score for the quality of service provided by their branch.

The scoring method used was a five-point scale on which each component was scored according to the degree to which that aspect of service at the branch was as the customer would expect. This method allowed for the gap between expectation and actual perception discussed earlier. The scale and its related scores were as follows:

	Score
Much better than I would expect	+5
Better than I would expect	+4
As I would expect	+3
Worse than I would expect	+2
Much worse than I would expect	+1

Establishing a Benchmark

Having devised a technique for measuring service quality in a quantified form, it remained only to test it and to establish a benchmark. A sample of 18,218 customers was selected from 16 branches of the Bank. Twelve of these were chosen as being representative of branches thought to be providing an average level of service. The remaining four were selected because it was felt that they offered widely different levels of service. These were used as test branches.

The benchmark graph (given as Figure 13.1) shows results for the 12 branches in aggregate. The maximum score possible on each aspect of service or on the overall level of service is +5; the benchmark score for the overall level of service was 3.61. The robustness of the benchmark was revealed when, after the survey had been running on a continuous basis for over a year, the results of more than 50 branches were aggregated and there was found to be a negligible deviation from the benchmark.

The four 'test' branches illustrated that the system was capable of discriminating between 'good' branches and 'bad'. Branch A (Figure 13.2) is consistently rated better than the benchmark, being rated unsatisfactory on only three features. Branch D (Figure 13.5) is well below the benchmark on all aspects, whereas branches B and C (Figures 13.3 and 13.4) show a broad similarity to the norm. These branches are discussed in more detail below.

Results

Branch A

This branch achieved a particularly high score on the general overall level of service of 3.80 and, as such, it remains one of the higher scoring branches. On only 3 of the 24 individual aspects of service measured does it fall short of the benchmark. Clearly, customers were well satisfied with the knowledge of the staff, with communication (especially the friendliness and cheerfulness of the staff and their

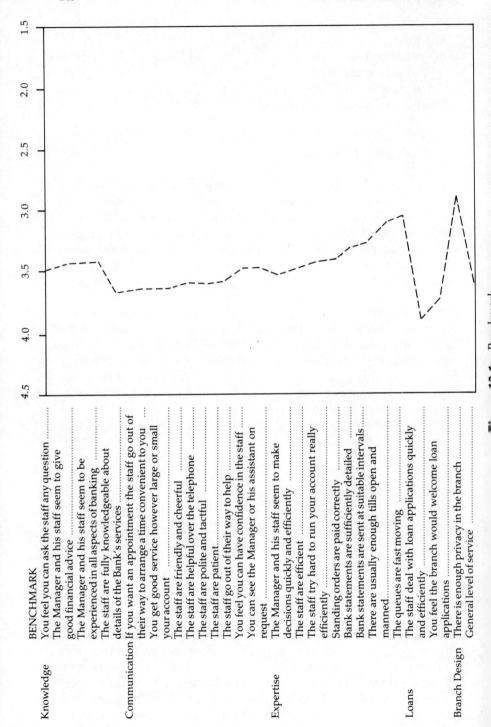

Fig. 10.1 Benchmark

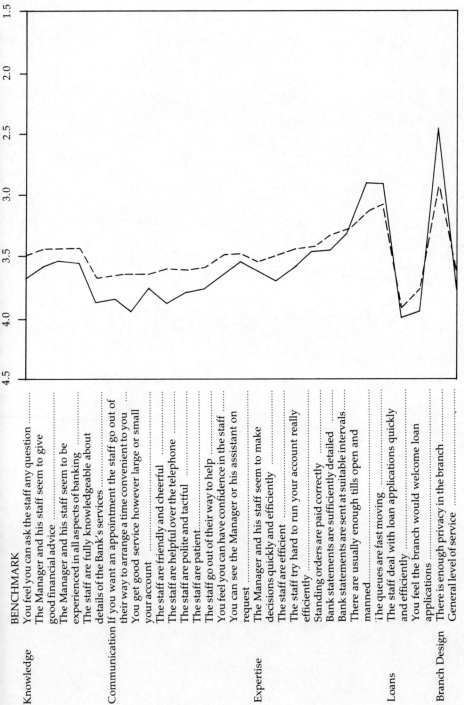

BENCHMARK

Knowledge
You feel you can ask the staff any question
The Manager and his staff seem to give good financial advice
The Manager and his staff seem to be experienced in all aspects of banking
The staff are fully knowledgeable about details of the Bank's services

Communication
If you want an appointment the staff go out of their way to arrange a time convenient to you
You get good service however large or small your account
The staff are friendly and cheerful
The staff are helpful over the telephone
The staff are polite and tactful
The staff are patient
The staff go out of their way to help
You feel you can have confidence in the staff
You can see the Manager or his assistant on request

Expertise
The Manager and his staff seem to make decisions quickly and efficiently
The staff are efficient
The staff try hard to run your account really efficiently
Standing orders are paid correctly
Bank statements are sufficiently detailed
Bank statements are sent at suitable intervals.
There are usually enough tills open and manned

Loans
The queues are fast moving
The staff deal with loan applications quickly and efficiently
You feel the branch would welcome loan applications

Branch Design
There is enough privacy in the branch
General level of service

Figure 13.2 *Branch A*

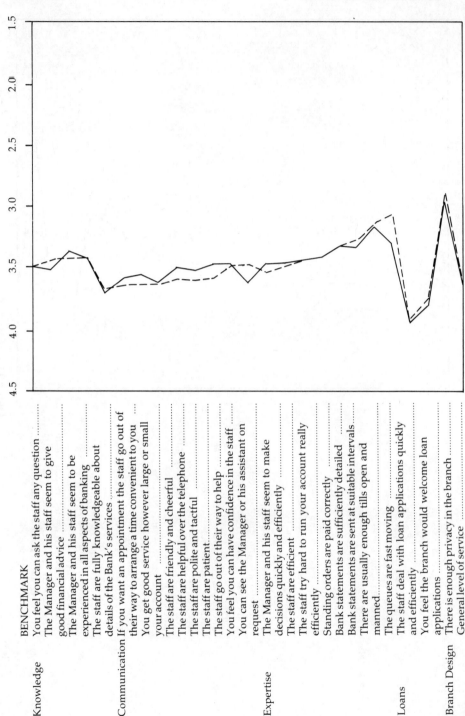

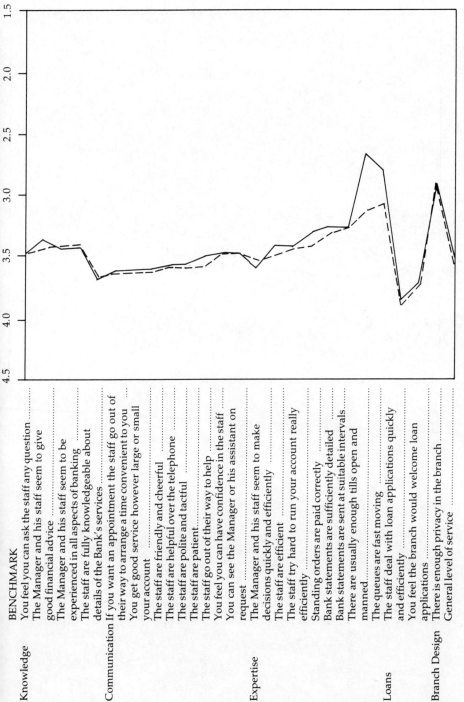

Knowledge BENCHMARK
You feel you can ask the staff any question
The Manager and his staff seem to give good financial advice
The Manager and his staff seem to be experienced in all aspects of banking
The staff are fully knowledgeable about details of the Bank's services

Communication If you want an appointment the staff go out of their way to arrange a time convenient to you
You get good service however large or small your account
The staff are friendly and cheerful
The staff are helpful over the telephone
The staff are polite and tactful
The staff are patient
The staff go out of their way to help
You feel you can have confidence in the staff
You can see the Manager or his assistant on request

Expertise The Manager and his staff seem to make decisions quickly and efficiently
The staff are efficient
The staff try hard to run your account really efficiently
Standing orders are paid correctly
Bank statements are sufficiently detailed
Bank statements are sent at suitable intervals
There are usually enough tills open and manned
The queues are fast moving

Loans The staff deal with loan applications quickly and efficiently
You feel the branch would welcome loan applications

Branch Design There is enough privacy in the branch
General level of service

Figure 13.4 *Branch C*

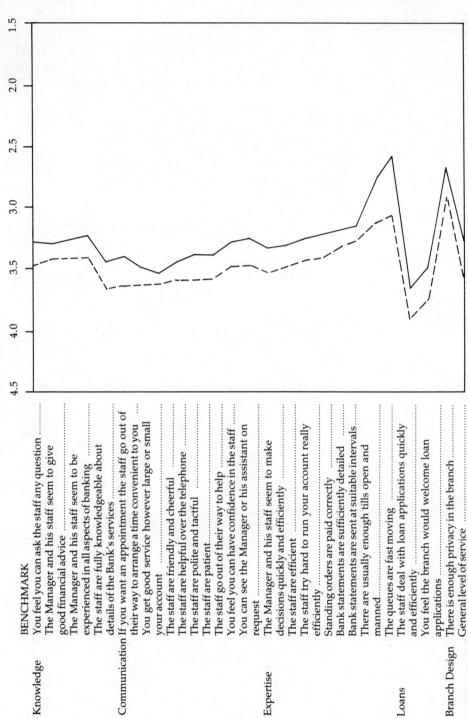

politeness and tactfulness) and with the willingness of the branch to lend money. Whilst most aspects of expertise scored above the benchmark, customers were less satisfied with the number of tills open and manned, with the speed of movement of queues and with the degree of privacy afforded by the branch. Subsequent experience of surveying a number of branches has shown that it is on these three particular aspects that a branch stands or falls.

Queuing in branches is a frequently mentioned problem and, in the open-ended questions on the questionnaire, respondents have been quick to offer remedies. However, in those branches where special queuing systems exist, criticism is minimised and scores for 'the queues are fast moving' are generally above the benchmark. With regard to the number of tills open and manned, there are usually two issues: there may indeed be an insufficient number of tills in use, but often it is the absence of specific tills for 'business people' making large cash deposits which reduces the speed of service and so increases the length of queues. At branches where there are tills set aside for cash withdrawals only, the scores for tills being open and manned are appreciably better.

Earlier research into branch design had indicated that the degree of privacy available to customers was of critical importance and it was to be anticipated that scores for privacy would reveal that this was not always as good as customers would expect. It has now become an unwritten policy that the design of new branches (or refurbished branches where space allows) should incorporate a number of private interview rooms.

Branch B

On most aspects of service, this branch was as good as, or marginally worse than, the benchmark. It was mainly on the people-related aspects that the branch was seen to under-perform. Scores below the level of the benchmark were given for the helpfulness of the staff, for their experience and for some of the more social aspects of communication—the friendliness and cheerfulness of staff, their politeness and tactfulness and their patience. On the generally contentious dimensions of queuing and privacy, the branch scored better than any of the other test branches.

Branch C

The scores for this branch mirror closely the service profile of the benchmark, although at a slightly lower level. Only two aspects were given scores which were above the benchmark. The manager and his staff were seen to be experienced in all aspects of banking and the manager and his staff seemed to make decisions quickly and efficiently. The number of tills open and manned was, however, judged to be less than satisfactory.

Branch D

This is one of the few branches to be surveyed which has had scores on all the service attributes which have been significantly below the benchmark. It achieved a score of 3.36 on the general overall level of service, compared to a benchmark score of 3.61. It may be that the low scores were the result of an 'inverse halo effect'. Perhaps only one or two things were wrong, but they were wrong to a degree which seriously coloured customers' views of all the other aspects of service. At the time of the survey, the banking hall, although lofty and impressive, afforded little space for customers and, as a consequence, orderly queuing was almost impossible and privacy negligible. These points were made by respondents in the open-ended questions. A substantial refurbishment of the branch has done much to improve the quality of service available.

Implementation

By this stage it has been demonstrated that the system is capable of fulfilling the objectives established at the outset. Regular surveys of branches were commenced in 1981 at the rate of four per month and the performance of a large number of branches has now been evaluated.

The results of each branch are presented to the senior head office manager responsible for the branch network. The performance of the branch on the 24 aspects of service is shown in tables and graphs and is accompanied by a brief written commentary highlighting strengths and weaknesses. The report is passed to the head office official within whose geographic region the branch falls and it is his task to communicate the results to the branch manager who, in turn, discusses them with his staff.

In the early days of the development of the survey, it was necessary to reassure branch managers that the survey results would be used in a positive and constructive manner. It has already been stated that the quality of service offered and the perceived quality received is dependent upon the performance of people. If that performance is to be improved, it is more readily achieved through teamwork, co-operation, a sense of common purpose and a willingness to learn. The strengths of each branch must be emphasised and built upon; weaknesses must be exposed but ways should be sought to make improvements which are effected not by cataclysmic change, but gradually.

Benefits

The introduction of a system of quality measurement and monitoring yielded a number of benefits to Yorkshire Bank, some of which had not been anticipated:

- It has been possible to identify the service strengths and weaknesses of a significant part of the organisation. The results of surveys have been used to guide head office management when deciding upon branch design and refurbishment; this has influenced the introduction of special queuing systems, the number of tills, the provision of private interview rooms and modifications to the design and positioning of tills to give customers greater privacy at the counter.
- Management has available documented and factual evidence when reviewing with branch managers or their staff the quality of service which is being offered. Moreover, it is not a subjective judgement which has been made but rather is it the distillation of the views of a sizeable proportion of the branch's customer base. It cannot be ignored.
- The results of the surveys have given rise to modifications being made to the content of training courses. After the survey had been running for a year, a working party was established to review training, to visit other organisations with reputations for offering high levels of customer care and to research the attitudes of staff to a number of matters relating to the quality of service they delivered.
- Finally, the introduction of the system had the psychological advantage of focusing the minds of all staff on the quality of service which they and their colleagues were delivering.

14

Ensuring Quality of Service for Sainsbury's Customers

'A man without a smiling face must not open a shop.'
Chinese proverb

OWEN THOMAS, Director of Personnel Services, J. Sainsbury plc.

Ask any housewife to name those retail organisations which epitomise quality and Sainsbury's would undoubtedly feature on most shortlists. Ever since the company was founded way back in 1869 a key cornerstone in its policy has been to ensure that shopping at one of its branches would be a pleasant experience. As the standard of living has continued to increase, so the proportion of the British public who demand more than simply the lowest prices has also continued to increase and, perhaps not surprisingly, Sainsbury's has expanded to meet a major part of the need that it has been largely instrumental in generating. The results have been nothing if not staggering with the last set of financial figures revealing a continuing healthy profit on an annual turnover of over three billion pounds. The group continues to expand and, as we shall see, the form of that expansion does, to a large extent, reflect feedback that the company secures on what shoppers regard as the right shopping environment.

What the editor found most revealing about this chapter was the material it contains relating to the extent to which the top management of Sainsbury's sees one of its prime tasks as on-the-spot monitoring of just what is happening in the stores. The man-hours involved and the associated financial investment represented by those highly paid man-hours must be huge, but it is quite clear that the organisation sets great store on the insights secured from these visits. Given that the group currently employs 62,000 people, it is apparent that ensuring a quality service demands a substantial training effort and it is, therefore, entirely appropriate that this chapter has been contributed by the individual responsible for this function along with staff selection and recruitment. A fundamental belief that staff skills and attitudes are critical in support of the service ethic ensures that they have a high priority in such a challenging and competitive environment. Before taking on board his present post Owen had, for eight years, managed the distribution and food packaging depots which are an integral part of Sainsbury's sophisticated re-supply system. Doubtless his previous career in the Royal Navy was a good training ground for both activities.

* * *

More than six million customers have come to expect, as a natural course of events, that buying good food will cost less at Sainsbury's. They also expect their expedition to be conducted in a comfortable and attentive environment and to emerge from it in a contented frame of mind. From Sainsbury's point of view, the continuing success of the business depends upon customers achieving those objectives, returning to shop again and again and spreading a rich message about what they have found and the way in which they have been treated.

These two stances are very different in character. From the customer's point of view, the requirement is quite simply expressed. From Sainsbury's point of view meeting that requirement is extremely complex and leads immediately to the thought that the term 'customer service' is a misnomer or at best an over-simplification of a process which involves concern that the customer be foremost in every part of the business. The customer care ethic has to be all-pervading: it has to influence directly those things from the location and nature of stores they build, the products they offer and the staff they recruit to the labelling on the product, the design of shopping trolleys and the lighting of the store. The service of retailing is a special position, very different from manufacturing, with the competitiveness of the industry and the enormous choice available to the customer demanding that all Sainsbury's staff are the 'sales force' and that the sum of its many parts forms the best possible customer interface.

This initial and continuing concern for the customer is, as might be expected, clearly focused amongst the corporate objectives:

> To provide unrivalled value to our customers in the quality of the goods we sell, in the competitiveness of our prices and in the range of choices we offer.
>
> In our stores, to achieve the highest standards of cleanliness and hygiene, efficiency of operation, convenience and customer service, and thereby create as attractive and friendly a shopping environment as possible.

That these objectives are long-standing is a most important platform for the business because they lend a confidence of consistency which evolves only by improvement. This philosophy was evident at the foundation of the business in 1869 and has been the driving force ever since. At that time, the idea that good quality food could be sold at a reasonable price in clean, hygienic conditions was quite revolutionary.

By the 1880s, concern for the customer and the Founder's enterprise resulted in a wholly new concept of shopping as evidenced by these comments on a newly opened shop in Croydon:

The earlier shops had not been elaborate. This one was far more decorative, but designed above all to be easy to keep clean at the time when cleanliness was the exception in the retail food trade. The windows were framed with marble-faced pillars, wood and stained glass spandrels; the fascia was crowned with wrought iron and displayed the Sainsbury name in gilded glass. The floor was tiled, as were the walls and counter fronts, in the lush designs of the period, and the counter tops were made of marble slabs. The office was built of polished teak, the customer's side of the counter furnished with bentwood chairs.

It seems evident that J.J. Sainsbury had in mind one type of shop for the market street and another for the suburban branches. In the markets, much business would be done through open windows, on the pavements and from street stalls. In the suburban shops, though trade was done through the windows, the shop design was intended to attract customers into the shop where a greater variety of food was on sale. It was a matter of catering to a community's needs.

Development continued apace through the years until, in 1950, Sainsbury's opened the first self-service stores in the country, and a blueprint for the future emerged. Thus we see the purposeful development from trading through the front of the shop to Sainsbury's modern supermarkets and hypermarkets energised by market opportunity in the form of anticipating and satisfying consumer requirements against the backcloth of at first a steady and, more recently, a rapidly accelerating change of consumer pace and life style.

In the period from the first self-service shop in 1950, Sainsbury's turnover has increased from £16 million per annum to over £3 billion per annum and it is rated amongst the most successful food retailers in the world. It is now the twelfth largest company in the UK by market capitalisation and its average compound sales growth over the last decade has been at the rate of 11 per cent per annum and profit has increased on the same basis by over 17 per cent per annum.

These two major pressures of consumer expectation and rapid growth, combined with the competitive nature of the business and the need for volume throughput for re-financing, require a really professional management team with a dedication to nurturing the customer and all that means in terms of business planning. The strategy is converted to detailed application with an equal dedication—indeed passion—because 'retail is detail', in terms of both trading and all the activities which support it, is a truism, as is the need for quality of application.

How, then, does Sainsbury's determine and assure the quality of service to customers in a constantly changing market? First of all, Sainsbury's is in supermarketing because it offers an excellent food shopping experience. It is efficient and cost effective; it enables prices to be contained and at the same time offers a wide range and choice of product in attractive and comfortable conditions. That this is what the customer wants is supported by the growing volume of business, but housewives are much more discerning than simply to settle for that: their expectations are as wide-ranging as Sainsbury's products. Some of those expectations, and the way in which they are provided for, are exemplified by Sainsbury's reaction to the car-borne shopper, the tastes and flavours acquired by travel, by communication, the influence of the healthy eating lobby, and by increasingly sophisticated customers.

The first objective was to make the shopping experience more comfortable and we have seen larger stores, more checkouts, greater choice and significantly longer trading hours, with the volume of trade during the evening hours showing just how much the shopper welcomes the convenience of such opportunities.

Sainsbury's currently invests some £250 million a year to provide a better service, not only by building new, modern stores but also by extending, updating and refitting many older ones. Although the Company is over 100 years old, the average age of its stores is under 10 years. The following table shows the situation early in 1985:

Supermarkets—over 20,000 sq. ft. sales area		77
10,000–20,000 sq. ft. sales area		143
under 10,000 sq. ft. sales area		33
Small stores		18
	Total	271
New supermarket openings in 1984/85		15
Average size of new supermarkets (sq. ft.)		26,080
Average size of all supermarkets (sq. ft.)		16,900

Free surface car parking is provided for new stores whenever possible, since it is known that multistorey car parks are a disincentive. Special trolleys are provided for customers with babies and for the disabled. At the checkout, free bags are provided for a minimum purchase and a packing service is available. 'Cash only' and 'express' checkouts speed customers on their way, and wide access is provided for those in wheelchairs. Within the store, there is a feeling of spaciousness and cleanliness with good lighting and clear and informative labelling on nearly 10,000 products. A number of these products are now sold by reversion to service counters which enhances both choice and the personal aspect of service—bakeries, delicatessens, and some fresh fish counters, all of which add to the attractiveness of the shopping environment. This all helps the housewife to shop in the most convenient way and, whilst these factors, together with the price, present the most visible form of service, they are but the culmination of a massive activity of which the customer is unaware. This invisible activity starts with the design of the store and Sainsbury's has won many awards for imaginative architecture which is supportive of the local vernacular.

Product ranging and display are most carefully thought through, with buyers adopting an innovatory role in anticipating new customer needs as well as being immersed in the product quality aspects. The buyer's initiative in product development is a relatively new role assumed by progressive retailers such as Sainsbury's, Marks and Spencer, Mothercare and Habitat, who see the need to respond quickly to their customers' needs rather than merely buy what the customer-remote manufacturer chooses to make available. This activity is supported by a large and expert food technology resource which also inspects for quality at the point of manufacture.

The outward sign at the point of purchase is the house style representing very much the trading philosophy. Sainsbury's chief designer is quoted as saying, 'The Supermarket shopper does not have to be bombarded with confusing graphics to grasp a sales message. Simplicity and honesty in packaging can work especially when aided by a design policy that has a regard for the needs of the consumer. Our approach to design problems is a natural extention of the company's concern with quality . . . I consider our style no more than workmanlike and functional, a direct style that appeals to the man on the street and the thrifty housewife . . . its success depends on how much it fulfills its role of communication to the customer.'

Whilst every part of the business has an impact on customers in some way or another, there are two further principal areas of activity which are worthy of some explanation. Firstly, Sainsbury's customers buy well over 100 million items each week and the stores experience one of the highest intensities of trade in the food retailing industry— about twice that of their competitors. This calls for a swiftly reacting re-supply system. The time scale is tight and a high proportion of the half million orders on the distribution service is delivered daily within 12 hours, overnight. Orders from all the stores are transmitted to central computers in the early evening and printed out in the depots at around 10 p.m. daily. For perishable products, the orders are matched with goods which have been manutactured or picked in the field that day, arriving in the depots by 8 o'clock the same evening. All these goods will arrive in the shops next day by 7.30 in the morning: from field to customer in under 24 hours. For all products, the call is for a 98 per cent service level (goods delivered compared with goods ordered) to the stores on a daily basis. This, together with the stock already in the stores, ensures that goods are always available. This could not be achieved without significant investment—typically £20 million per annum—in computer systems, all designed to have goods in the right place at the right time for the customer.

Secondly, it is imperative that the customer perceive the staff to be knowledgeable and skilful if he or she is to be assured of value for money. There are professional personnel managers in every store who recruit the shop floor staff to an agreed specification and employ them on a variety of schedules so that staff availability matches the operational requirement and, importantly, the customer flow. There are detailed criteria for the recruitment of management, which is regionally or centrally controlled to ensure that standards are being achieved and maintained.

As well as having traditional trading values, Sainsbury's has long had a strong commitment to training and this is another area of very high investment. It recognises clearly that effective training is the means of giving the best service to the customer particularly in the environment of its extremely intensive trading, of gaining the best return on capital investment, of improving productivity which is such an important element in its business—or any other for that matter—of maintaining high standards and thereby energising its striving for excellence; and, most importantly, of facilitating the required changes in trading and operational methods, in customer requirements and in technology.

All training has an emphasis on customer service and there are also specific customer relations programmes. Training is staged and progressive, from the initial induction to checkout operator, with each store departmental manager undergoing courses before and after appointment and a carefully structured development programme to store manager and beyond, all designed to equip staff for optimum service to the customer and for professional management.

Checkout operators have to pass a test to a defined standard before completing their initial probationary period, with a strong appreciation of the customer interface. All shop-floor staff receive product knowledge instruction, the service areas of bakery and delicatessen requiring special customer relation skills. Management employees have a programme of technical and management skills training which they progress through as a matter of course and this leads, for example, to management and supervisors coming together for a residential course in effective teamwork prior to each new store opening. The degree of emphasis on the 'sharp' end can be seen in the attendance of all senior management in head office at a computer-aided workshop on the task of the store manager. The commitment to training is seen in the detailed monitoring at board level.

How does Sainsbury's set about determining how customers want to be treated, what they want to buy and whether they have the facility they want? Is it trading instinct or is it based on market research in various forms? In fact, it is more than merely a combination of both those approaches: it is market research, it is trading flair built on many years of experience and skilful trading, it is observation and direct contact with customers, and it is its own innovatory role. Sainsbury's sees it, of course, as most important that this latter role is anticipatory and not conditioning.

Directors visit stores every week, typically carrying out over 600 visits a year and they see and hear, on the shop-floor level, the reaction of customers. They also examine the operation in great detail, requiring to know immediately, for example, why even a single product in a store is not available to customers. Whilst regional management is constantly in touch at store level, it is the store manager who has the greatest opportunity to hear and see customer responses and this whole process supports and sometimes influences decisions flowing from factual data. Before opening every morning, the store manager will have all the detail at his fingertips. He will know the delivery situation; the date coding of perishable goods received, the state of goods displayed, the lines short of stock and staff availability; and he will carry out a thorough visual inspection of the store. He will see to it that immediate action is taken on any shortcomings.

In terms of market research, it is unwise to react to intermittent data and Sainsbury researchers work in a climate of market information and opinion within which averages and trends can be clearly seen and in which the various elements are brought neatly together to provide a sound platform from which corporate decisions can be taken in the interests of the consumer.

Research is both quantitative and qualitative. For example, facts on car ownership lead to the building of stores with adjacent car parks but this was qualified by the view that the average housewife distrusts multi-storey car parks. This work forms an integral part of the on-going efficiency and development of the Company and it is in two principal forms: firstly, a monitor on the current operation which leads to instant remedial action where necessary; and secondly, an opinion and data base for future action and corporate planning.

In the short term, there are daily reports to board level on a sample of stores showing the sales level, the level of display and the lines which have not been delivered. On a point of detail, shelf space is allocated to products to ensure that goods are always available to customers on busy trading days without replenishment: a display fill of 95 per cent is required and the reported state is relative to this: the depot service level, already discussed, ensures that this can be achieved. The report also shows the depot service level for the sample, which typically ranges from 95 to 99 per cent, as explained previously, as well as deliveries arriving late and any other problems such as wrong coding of goods. There are separate reports to board level of any problems with computer systems which may interfere with the re-supply efficiency: these might typically say that a system was 'down' for 15 minutes with resultant delay in orders being available in depots for assembly and despatch.

There are also unannounced customer service checks on a range of stores each week organised by Sainsbury's marketing services department. These cover typically 15 stores and report lines out of stock or poor replenishment as evidenced by gaps in the displays, proportion of checkouts manned, and average queue length. A typical summary report might show averages of 15 gaps, 80 per cent checkouts open and a queue length of 2.4 people. Individual store data are submitted and if, for example, the queue length is too great and all checkouts are not open, then the store manager is called upon to explain the reasons. The report also shows the availability of packers, of trolleys and baskets and the state of the high-volume displays, those less than 25 per cent full being reported. Again, this report is scrutinised at board level.

A further method of reviewing how well the needs of Sainsbury's customers are being met is through the analysis of letters and telephone calls, both complaining and complimentary. Well over 1,000 letters a week are received. These are co-ordinated by product groups and examined by buyers and line management. Where the goods are returned, they are analysed in the laboratory and trends and serious cases are then pursued by food technologists with suppliers for remedial action. Where complaints are justified, a gift token of an appropriate amount is sent to the customer. Every customer who writes or telephones receives a prompt reply and Sainsbury's feels it important to handle every complaint sympathetically.

Sainsbury's has a team of home economists who give talks to women's groups wherever there is a supermarket in the area. These talks, for which no charge is made, are on the theme of 'Value for Money' and may, for example, cover the nutritional value of certain product groups. A small team of experts also provides a free speaker service on wine. Overall, about 25,000 people attend these talks every year and Sainsbury's actively looks for feedback from the customers. In addition, there is a film about Sainsbury's which is available free on demand for showing to groups ranging from housewives to parent/ teacher groups. All these occasions are important opportunities to test opinion.

Separate meetings with groups of customers are organised on a

regular, qualitative research basis so that Sainsbury's understands
their wants and then observes and acts upon the emerging trends. A
typical conclusion drawn from such a survey might be, 'there are
distinct regional differences particularly with reference to pastry'.
Northerners prefer darker coloured pastry than any that the Sainsbury range offers which to them suggests 'crispness' and 'crunchi-
ness', whereas the converse is true for southerners who would
describe their ideal pastry shade as 'golden'. Products will be
developed with this firmly borne in mind.

   Competitors' prices, which undoubtedly have an influence on
where the thrifty housewife shops, are monitored regularly, as are
the special offers. These data are drawn from market research
companies and from Sainsbury's own surveys with the aim of
maintaining a competitive package for the customer.

   On a longer-term basis, once a year Sainsbury's conducts a
behaviour and attitude survey of housewives living within the
Company's catchment area. Whilst somewhat subjective, the results
are to be seen within trends and give a most useful indication of the
different ways in which housewives think about the Company and its
competitors. The results act as a guide to the action or emphasis
needed to attract more customers who will do the greater proportion
of their weekly or monthly shopping at Sainsbury's.

   Attitudes are measured by asking housewives to rate appropriate
factors on a five-point scale. Absolute values are not particularly
meaningful, but importance is attached to the relative scores for high
quality, low prices, value for money, freshness of product, cleanliness, friendly/helpful staff and pressure at the checkouts. Surveys are
taken amongst Sainsbury's 'main' customers and competitors' 'main'
customers. An extract from a recent survey showed:

	Sainsbury's main customer		A competitor's main customer	
	Sainsbury	Competitor	Competitor	Sainsbury
High quality	Very Good	Average	Very Good	Good
Value for money	Very Good	Average	Very Good	Good
Cleanliness	Very Good	Average	Very Good	Very Good
Friendly/ helpful staff	Good	Low	Good	Good

Regular research is also conducted on shoppers' habits, such as
where else they shop and what proportion they spend with each
retailer so that Sainsbury's has a clear view of the strength of the

competition and what it is that the competition offers that attracts the customer.

Data for all these sources are examined weekly by board-level committees. At these meetings, the results of visits to stores are reviewed, the research data are examined and immediate policy action decided: corrective action within existing policies will already have been taken. The longer-term issues and major policy decisions are taken at a higher level board committee or by the board as a whole. There is thus demonstrable commitment from top management in the Company to the efficiency of the business in satisfying customer needs.

It is in these ways that Sainsbury's maintains contact with customer opinion and is able to react quickly to identified requirements. As has been brought out above, the art is in using all the information available in a co-ordinated way to draw business-like conclusions and devise action plans to meet the needs of the customer. At the end of the day, it is the shopping environment, the goods on the shelf and the attitude of the staff which will please or displease the customer. That Sainsbury's customers find much to make them return again and again is shown by the movement in market share, which indicates that Sainsbury's is the leading food retailer in the country and the biggest seller of produce and off-licence products.

Customers see the business through its people as much as its products. Apart from the aforementioned extensive training, which imparts skill and confidence in dealing with customers, staff with qualifying service have a share in the profits and therefore a vested interest in efficiency and customer care.

Sainsbury's has a deep concern that its growth and its rate of growth should not erode the attributes and opportunities for customer care evident in a smaller business. That customer care extends to community responsibility can be seen in Sainsbury's sponsorship of the arts and its charitable work which is an extension of its concern for the quality of customer facility.

To summarise: the culture of a company decides the style, and direction and supermarketing in the Sainsbury way shows that the customer is the principal focus and beneficiary of the activity conducted in the many parts of the business. The culture is one of purposeful direction and detailed application of all aspects of customer service: it is the very heart of the business itself and the success of the business illustrates the customers' view of the results.

15

Quality Control in Thomas Cook

'Jonas acquired some reputation by travelling abroad,
but lost it all by travelling at home.'
Boswell's *Life of Johnson*, Vol. II

TIM BURFOOT, Market Research Manager, Thomas Cook Ltd.

It could be argued that the very large proportion of Britons who now
take at least one annual holiday abroad is primarily attributable to what
some would claim to be, at best, an unpredictable climate. In truth the
growth in this market can, to a large extent, be put down to the
activities of those companies which have pioneered the concept of the
package holiday. The original pioneering endeavour was, of course,
that of Thomas Cook himself who organised his first trip in 1841 on
behalf of churchgoers intent on travelling from Leicester to Loughborough. It seemed eminently sensible, therefore, to approach this
same company in 1986 for an indication of how they set about
ascertaining assessments from those who had holidayed with them.
Subsequent contact revealed that they now also assess how their retail
customers judge the service they receive, and so both topics are
covered in what follows.

To any reader whose holiday has contained some unpleasant
experience it would seem self-evident that the travel companies ought
to be concerned with this aspect of their business. 'Once bitten twice
shy' must be an adage that fits this industry more accurately than any
other. Here more than anywhere a poor experience is likely to have a
deleterious impact upon the re-booking rate, so all the more reason for
discovering just what holidaymakers felt about their two-week stay in
Marbella, for example. How did they rate the hotel? How good was the
courier at performing her job? Was the food considered to be excellent
or dreadful? As we shall see, Thomas Cook addresses these and other
issues on a routine basis on the supposition that, if it wants to be
around in another 145 years, it must secure such feedback.

The system relating to the retail side of Thomas Cook's business was,
in fact, devised and implemented by Tim Burfoot who carried overall
responsibility for all British market research and some of that on a range
of international projects. Prior to taking up his present post he had
been a product group manager for Premier Percussion, with special
responsibility for the international marketing of professional products.
To some extent this could be seen to be a natural development of his
university studies which involved the unusual combination of English,
music and comparative religion.

★ ★ ★

Background

The main summer holiday holds a unique place in the minds of the majority of consumers and appears to be laden with a range of symbolic referents which are seldom found amongst more 'product' based goods and services. Independent research conducted by Thomas Cook indicates that the summer holiday, or indeed the main holiday of the year regardless of departure date, is seen very much in terms of a reward system. That is to say, unlike the purchase of a motor car, audio system or white goods which may be purchased in response to peer or social group pressure to maintain an implicit level of status, the summer holiday is motivated by a sense of 'reward of living'. In other words, the holiday, when viewed at a conceptual level, appears to be regarded as a reward for surviving the rigours and uncertainties of daily life. It is, perhaps, not insignificant that the number of package holidays taken abroad continued to grow throughout the early 1980s at a time when the recession was biting deeply. At a time of increased insecurity and uncertainty the reward ethic seems to have gained ground.

A second consideration in the broad sphere of packaged holidays is that the 'holiday' is sold as a concept or idea rather than as a defined product or service. The holiday brochure is a means of describing a variety of accommodation types in a range of destinations but, in addition, information is provided on transport and the resorts. Rather than providing a detailed understanding of what the holiday will be like, it fosters and enhances the idea of taking a holiday.

Although the holiday may have been bought in January, the promise is not fulfilled until perhaps July or August, which contributes to the sense of anticipation. It is primarily for these reasons that any company involved in the sale of package holidays must do all it can to minimise the risk of providing the consumer with an inappropriate holiday content in terms of resort, representation, accommodation or transport.

It is against this background that quality control in the package holiday industry is maintained. The Thomas Cook Holidays customer satisfaction questionnaire is handed to clients at the end of their holiday on the coach transfer from the hotel to the airport. Questions of a general nature are asked about the holiday and specific aspects of the holiday experience are covered in some detail.

As can be seen from the questionnaire which is reproduced in Table 15.1, the first section solicits factual information relating to resort, accommodation, airline, departure airport and date of the outward flight from the UK. These are all key filters for the analysis, although the primary requirement is for information about the hotels within

Table 15.1

Dear Holidaymaker,
One of our main priorities is to maintain and, where need be, improve the standard of holidays we offer the public. Please help us to achieve this aim by spending a few moments to complete this questionnaire. The results are carefully scrutinized and action taken wherever necessary.
Unfortunately, it is not possible to reply to questionnaires individually. If you have any particular comments to make, which you feel require a personal reply, please write to our Customer Relations Department.
We hope that you enjoyed your holiday.

PLEASE MARK ALL YOUR ANSWERS AS CLEARLY AS POSSIBLE AND RETURN IT TO OUR REPRESENTATIVE ON COMPLETION

---

1. Name of resort

2a. Name of hotel/villa/apartment

2b. If you took a two-centre holdiay in Tenerife, name your second resort

2c. and hotel

3. With which airline did you travel?

4a. Name of UK departure airport

4b. Date of your outward
    flight from UK   /   /   198

5a. Were you satisfied with the pre-departure administration provided by Thomas Cook Holidays?

    Yes☐   No☐

5b. If you answered NO, why were you dissatisfied?

6a Were our brochure descriptions of your hotel/resort adequate?

    Yes☐   No☐

6b. If you answered NO, in what way was the brochure inadequate?

7a. Did your holiday live up to your expectations?

    Yes☐   No☐

Table 15.1 *contd.*

7b. If you answered NO, please explain why

---

8   How do you view our key rating for your holiday hotel/villa/ apartment?

      Correct   □

      Too High   □

      Too Low   □

9. Have you ever taken a Thomas Cook holiday before?

    Yes □   No □

10. Why did you choose Thomas Cook Holidays this time?

---

11. How likely are you to choose Thomas Cook Holidays again for a future holiday?

      Definitely   □

      Probably   □

      Possibly   □

      Unlikely   □

PLEASE RATE THE FOLLOWING ASPECTS OF YOUR HOLIDAY BY TICKING ONE BOX FOR EACH STATEMENT THAT APPLIED TO YOU

To be answered by everyone	Exc.	Very Good	Good	Fair	Poor
• Airport check-in facilities	□	□	□	□	□
• Inflight catering	□	□	□	□	□
• Inflight service	□	□	□	□	□
• Transfer arrangements from airport to accommodation	□	□	□	□	□
• Thomas Cook Holidays optional excursions offered by our Representative (answer only if taken)	□	□	□	□	□
• Helpfulness and quality of the service of Representative	□	□	□	□	□
• Quality of information on Thomas Cook Holidays noticeboard and in excursion binder	□	□	□	□	□
• Hotel/villa/apartment overall	□	□	□	□	□
• Situation of hotel/villa/apartment	□	□	□	□	□
• Comfort of accommodation	□	□	□	□	□
• Chambermaid/maid service	□	□	□	□	□
• Room maintenance	□	□	□	□	□
• If there are children in your party, how do you rate the facilities provided for them?	□	□	□	□	□
• The resort in general	□	□	□	□	□
• Weather during your holiday	□	□	□	□	□
• Value for money of holiday overall	□	□	□	□	□
• Taking all aspects into account, how would you rate your holiday overall?	□	□	□	□	□

Table 15.1   *contd.*

ANSWER ONLY IF YOU STAYED IN AN HOTEL	Exc.	Very Good	Good	Fair	Poor
• Meals in hotel	☐	☐	☐	☐	☐
• Waiter/buffet service in dining room	☐	☐	☐	☐	☐
• Attitude and helpfulness at reception desk	☐	☐	☐	☐	☐
• Hotel bar service	☐	☐	☐	☐	☐
• Entertainment (if advertised in brochure)	☐	☐	☐	☐	☐

ANSWER ONLY IF YOU STAYED IN A VILLA/APARTMENT					
• Cooking facilites	☐	☐	☐	☐	☐
• Eating/cooking utensils	☐	☐	☐	☐	☐
• Groceries provided on arrival (if advertised)	☐	☐	☐	☐	☐

ANSWER ONLY IF YOU WERE ON A WINTERSPORTS HOLIDAY					
• Standard of hire skis and boots available (answer only if hired)	☐	☐	☐	☐	☐
• Efficiency of ski lift system	☐	☐	☐	☐	☐
• Standard of tuition of ski school (answer only if used)	☐	☐	☐	☐	☐
• Range of skiing in resort	☐	☐	☐	☐	☐
• Snow conditions	☐	☐	☐	☐	☐
• Apres-ski/evening entertainment in resort	☐	☐	☐	☐	☐

In addition to downhill skiing, which of these wintersports activities did you participate in during the holiday?

• Tobogganing ☐   Cross-country skiing ☐   Skating ☐   Walking ☐

TO BE ANSWERED BY EVERYONE
Are there any other points you would like to mention that haven't been covered by this questionnaire?

_____

_____

_____

THANK YOU VERY MUCH FOR YOUR HELP

the resort. Questions 5a–8 seek respondents' views on the accuracy of the information provided by Thomas Cook Holidays prior to the holiday departure. This material is particularly important given the unique position of holidays as a product which is bought without reference to the actual holiday experience. Tour operators rely on the brochure as a means of persuasion and information about both hotels and resorts. Obviously it needs to be accurate and helpful bearing in mind that the package holiday buyer has an inherent suspicion that the brochure descriptions are biased and the photographs are invariably taken so as to show hotels in the best possible light. Questions 9–11 provide data on frequency and reasons for using Thomas Cook Holidays.

It can be seen from the questionnaire that questions relating to specific features of the hotel and the perceived quality of resort representation are dealt with by means of a rating scale and it is these questions which constitute the bulk of the questionnaire.

Quality control in the package holiday industry performs two functions. Firstly, it contributes to tactical decisions taken during the season when action can be taken to improve poor ratings. Secondly, it has a direct effect on the planning process, particularly with respect to the forward contracting of accommodation. For obvious reasons, the year is divided into two seasons: summer, from April to October inclusive, and winter, from November to March—and planning cycles are necessarily long. For example, brochures for the summer season are launched in October so contracting must take place during the early part of one year for the summer season the following year.

Although the processing of the questionnaires is continuous, an early-season report is produced four weeks after the start of the programme. This provides early indications of any problems with accommodation, transport arrangements or resort representation. Such problems could include poor maid service or poor food at the hotel, airport transfer not running or poor service from the operator's own resort representative. The data are used to take corrective action where appropriate and this can involve a wide range of personnel. Product managers look after the programme as a whole and respond to clients' views on brochure descriptions and resort facilities. Contractors have the responsibility of ensuring that hotels meet the required levels of service and comfort and they may have to take action at specific properties. Resort representatives, or couriers as they are more commonly known, are the responsibility of overseas service managers who may have to take action with any representative who is in receipt of poor ratings. Resort representatives are not employed on a long-term basis but on seasonal contracts which can cause occasional difficulties.

A second wave of analysis is conducted at the mid-season point. This is used in much the same way as the first wave but it does also provide an opportunity to assess the effects of corrective action taken following the earlier analysis and it does, of course, serve to identify any new sources of difficulty. The report format shows the various aspects of the holiday in rows and property and region breaks in columns. One such typical report is shown in Table 15.2, this being

Table 15.2 . *Thomas Cook Holidays — Winter Sun 1985/86 — Villas/Apartment Analysis*

SUMMARY OF HOLIDAY ATTRIBUTES

Base: Total Sample

VILLAS/APARTMENTS

	Holidays Total	Villas & Apts. Total	Majorca RESORT Total	Puerto Pollensa TOWN Total	Daina Apts. PROPERTY	Cala San Vicente TOWN Total	Ca'n Botana Villas PROPERTY	Costa del Sol RESORT Total	Estepona TOWN Total	Vila-Cana Apts. PROPERTY	Marbella TOWN Total	Melia Jardines del Mar PROPERTY	Fuengirola TOWN Total	Las Palmeras Sol Apts. PROPERTY	Nerja TOWN Total	El Capistrano Apts. PROPERTY
Total	1893	544	102	26	26	21	21	22	8	8	4	4	4	4	6	6
Airport check-in facilities	69	68	74	75	75	71	71	58	66	66	63	63	50	50	50	50
Inflight catering	56	57	56	68	68	57	57	48	50	50	63	63	44	44	38	38
Inflight service	64	63	61	71	71	60	60	65	68	68	63	63	69	69	60	60
Transfer arrangements	74	71	75	84	84	79	79	75	69	69	88	88	63	63	83	83
Optional excursions	68	62	73	88	88	88	88	50	50	50	75	75	63	63	1	1
Helpfulness/quality of our Representative	80	78	82	92	92	86	86	81	88	88	94	94	75	75	65	65
Quality of information on noticeboards and in excursion binder	71	69	70	73	73	65	65	66	69	69	83	83	67	67	26	26
Hotel/villa/apartment overall	72	72	78	85	85	86	86	67	78	78	63	63	32	32	79	79
Situation of hotel/villa/apartment	75	70	71	69	69	76	76	75	75	75	81	81	75	75	70	70
Comfort of accommodation	71	66	73	82	82	79	79	65	72	72	57	57	44	44	75	75
Chambermaid/maid service	73	67	67	83	83	57	57	64	54	54	81	81	44	44	79	79
Room maintenance	68	62	64	78	78	62	62	60	61	61	63	63	44	44	67	67
Special arrangements for children	53	50	45	50	50	50	50	47	38	38			100	100	42	42

MID-SEASON 1985/86

for Spanish villa and apartment holidays featured in the Winter Sun brochure. Separate tables are produced for hotels, villas and apartments and these show, from left to right, the total score for all holidays taken in the season to date. This is used as a benchmark against which all resort and property ratings can be measured. The second column shows the total for all villa and apartment holidays which is compared firstly to the scores for all holidays and secondly is used as a benchmark for villa and apartment holidays. The remaining columns show the data broken down to the lowest level giving the country or resort area first, individual towns second and specific properties third. In this particular case each resort is associated with only a single set of properties. In the larger summer brochure a resort could well feature several hotels or rental properties, in which case the resort index provides a benchmark against which each facility can be meaningfully contrasted. The rating scale used to derive the computed scores is:

Excellent	100
Very Good	75
Good	50
Fair	25
Poor	0

An acceptable level of performance is generally considered to be 60 and action is always taken when scores fall below this level. The first row, marked 'TOTAL' is the number of respondents who completed questionnaires. The particular example shown relates to winter villa and apartment holidays which obviously feature far fewer customers than do the summer programmes. However, attention is always paid to the sample size when determining courses of action. A further factor which contributes to the decisions about corrective action is the weather experienced on the holiday. Research has shown that respondents who suffered poor weather while on holiday are more likely to hold poor views of other aspects of the total experience.

At the end of the season an analysis is carried out both on the second half of the programme to ensure that previous action taken has been effective and on the season as a whole from which a plan of action is constructed for future product development. Product managers use these data to assist in rephrasing descriptions of resorts and properties used in the brochures and to determine, in conjunction with contract managers, which properties to retain and which to suspend from future programmes. The process of quality control in package holidays is continuous and vital for companies buying rooms and services overseas. It is important that the sample base be maintained at the highest possible level to ensure that the results are credible and of statistical significance. In this respect Thomas Cook currently achieves a response rate of 60 to 65 per cent which ensures that all resorts and properties are represented in the results. Because of the wide range of products which need to be audited for quality there tends to be a wide number of questionnaires covering the specific needs of each product area.

The routinised use of this questionnaire now represents a key element in our total quality control programme. The insights gained from it are valuable and have, undoubtedly, contributed to ensuring that Thomas Cook holidays continue to be viewed as offering good value for money. Only by ensuring that our customers are satisfied can we hope to see them rebook with us.

So successful has the scheme been that we have recently introduced an evaluation procedure for our retail outlets. Here the emphasis is, of course, on different issues but the underlying philosophy is the same, i.e. the determination of comparative standards and the identification of areas where remedial action is called for.

Quality Control in Retail Travel Shops

Whilst it is relatively easy to administer quality control questionnaires to holiday takers in the resort by utilising the coach transfer or whole-plane charter as a distribution point, it is clearly far more difficult to monitor performance in retail travel shops. There is a need not only to monitor the quality of the package holidays bought from an operator's brochure, but also to ensure that the retail promise is fulfilled. This latter poses the additional difficulty of being primarily associated with service values as the travel agency service is perceived to be first and foremost the source and supply of clear and unbiased information about resorts, hotels and tour operators which will enable the customer to choose the holiday that will most accurately meet his needs. Only secondarily are travel agents thought of as a medium through which the holiday can be booked. Independent research indicates that the travel agent is in ascendancy during the selection process as a source of information as described above. Once a booking has been completed, though, it is the tour operator who takes the stage, leaving the travel agent as a subsidiary player.

Thomas Cook is the first UK travel agent to develop a system of quality auditing which reflects the complexity of a tour operator's system. It has done so for two specific reasons. Firstly, there is a need to obtain some feedback on the quality of information provided to the client prior to booking. This consideration has a clear impact on customer care and provides some measurement of a number of subjective issues. Could we have provided videos showing different resorts, for example, or should we have been in a position to provide information on the most appropriate destination for young couples, families, singles, and so forth? Secondly, travel agents negotiate levels of commission from tour operators which are usually based on the level of service and sales support provided to agency staff. The opportunity has been seized to ask customers a series of questions similar to those asked by the tour operator in the resort. These are aimed at determining the views held about the holiday itself. This information can then be used as part of the negotiating process, as it is clearly important for a large multiple retailer to guarantee the quality of the products it offers to the public.

The Thomas Cook retail quality control questionnaire (see Table 15.3) is mailed to customers ten to fourteen days after they have returned from their holiday, the despatch date being routinely determined from the original holiday booking receipt. Questionnaires are packaged to clients as part of a broader customer care and direct mail programme known as Travel Masters. This system enables us to build relationships with customers based upon the emphasis that Thomas Cook places on ensuring that the most appropriate holidays are provided for different people. The inclusion of the questionnaire in this mailing helps maximise the return rate, the rationale being that the customer can be persuaded to complete such a document more easily if he feels it to be part of a complete programme and that he has an important part to play in decisions regarding the holidays being sold.

As with the holiday questionnaire, the data are processed on a seasonal basis using the same calendar breaks for summer and winter. However, it is not as important that information be made available throughout the season and, consequently, a single analysis is produced at the end of the season. The results are used as the basis for negotiation with tour operators, for enhancements to customer care and information provision at branch level, and for booklets about different hotels and resorts which are published by Thomas Cook to help customers with their choice of holiday destination.

All in all, this extension to our monitoring programme is providing us with valuable insights into where our performance can be improved. Holidays represent for many families by far the single biggest item of expenditure in a year. Our efforts at measuring how well we contribute to the value of that investment are substantial. We anticipate that customers will benefit directly but, clearly, we fully recognise that this year's satisfied customer is next year's prospective client.

Table 15.3   *Thomas Cook*

Dear Customer

It is one of our main priorities to maintain high standards in the holidays we sell. Please help us to ensure that the operators and resorts we recommend meet these standards by spending a few moments to complete this questionnaire.
We hope that you enjoyed your holiday.

Tim Burfoot
Market Research Manager
Thomas Cook Ltd.

PLEASE USE THE PENCIL PROVIDED

SECTION 1: TRAVEL AGENT

Q1   To which of these age groups do you belong?

24 or under	☐	45-54	☐
25-34	☐	55-64	☐
35-44	☐	65 +	☐

Q2   What is the occupation of the chief wage earner? (if retired please state previous occupation)

Q3   Did we provide enough information to help you select the right holiday?
Yes   ☐
No   ☐

Q4   Below are some examples of holiday information. Of these, which would you have liked Thomas Cook to provide? (You may tick more than one)
Resort videos   ☐
Resort fact sheets   ☐
Information on the tour operator   ☐
Information about the operators resort representatives and services   ☐
Advice on alternative tour operators covering the same resort   ☐
Special advice on the right resort for singles, young couples, young families
etc.   ☐

Q5   How could we have improved our service as a travel agent?

SECTION II: RESORT

Q6   What was the name of the resort you stayed at this year?

Table 15.3 *Thomas Cook contd.*

	Very Good	Good	Fair	Poor	Very Poor
Q7 What was your opinion of the facilities for eating out in the resort?	☐	☐	☐	☐	☐
Q8 What was your opinion of the beach/lido facilities in the resort?	☐	☐	☐	☐	☐
Q9 How would you rate the nightlife in the resort? (Answer only if you sampled it)	☐	☐	☐	☐	☐

SECTION III: THE HOTEL/VILLA/APARTMENT

Q10   What was the name of your hotel/villa/apartment?_____

Q11   What type of accommodation was this   Hotel ☐   Villa ☐   Apartment ☐

Q12   Below is a list of various aspects of holiday accommodation. Please rate your accommodation on each aspect

	Very Good	Good	Fair	Poor	Very Poor
The situation of the hotel/villa/apartment	☐	☐	☐	☐	☐
Comfort of accommodation	☐	☐	☐	☐	☐
Maid/Chambermaid service	☐	☐	☐	☐	☐
Room maintenance (eg decoration, fittings, etc)	☐	☐	☐	☐	☐
Special arrangements for children (if used)	☐	☐	☐	☐	☐
HOTEL					
Meals in the hotel	☐	☐	☐	☐	☐
Waiter/buffet service in dining room	☐	☐	☐	☐	☐
Attitude/helpfulness at reception	☐	☐	☐	☐	☐
Hotel bar service	☐	☐	☐	☐	☐
Entertainment	☐	☐	☐	☐	☐
VILLA/APARTMENTS ONLY					
Q13 Cooking facilities	☐	☐	☐	☐	☐
Eating/cooking utensils	☐	☐	☐	☐	☐
Groceries provided on arrival — if advertised	☐	☐	☐	☐	☐
Cleanliness on arrival	☐	☐	☐	☐	☐
Q14 How would you rate the quality of the accommodation overall?	☐	☐	☐	☐	☐
Q15 How far do you think the accommodation was good value for money?	☐	☐	☐	☐	☐

Table 15.3 *Thomas Cook contd.*

SECTION IV: TOUR OPERATOR

Q16 What was the name of the tour operator with which you took your holiday?

____

Q17 Excluding the holiday you have recently taken, how many holidays have you taken with this operator, in the last 2 years?

None ☐ 1-2 ☐ 3-5 ☐

Q18 Why did you choose this particular tour operator for your holiday this year? You may mark more than one.

Price	☐	Past experience	☐
Convenient flight times	☐	Recommendation of friends/relatives	☐
Convenient departure dates	☐	Recommendation of travel agent	☐
Good brochure	☐		

	Very Good	Good	Fair	Poor	Very Poor
Q19 What was the quality of the pre-departure administration offered by the tour operator?	☐	☐	☐	☐	☐
Q20 How accurate was the brochure description of your					
Hotel?	☐	☐	☐	☐	☐
Resort?	☐	☐	☐	☐	☐

Q21 If you travelled with an airline, which one was it? ______________________________

	Very Good	Good	Fair	Poor	Very Poor
Q22 How would you rate the quality of the inflight service and catering?	☐	☐	☐	☐	☐
Q23 How would you rate the transfer arrangements from the airport to your hotel/villa/apartment?	☐	☐	☐	☐	☐
Q24 How would you rate the service you received from the resort representative?	☐	☐	☐	☐	☐
Q25 How likely are you to choose the same tour operator for a holiday next year?	☐	☐	☐	☐	☐
Q26 Taking all aspects into account, how would you rate your holiday overall?	☐	☐	☐	☐	☐

Why do you say this?

____

HOSPITALITY

16

The Sheraton Guest Experience

'On from room to room I stray
Yet mine host can ne'er espy,
And I know not to this day,
Whether guest or captive I.'

World Strangeness
Sir William Watson

MIA TOUZIN, Manager, Manpower Development and Training, Sheraton Management Corporation.

Anyone whose business involves staying overnight in hotel rooms will be familiar with the forms which appear in the room on which observations on service are solicited. Originally I had anticipated that the planned chapter on quality control practice in hotels would involve little more than a presentation of some of the results emerging from an analysis of these forms. In the event, when I made contact with the Sheraton Corporation, it transpired that they had a somewhat more interesting story to tell. Like all international hotel chains they have come to the conclusion that their customers take high-quality decor and facilities for granted. What will differentiate one hotel from another will be the extent to which its customers feel they have been on the receiving end of a pleasant personal experience. Sheraton have, therefore, devoted a good deal of energy towards attempting to improve this aspect of personal service and in what follows the various annual campaigns devoted to it are described.

Given the emphasis such a commitment places on staff training, it is appropriate that the chapter is contributed by the person responsible for the manpower development and training function at Sheraton. In that role she has been heavily involved in the last two quality campaigns which covered all 60 Sheraton hotels in 38 countries in Europe, Africa, The Middle East and S.E. Asia. Prior to taking up her present post in 1984 she had worked as the Human Resources Manager with Holiday Inns, Europe, in which post she was responsible for the personnel and training function in 45 hotels in ten countries. She obviously possesses qualifications in hotel administration but her ability to operate so readily across frontiers is helped by a fluency in six European languages.

★ ★ ★

181

What is the best 'Quality Guest Experience' in the Sheraton hotels? How do we define Quality? How do we ensure that what we give is what our guests want? What makes our guests return? Does it make a difference to the 'bottom line'? To answer those questions, I need to familiarise you with:

- the Sheraton Story
- the Quality Improvement Programmes
- their history (1981–1984)
- the results to date
- what we have learnt so far—and
- where we are going next!

The Sheraton Story

The Sheraton Corporation is one of the largest international luxury hotel companies in the world. There are currently 488 hotels in almost 60 countries worldwide, and every eight days Sheraton opens a new hotel somewhere in the world.

It all began in 1937 when the founder of Sheraton, Ernest Henderson, purchased a 200-room motor inn at Springfield, Massachusetts. Two years later three further hotels were acquired in Boston. One was named Sheraton and the rooftop sign was in such good condition that, rather than take it down, the name was retained and so Sheraton was born. In its formative years Sheraton expanded relatively slowly. It became an international organisation in 1949 as a consequence of the acquisition of two hotel chains in Canada. In those early days Sheraton purchased existing hotels, but in 1957 the company achieved another milestone when it designed and built The Philadelphia Sheraton.

The first properties acquired outside the Continental United States were four hotels in Honolulu in 1959, and in 1961 a hotel was purchased in Israel. The Franchise Division was formed in 1962 and in 1963 the corporate name appeared for the first time in Latin America. In its first 30 years of operations, Sheraton gained a foothold in ten countries. It was then considered more of a real estate company than a hotel management company.

In 1968 Sheraton became a wholly-owned subsidiary of International Telephone and Telegraph Corporation (ITT), then under the dynamic leadership of Harold S. Geneen, and the company's expansion really took off. Howard P. 'Bud' James was brought in as President and Chief Operating Officer. He immediately changed the corporation's operating philosophy from one of a real estate organisation involved in the building, owning and managing of hotels to one of a hotel management company where the emphasis was on managing, rather than owning, de luxe hotels throughout the world. James predicted that it would take ten years to accomplish his new mode of operating. It took, in fact, just eight years.

Today, Sheraton is the fastest growing international luxury hotel company in the world. It operates on the basis of five geographical operating divisions: North America; Latin America; Europe; Africa, the Middle East and South Asia; Hawaii and Japan and the Far East. The Franchise Division operates more than 300 Sheraton properties in North America. In 1983, John Kapioltas was appointed President and Chief Operating Officer of the Sheraton Corporation, and a year later he was appointed Chairman.

Sheraton's marketing force, which provides one of the toughest marketing muscles in the business, is distributed among major sales centres around the world. The company also operates in some of the world's most exotic locations as, for example:

- four Nile Cruise ships in Egypt that cruise between Aswan and Luxor;
- the spectacular 1,800-room Sheraton-Waikiki Hotel which is one of Hawaii's largest convention hotels;
- the elegant Sheraton St. Regis at 55th and 5th in the heart of The Big Apple, New York; and
- spectacular Sheraton properties in Australia and Latin America.

Sheraton offers aggressive management training schemes for hotel career students, and it maintains one of the world's most professional teams of hotel operators.

Quality Improvement Programme

With the rapid rate of international expansion, Sheraton was faced with the major challenge of maintaining and improving the quality image throughout the company's network of five-star de luxe hotels. The answer lay in a Sheraton Quality Improvement Programme that would infiltrate through every department in every Sheraton hotel in the Europe, Africa, Middle East and South Asia Division (EAME & SA).

The impetus for the campaign came from Sheraton's parent company, ITT, Inc. A highly motivated Quality Improvement Department directing Quality Improvement Committees is maintained throughout ITT's worldwide network of companies. ITT defines quality for its units as: 'Conformance to an established requirement, specification or purpose'. Sheraton took its quality programme from there.

Each year since 1981, when the programme was first introduced to Sheraton hotels in Europe, Africa, the Middle East and South Asia, we have mounted a Quality Improvement Programme around a particular theme:

Quality Improvement Teams
The inaugural 1981 programme involved the setting up of Quality Improvement Teams in each hotel. The minutes of each meeting were circulated among all hotels thereby spreading ideas for good practice around the division.

Q'Lympics Campaign
The 1982 Quality Programme centred on the Q'Lympics Campaign which introduced a competitive element aimed at stimulating creativity.

Sher-a-thon Relay Race
The 1983 programme involved a Quality Management Team of six divisional department heads who established a major goal for each of their departments. These six goals were the basis of the six relay races run throughout the year.

A Hand in Quality
In 1984, A Hand in Quality campaign was introduced to carry on the momentum of the competitive spirit and will to excel. The 1984 campaign focused on self-audit.

Back to Basics
In 1985, the Quality Campaign went back to the basics. It required our staff to find out the meaning of quality from our guests, and then the staff were required to find ways of meeting the guests' needs.

The 1986 Quality Campaign is based on some of the findings of the 1985 Quality Campaign. In 1985, we established that our guests were demanding a more personal service. This was the criterion for repeat guests. The 1986 Quality Campaign is aimed at measuring our approach to meeting guest satisfaction. Let us now look at the campaigns in more detail.

1981: Quality Improvement Teams

The duties of the QI Team were:

1. To instil the concept of quality in all employees by involvement in:
   - staff induction programmes
   - training programmes
   - staff newsletters
   - award and incentive programmes
2. To collect information on the operation of the hotel through:
   - guest comment forms
   - inspection reports
   - quality audit reports

- department log books
- observation (as, for example, the inspection of guest rooms)
- safety and accident reports

—and to recommend appropriate actions to the management.

1982: The Q'Lympics Campaign

In 1982 the Q'Lympics Campaign was launched in the Europe, Africa, Middle East and South Asia Division (EAME & SA). It was a campaign designed to stimulate quality awareness by introducing the element of competition. The emphasis of this campaign was creativity. The programme proved to be an outstanding success. EAME & SA hotels submitted a total of 402 entries, providing a host of new ideas for improving and maintaining the quality levels in all aspects of our operations.

The Q'Lympics '82 Campaign was introduced to each hotel, with an impressive audio-visual presentation which was shown to all general managers and quality teams in the division. A special edition of the Q'Tips Newspaper was published to coincide with the launch of the campaign which was given extra momentum with the help of banners, stickers and letterheads which were given massive exposure in all back-of-house areas. There were competition entry forms, as well as an attractive Q'Lympics '82 calendar featuring catchy quality slogans for each month.

A Quality Handbook, with an easy-to-read breakdown of all aspects of quality improvement in the division, was distributed to each hotel in EAME & SA. Each quarter there were three competition categories. In January, for example, they were Public Relations, Sales and Food and Beverage. Each hotel in Europe, Africa, Middle East and South Asia was required to enter one of the three categories in the competition which required them to describe how they would improve and maintain the quality levels in the given category.

The best three submissions were then awarded Q'Lympics gold, silver and bronze medals. Each month the winning entries were circulated to all the hotels in the division in an effort to improve their quality programmes. The whole process was repeated each month, but for different categories. By the end of 1982, points were totalled, and three hotels were declared overall gold, silver and bronze medal winners.

Among the multitude of creative new ideas that emerged there were a number of unusual food promotion themes, including:

- using areas in the hotel not previously used for producing revenue, e.g. swimming pool area and car park;

- utilising the national food or entertainment skills of our, generally, multinational employees, e.g. Philippine food with traditional dances.

One of the most innovative ideas to come out of the 1982 campaign was the introduction of the 'Q-Box'. Although ostensibly no more than a box of easily accessible cards containing hundreds of quality improvement ideas the benefits of such a simple concept have been phenomenal.

Ideas documented on the cards ranged from the Dubai Sheraton's suggestion for a campaign to pay extra attention to children of families in the restaurant to the Tel Aviv Sheraton's 'Gold Carpet Service' for the business executive. Several top floors are reserved as a special 'hotel within a hotel' and there is a separate check-in, champagne on arrival, secretarial services and a separate lounge serving morning coffee. The 'Q-Box' continues to be widely used throughout the division by all hotels looking for new ideas.

1983: Sher-a-thon Relay Races

Following through on the competitive spirit of Q'Lympics, the 1983 Sher-a-thon Relay Race was introduced. The divisional quality management team, along with the six divisional functional department heads, established a major goal for each of their departments. These six goals constituted the basis of the six relay races which were run throughout 1983. The emphasis of this campaign was implementation. The unit quality improvement team reported on a quarterly basis the progress by each department towards the achievement of the established goal. These entries were judged by experts and the points given were recorded on a colourful race track. The winners of each category received a 'Golden Baton'. At the end of the year the batons were permanently awarded to the hotels with the highest result. A special award was given to the Grand Winner. Participation during 1983 resulted in 430 entries from over 40 hotels.

The Competition

The six divisional departments organising individual departmental races were:

- Sales and Marketing
- Food and Beverage

- Rooms Department (Front Office, Housekeeping, Reservations)
- Maintenance
- Personnel and Training
- Controllers

For each department's race there were:

- the major goal for 1983
- the criteria for measurement of each relay

The Food and Beverage Department's major goal, for example, was to 'Increase the profitability of the restaurant, serving the highest number of covers per day, through the improvement of quality of service, product and facility.'

The measurements which in all cases were compared to Actual '82 and Budget '83 figures in local currency were:

- number of total covers served by that restaurant
- average bill of the restaurant
- ratio of number of covers served in the restaurant to the house count (guests in hotel)

These steps had to be supported each quarter by a brief description of the various steps taken to achieve this 1983 quality goal.

The Personnel and Training Department's quality goal was 'To improve employee productivity and quality guest experience' through:

- the hotel training plan
- control of employee absenteeism
- analysis of work methods
- other methods appropriate to the individual hotel

The measurements, again compared to Actual '82 and Budget '83 in local currency, were:

- total revenue per full-time employee
- ratio of salaries and benefits to total revenue
- ratio of total benefit to total salaries

The figures had to be supported, as for Food and Beverage, by a brief description, every quarter, of the steps taken to achieve the goal.

1984: A Hand in Quality

This campaign was designed to carry on the momentum of the competitive spirit and will to excel. The 1984 campaign focused on self-audit. Each unit quality improvement team was presented with a choice of goals for each department. These goals were established by Sheraton Management Corporation department heads and reflected the themes and subjects at the recent Departmental Conferences. Quarterly submissions of the work prepared by each unit were submitted for judgement and each employee of the quarterly winning team received a letter of appreciation and a certificate signed by the Divisional President.

Each EAME & SA hotel received a set of glossy Q Cards for each department outlining the six set tasks, four of which had to be completed during 1984. The Q Cards '84 covered Controllers, Food and Beverage, Rooms, Personnel and Training, Maintenance and Sales and Marketing functions. By the end of 1984, a total of 606 entries had been received in the divisional headquarters from 50 hotels. The entries were judged on a scale where the maximum possible number of points for *presentation* was 5, that for the *concept* 10, with *results*, naturally, featuring the highest potential of 15. Each set of Q Cards included one Gold Q Card that could be played only once and when it was used it would double the score.

The Sheraton Europe, Africa, Middle East and South Asia hotels quality campaigns had evolved into the most outstanding quality improvements effort ever seen in any hotel company and were probably far superior to those in many other industries. The quality of entries, in terms of both content and presentation, has risen continuously and has involved a substantial effort from the participating teams and individuals. The judging of over six hundred entries demanded and deserved an almost equal effort.

That, then, was the history of the Quality Improvement Programmes up until December 1984. What had we achieved? The answer was, we were winning and we were also losing. The first achievement of the campaigns was that they had brought a sense of quality, creativity, enthusiasm and competitiveness into the day-to-day operations of the hotels throughout the division which by now encompassed 38 countries. The campaigns also created recognition and visibility for the quality efforts in the hotels on the part of the senior divisional executives. This recognition had demanded the participation of our general managers and therefore the word 'Quality' had a new meaning in the division. As a consequence the results of these various efforts were passed on to Sheraton guests.

However, the Quality Campaigns were not without their problems at both the hotel and the divisional headquarters at Denham Place, England. The Quality Campaigns necessitated many man-hours of effort at the hotels not only in the creation of ideas but also in the subsequent preparation of the presentation of the ideas to senior management. Indeed, some hotels with more money to spend than others contracted out their presentations, converting an ideas competition into one where the emphasis was on presentation.

The hotels had also begun to complain that the Quality Campaigns resulted in too much time being diverted from the actual operation of the hotel. The programmes, claimed the hotels, had mainly remained at management level and employees below that level were rarely involved. This resulted in some of the programmes not being fully implemented.

We were also faced with the inevitable fact of life that we have one winner and 59 losers in the various competitions. We reached a point where some general managers were asking for a 'rest' from the campaigns. Their comments included: 'We can't think of anything else creative; we haven't got the time.' Some general managers even claimed that they were presenting ideas that were not really very practical.

We were, therefore, faced with having to make a decision in the middle of 1984 as to whether or not we should continue with the Quality Programmes. The first point on which everyone was agreed—general managers and divisional headquarters staff alike—was that we had established an excellent communications tool with the Quality Teams. It was also widely accepted that our Quality Campaigns had been primarily targeted at improving the facilities of our hotels, i.e. lobbies, restaurants, menus and rooms.

The industry had, however, evolved to the point where our discriminating business traveller, who is the bread and butter of our business, was beginning to take all these facilities for granted. This sophisticated traveller wanted something more from a five-star de luxe hotel. Consequently, we would base our future Quality Campaigns on the new needs of our sophisticated guests. Once we had established those needs, we then had to decide, as operators, what we should do.

1985: Back to Basics

The objective for the campaign was to define and enhance the role of each department in providing a Quality Guest Experience that would influence the competitiveness of Sheraton EAME & SA in each hotel's local marketplace and as a division. The rationale was to use internal means to develop and share creative, effective methods and presentations, and:

- to involve all departments, back as well as front of house, in order to build team spirit within the hotel and get the message of Quality Guest Experience into all areas;
- to aim at competing as a hotel against the competition, rather than against other Sheraton hotels.

This campaign comprised two complementary component parts:

- We went back to the guest and asked him why he would decide to return (or not to return) to a Sheraton hotel. In other words, we were looking for specific answers to such questions as, what is personal service? What does quality mean to you? And what makes you remember one Sheraton hotel over that of a competitor?
- A great deal of the guest research was actually carried out by the rank and file staff of the hotel. This gave all members of staff, from the most junior ranks up, a first-hand knowledge of the feelings of Sheraton guests. This exercise had a particularly effective advantage for the rank and file employees. They experienced a sense of pride as a consequence of representing the company to guests. They also had the feeling that they personally wanted to help the guest. The second part of the 1985 Quality Campaign was, therefore, addressed to ways in which our employees could improve the guest experience at a Sheraton hotel. Based on their own research, our employees now knew why they were doing what they were doing; they also recognised that their 'new' ways were important to management and they were beginning to realise that what is Quality to one guest may not be Quality to another.

This time we changed the procedure from individual executives judging entries on their own to a one-day conference. Executives and invited representatives from the general managers would judge the entries together in groups. This conference in itself became a forum for:

- ensuring that headquarters personnel were fully aware of what the hotels were doing and could make the hotels feel that their entry was made visible, during subsequent field trips;
- a brainstorming session on quality among experienced executives who, because of travel schedules, rarely have the opportunity to spend a full day together, talking about ideas and concepts.

What, then, were the results of the 1985 Quality Campaign? It was successful both from the guest's point of view and also when viewed from the perspective of Sheraton management. A few examples will illustrate the range of initiatives which stemmed directly from the campaign.

In *Abu Dhabi*, a computer was installed in the lobby next to a Guest Relations Officer. Guests were invited to make their comments during an informal interview with the Guest Relations Officer. The results were positively staggering! Guest responses increased to 4,000 in a given month as against the previous average of around 200. Sheraton guests were enthusiastic about the attention the company and its staff were devoting to them. Guests were questioned at airport lounges, in Sheraton lobbies and restaurants and they were invited to sit in on quality team meetings or asked to speak at staff meetings. Every guest who was asked to participate in one form or another accepted the invitation with enthusiasm.

In *Oslo*, the Sheraton Oslo Fjord Hotel actually invited guests who were staying with the competition to attend a Sheraton luncheon to discuss our competitor's quality and what had induced them to stay there. Several such luncheons were organised and all the guests, without exception, accepted the invitation. Several months after the initial function these same individuals were invited to a follow-up luncheon. As they had been so generous of their time and so forthcoming with information, we felt it only proper to provide them with feedback on what we had done with their comments. It should perhaps be stressed that these luncheons were most definitely not a crude attempt to lure these guests to our hotel and, indeed, were not seen to be so. We simply wanted to know what we could and should do better than our competitors.

In *Dhaka*, the Dhaka Sheraton turned a major refurbishment programme, which necessarily caused unending inconvenience to guests, into an advantage. Temporary power cuts, temporary water cuts and the sound of drills echoing through the hallways virtually removed all semblance of luxury. But the hotel took it all in its stride—with humour. As a consequence, the hotel guests took it in their stride. Management arranged children's parties which included Dhaka Sheraton staff members dressing up as Mickey Mouse and ET. Sports competitions were organised and amusing posters mocking the current conditions of the hotel were displayed prominently in the public areas. One direct consequence was that one positive story after another appeared in the local press, which in turn prompted the local market to increase its utilisation of the hotel.

From the employees' standpoint significant gains were also achieved as evidenced by significant reductions in staff turnover and absenteeism throughout the division in 1985. The general managers voiced overall enthusiasm for the 1985 Quality Campaign, a typical quote being: 'We haven't done enough on this campaign, but we believe in it and we want to do it again using the experience in Listening and Responding that we have shared during this conference'. They had in effect taken over ownership of the programme: both the concept and the activities. We now had full commitment and understanding from the top.

The Quality Programme for 1986 is based primarily on the work of the 1985 campaign. It has been structured into two phases:

Phase I

- Propose five methods of measuring guest satisfaction in the hotel using the guidelines introduced in the 1985 Quality Campaign. These guidelines include guest surveys, competitor shopping, staff training and working conditions.
- Review management support for all guest contact personnel. What do they need in order better to satisfy the guest?

Phase II

- Demonstrate the results from Phase I.

Conclusion

The Quality Campaigns in the Europe, Africa, Middle East and South Asia Division have undoubtedly been successful. Dividends will be reaped from them for many years into the future. Our guests have been winners, our employees have been winners and our management and owners have been more than satisfied with the programmes. It is the corporation's intention to continue these highly motivating and resourceful quality campaigns in order to reach an even higher level of guest satisfaction for the 1990s. So how did we do in 1986? Ask us in 1987!

17

The Good Food Guide

'Shall we never learn the worthlessness of other
peoples' views of food? There is no authoritative
body of comment on food. Like all the deeper
personal problems of life, you must face it alone.'

The Colby Essays, Vol. 2
Frank Moore Colby

JEREMY ROUND, Assistant Editor, The Good Food Guide.

One of the most visible signs of increased potential customer concern
with levels of service has been the growth of the 'Guide' style of
publications. The public, or at least a part of it, has taken these to their
heart to the extent that a good entry can have a quite dramatic impact
upon business. Indeed, my only reservation about this particular form
of development is that it can be too successful. To frequent a restaurant
for a number of years prior to it receiving its seal of approval and then
to find one is subsequently obliged to book days or even weeks ahead
can be galling in the extreme, but then one cannot have everything.
Although a variety of publications exist, not all carry the same degree of
credibility. What is certain is that *The Good Food Guide* is a tried and
trusted companion in many households. A part of the explanation must
lie in the fact that it emanates from the Consumers' Association stable
and to that extent is inevitably associated in the public's mind with a
detached but professional set of appraisals. In fact, as we shall see, the
Guide does not rely solely on a good progeny. The effort involved in
ensuring that the annual publication keeps track of culinary developments nationwide is immense. It represents a nice balance between a
professional and well coordinated set of headquarters-based activities,
with an enormous monitoring by self-selected or designated judges of
what constitutes good food. It is most certainly the case that the
emergence of the Guide has contributed to the overall improvement of
the 'eating out' experience even though many restaurateurs must await
its publication with a certain amount of trepidation.

Jeremy Round is another of those individuals with a less than normal
background. He dropped out of university half-way through a degree
in English and Philosophy to find out how far round the world he could
hitchhike on £10. Apparently it got him as far as Istanbul where he
taught English for 18 months before returning to complete his studies.
For the next three and a half years he worked as a courier for Rambler
Holidays in Turkey while at the same time compiling a guidebook to
the Aegean and Mediterranean coasts of that country. This is to be
published next year. He then won a course at Prue Leith's School as a

prize in the first *Guardian*/Mouton Cadet cookery competition and
subsequently joined the Guide in 1984. He also contributes pieces to
various magazines and has recently completed another book, this one
on Regional Turkish Cookery.

* * *

The birth of *The Good Food Guide* can be traced back to an article by
Raymond Postgate published in the 1949 *Leader Magazine* entitled
'Society for the Prevention of Cruelty to Food' (Postgate 1949). The
following year, The Good Food Club was launched with a membership form in the same magazine inviting restaurant recommendations from readers. The declared aims of the enterprise were:

- To raise the standard of cooking in Britain, and to keep prices
  reasonable.
- To encourage the drinking of good wine and the proper care of beer.
- To earn foreign currency by improving British hospitality and by offering
  overseas visitors guidance, not official puffs.
- To reward enterprise and courtesy.
- To do ourselves a bit of good, in due course, by publishing an
  annual which would make our holidays, travel, and evenings out
  enjoyable.

To potential reporters, Postgate suggested that they think of five
questions when assessing a restaurant: 'Is the cooking good and
ample? Is the price reasonable? Is the drink good and ample? Is *its*
price right? Did you find the service courteous and adequate?' Even at
this early stage it was stated that recommendations could not be
accepted from interested parties such as caterers, and that the book
would not be able to accept advertising from hotels or restaurants.

The first edition, which was published in 1951, contained 500
entries and sold 5,000 copies. The principles by which restaurants are
assessed, and the annual entries compiled, remain remarkably
similar, although sales are now ten times as great and the number of
entries about double.

The Good Food Guide is now an in-house publication of the
Consumers' Association. The assistant editor and an editorial
assistant are full-time staff appointed by the CA and two staff, the
editor and his senior assistant editor/chief inspector, are on short-
term contracts. Other staff are taken on as necessary to cover various
activities apart from the work on the main Guide which is undertaken
by the office throughout the year. This *ad hoc* work, which could be
related to new titles or research projects, is always undertaken on a
temporary basis, however senior the level of involvement.

The editorial assistant and assistant editor take care of the office system which mainly involves the management of the large volume of correspondence that is received each day and the gathering of precise factual information—opening times and so on—from the restaurants that are to be included in each new edition. The senior assistant editor is responsible for generating the lists of restaurants to be considered for inclusion each year, arranging for the most likely ones to be inspected, and assimilating the qualitative information received from public reporters and inspectors. The editor bears the final responsibility for the decision to include or exclude particular restaurants from the Guide. He it is who is responsible for the words that appear in the book although he actually writes only around 60 per cent of the material. He also writes most of the columns that the Guide provides each week for the *Guardian*'s Food and Drink page which is, coincidentally, edited at the time of writing by Christopher Driver, himself a former Good Food Guide editor. The editor is, of course, the public voice of the Guide.

There are about 400 voluntary Good Food Guide inspectors up and down the country who report in depth on meals they happen to partake of when eating out. They keep an eye on the restaurant scene of the areas in which they live, and are available to inspect officially, at the Guide's expense, any places about which the Guide cannot otherwise come to a firm decision, or about which a more tutored opinion than that to be deduced from public reports is thought necessary. They have, for the most part, been selected over the years from the most regular, reliable and perceptive public reporters. Almost without exception they are enthusiastic amateurs who care deeply about the standards of food and drink available in British restaurants and are willing to work very hard with no remuneration toward the promotion of excellence in this field. No-one actively involved in the restaurant trade is accepted as a voluntary inspector, although one or two are ex-restaurateurs or ex-chefs. In addition to voluntary inspectors, the Guide is in touch with a large number of expert consultants in a variety of specialised fields ranging from English cheeses to Chinese cookery techniques. These individuals advise when necessary—for the most part out of goodwill rather than for payment.

The Consumers' Association has charitable status—all profit is ploughed back into research within the organisation. The Good Food Guide just manages to support itself—making as much money as it spends. Its inspection budget is necessarily small compared with the cost of combined staff salaries and office overheads, but—with a day's post containing anywhere between 50 and 200 unsolicited public restaurant reports—the office benefits from about one million pounds' worth of 'free' restaurant information per year from its correspondents. In contrast the budget for commissioned inspections is in the order of £35,000. The editor and senior assistant editor inspect:

- establishments that seem likely to rate particularly highly;
- seemingly interesting places about which public reporters and/or voluntary inspectors are at odds;
- other places selected at random from across the country in order to ensure that ratings retain their consistency.

The Guide office uses a computer database designed to its own specification. Information is stored and kept readily accessible according to the very flexible requirements of a semi-journalistic operation. The basic office system is to process the post received each day. This includes the unsolicited reports from members of the public, unsolicited reports from voluntary inspectors, and commissioned inspections from voluntary inspectors, specialist consultants, or the editor or senior assistant editor. This material is input directly into the database in order to render it easily analysable when the decisions are being made about which establishments to include in the next edition of the book. The information 'filed' in the database also forms the basis for each written entry in the Guide.

The database has each report entered into it in two ways:

- as an abstract of the report held against the name of the restaurant and the name of the reporter (the statistical 'meat' of the system);
- as 'memo-style' notes to be used for compilation of the final entry for that restaurant in the next edition of the book (the journalistic 'bones' of the Guide).

Each report is read by the senior assistant editor or editor, who marks the points that will be especially useful when deciding whether the particular establishment should be included in the Guide: along with the passages of prose that will be most helpful to the writers when they are compiling the Guide.

The annotated post is then entered into the database by temporary freelancers who have secretarial skills, some writing ability, and sound food knowledge. Many are professional people in fields that do not operate along 9–5 lines: as, for example, opera singers and cookery teachers. Many of these are also voluntary inspectors. Part of the 'entering process' involves acknowledging the report which involves thanking the correspondent and offering, by way of small recompense for trouble taken, a list of amendments to information in the last Guide and recommendations for new places to eat that have not so far gained an entry.

Each 'post logger' works for a three-hour stretch only. Two computer terminals are available full-time to loggers, but on average only one is in operation each day (i.e. two three-hour sessions). At particularly busy times of the year both terminals, and sometimes an extra one, are kept busy with constant shifts of loggers. These busy times generally follow holiday periods such as the Christmas and New Year break, when reporters are particularly active.

Acknowledging post and logging it onto the database is a year-round activity, and the most essential function of the office. The mechanics of organising the body of part-time freelance labour outlined above, and liaising with the computer department of the CA, on whom the smooth running of the whole system depends, is the province of the assistant editor and her assistant.

The Good Food Guide is published in the late autumn of each year and so must be sent to the typesetters at the end of each summer. The writing starts in May and gathers speed up to the final copy date. Logistical decisions about the writing (i.e. who is going to write what) are undertaken by the editor. He commissions feature articles early in the year, then builds up a steady band of reliable, food-knowledgeable freelance writers throughout the early spring, on whom he will call as the pace of the operation increases and deadlines approach. He negotiates their rates of pay on an individual basis and pays them per entry.

The factual information about each restaurant included in the Guide is gathered from the establishments themselves by means of a formal questionnaire. The information from the questionnaires is entered into the computer by a data-entry clerk who does nothing else for the months of late spring and summer. When the writing of the prose part of each entry is complete, the right buttons are pressed to obtain a separate print-out of the relevant factual information ordered for the typesetter's convenience. Hard copies of both the rubric and the prose description/evaluation are then given to the CA in-house sub-editorial department who mark it up for the typesetter and at the same time check for factual accuracy against printed material received from the restaurant itself as, for example, menus. Any queries are brought up with the specific author of each entry and with the editor.

Punctilious verification of facts is one aspect of its work on which the CA prides itself throughout the whole organisation. Just as the writers of the entries make every effort to reflect precisely the judgements of those reporters and inspectors who have had something to say about each establishment over the year, so the sub-editors make every effort to check the factual content. They also double-check that the writers have not been swayed by either their own unsubstantiated opinions, or the subjectivity of any particular reporter. The sub-editorial department is careful to ensure that each entry err on the side of the optimistic understatement rather than that it be in any way construable as unfair. Of course, this is not to say that entries are not often thought unfair—either by the proprietors or chefs of the establishments involved or by later reporters. The positive and negative responses of reporters and inspectors and, to some extent, restaurateurs to each year's edition form the basis for the following year's entry or lack of one.

A month or so after publication, the senior assistant editor calls up print-outs of all the restaurants on the system and determines how each should be regarded with respect to the following year's inspectoral shortlist. A draft shortlist is developed but, as he and the editor annotate each day's post, they constantly amend this list. By early spring a shortlist exists which can be sent out to all inspectors in a region. The inspectors bring their local knowledge to bear on the list and hone it down further.

A waiting game then starts during which the office tries to delay for as long as possible the commissioning of inspections on the various establishments. The hope is that enough public reports will have been received upon which to base a firm, fair and up-to-date opinion, but at the same time an eye is kept on the next Guide's schedules, and the ever-diminishing budget.

The Good Food Guide contains entries for around 1,000 restaurants grouped alphabetically by the name of the habitation in which the establishment is to be found, under the general headings: London, England, Scotland, Wales, Channel Islands, Isle of Man, Northern Ireland. Other sections may be included from time to time: the Republic of Ireland, France's Channel Ports and Paris have, for example, featured in recent editions. These will change from year to year, and are tending to be seen in editorial terms more as 'feature interest' than as an integral part of the main listings.

The Guide is indexed by restaurant name, and includes a full set of maps plotting the whereabouts of each establishment listed. The prose entry describes the establishment, its setting, the decor, the ambience, the menu, the wine list and the style of cooking; it also features an evaluation of the quality of the ingredients, cooking, and service. The rubric section gives full address and telephone number, opening times and days, explains the establishment's methods of applying service and other extra charges, and lists the facilities in words rather than as a succession of symbols. The restaurant is accorded a rating by the editor out of a possible twenty marks. This enables the reader to see immediately what category of establishment is being described and how it compares in our estimation with other establishments of a similar type. The fictitious Guide entry (Table 17.1) illustrates the format.

Table 17.1 *How to Read a Guide Entry*

TORQUAY Devon[1]   map 17[2]

▲ *Fawlty Towers* [3] [12/20][4]

---

16 Elwood Avenue[5]
TORQUAY (0803) 777[6]
behind Scala Cinema[7]   X   □Real Food[9]£11-£18[10]

(main text)[11]
CELLARMAN'S CHOICE:[12]
Approvers: John Cleese, Andrew Sachs, Monty Python, Connie Booth, Prunella Scales[13]

CHEF: Kurt and Terry PROPRIETOR: Basil Fawlty[14]
OPEN: Mon to Sat[15] CLOSED: Aug[16] MEALS: 12 to 2, 7 to 9[17] Must book[18]
PRICES: L£7 (£11), Set D£12 (£18)[19] CARDS: Access, Amex, Diner, Visa[20]
SEATS: 72 (private parties 26)[21] 4 tables outside. Vegetarian meals[22] Car park. Jacket and tie preferred[23] No smoking area[24] Children's helpings. No children under 16[25] Wheelchair access (2 steps: also WC)[26] Classical music[27]
ACCOMMODATION: 14 room (all with bath/shower) B&B from £12 to £33[28] No pets[29]
Afternoon teas. Indoor swimming pool. Garden. Tennis (GHG)[30]

---

[1]   The town and county (in the London section, restaurants are listed alphabetically by name rather than geographically).
[2]   The map reference. The maps are to be found at the front of the Guide.
[3]   The name of the restaurant. ▲ by name denotes that it has rooms.
[4]   The Guide rating out of 20.
[5]   The restaurant's address.
[6]   The restaurant's telephone number including its STD code.
[7]   Any special directions in case the restaurant is hard to find.
[8]   This symbol is only awarded to restaurants with exceptionally fine wine lists.
[9]   Real Food denotes a restaurant that does not use processed food.
[10] This is the price of the meal calculated by the Guide to include three courses, half a bottle of house wine and any hidden extras.
[11] The text is based on reports sent in by readers during the last Guide year, confirmed by commissioned, anonymous inpsections.
[12] Some entries conclude with a CELLARMAN'S CHOICE. This is a wine, usually more expensive than the house wine, that the restaurateur assures us will be in stock during 1985, and that we would recommend as suitable for the kind of food served, if you do not want to order the house wine.
[13] These are the names of readers who have eaten here and approved its inclusion in the Guide. Only restaurants scoring 12 or more have the names attached.
[14] On restaurants scoring 12 or more we list the names of the chef and the owner, so that any change in management will be instantly detectable. It is also an acknowledgement of their standing in the profession.
[15] This indicates the days of the week the restaurant is open.
[16] This indicates any annual closures.
[17] These are the times of first and last orders for meals.
[18] It is always advisable to book before going to a restaurant even if it does not specifically say so. If you book and then cannot go, please remember to phone the restaurant to cancel.
[19] These are calculations of the typical prices for lunch (L) and dinner (D), showing variations for set meals where applicable. The first price includes only the prices given on the menu; the second price in brackets is the real cost when all the extras and wines and service have been included.
[20] These are the credit cards accepted by the restaurant.
[21] Not all restaurants will take private parties. The maximum number of people in a party is given.

Table 17.1   *How to Read a Guide Entry contd.*

[22] Many restaurants claim to cater for vegetarians but in fact do not. It is always advisable to explain when you book if you do not want meat.

[23] Jackets and ties are compulsory in very few rstaurants and this is specified; otherwise it means the proprietor prefers smart dress.

[24] The no smoking arrangements are notified to us by the restaurants.

[25] Many restaurants and hotels are not keen on children. Where it says children's helpings it indicates that they don't mind. Any limitations on age are specified.

[26] Wheelchair access means that the entrance is 33 inches wide and the passages four feet across. Where there are steps it will say so. If it says 'also wc', then the toilet facilities are suitable for disabled people.

[27] If a restaurant plays music, this is indicated. Many diners positively dislike it.

[28] The price for rooms is as notified to us by the hotels. The first price is for one person in a single room, the second price is for two people in a double room.

[29] Some hotels will allow pets in bedrooms only. Best to check first.

[30] [GHG] denotes that this establishment is also listed in the 1985 edition of our sister guide, *The Good Hotel Guide*. A list of these, and also of those establishments listed in the 1985 editions of *The Good Pub Guide* and *Which? Wine Guide*, are given at the back of the book.

As well as The Good Food Guide, the same office produces, as from 1986, a Budget Good Food Guide which covers establishments where it is easy to eat for around £5 a head, and a Good Food Directory to shops and suppliers. Other projects are planned as one-offs for future years.

18

Customer Satisfaction with Package Holidays

'One of the main troubles about going to Europe is that no-one wants to hear about your trip when you get back home. Your friends and relatives are ripe with jealousy and are not only sorry you went to Europe but deeply regret that you came back.'

Vogue, 1 April 1954
Art Buchwald

DR. BARBARA LEWIS, Senior Lecturer in Marketing at UMIST and **MIKE OWTRAM,** ICI.

The annual holiday which is so much a feature of British life is now taken abroad by some 14 million of us. For many families such an investment represents one of the largest single financial outlays and most expect to be able to look back on it with fond memories rather than anticipate a cheque in recompense for something having gone wrong. An early UMIST project revealed that many of the firms engaged in providing package holidays made surprisingly very little effort to ascertain what their clients thought of the package they had experienced. It does seem entirely reasonable to speculate that, when the expenditure incurred is not mirrored in a holiday that lives up to one's expectations, there is a natural tendency not to browse through that company's brochure for several years following. In many situations a most unfortunate accident is frequently no more than an untoward incident which, but for a variety of circumstances coming together, would have engendered no great excitement. Most of us, for example, have probably been very close to being involved in a fatal accident had circumstances been but marginally different. The same is true of things that go wrong with holidays. The logic of ascertaining travellers' views is not, therefore, to find out about things going dramatically wrong. Rather it is to have a monitoring facility which provides insight into how different aspects of these important episodes in our lives live up to what is expected.

Barbara was able to persuade one large tour operator to allow her to experiment with more sensitive monitoring systems than those typically found in the travel industry. An important feature was the opportunity to question holidaymakers both prior to and following their overseas trip, thereby enabling insight to be gained into the difference between the expectation and the reality.

This study is one of a number in which Barbara and a collection of research students have brought marketing concepts to bear on service industry issues. These have included, among others, the marketing of nursing as a career; kidney donorship; and a number of marketing issues in banking. She is, in fact, the editor of the *International Journal of Bank Marketing*. Mike, like Barbara before him, graduated in Management Sciences from UMIST and elected to pursue postgraduate research in the same department. Upon completion of this project he went on to secure a marketing traineeship with ICI where he is presently employed.

★ ★ ★

The Growth of International Tourism and Package Holidays

Package holidays comprise one, albeit a major, element of the tourism industry. Tourism has recently been defined to denote the temporary short-term movement of people to destinations outside the places where they normally live and work and their activities during the stay at these destinations (Burkart and Medlik 1981). International tourism, for business and non-business reasons, has increased from 55 million trips in 1958 to a present level in excess of 300 million trips a year worldwide. In 1983, UK residents alone took 19 million trips abroad of which 73 per cent were for a holiday and 5 per cent combined a holiday with visiting friends or relatives (English Tourist Board 1983).

Holidays abroad may be divided into inclusive tours, more popularly referred to as package holidays, and independent holidays. The first tour operator was Thomas Cook who, in 1841, ran a day excursion from Leicester to Loughborough for one shilling when he chartered 570 seats on a train to take supporters to a political meeting. The first air inclusive tour was offered as recently as 1950 and the subsequent growth in this form of holiday has both accompanied and caused the growth in the foreign holiday market.

Overseas holidays by UK residents increased by 18 per cent per annum in the 1960s (Economist Intelligence Unit 1984), and by over 10 per cent per annum in more recent years. Two-thirds of British expenditure on all holidays is presently spent on holidays abroad as compared with 27 per cent in 1960 (British Tourist Authority 1984). The number of holiday visits of four nights or more taken abroad by British residents was 5.7 million in 1970. By 1984 this figure had reached 15.0 million which represents an annual expenditure, including fares, of over five billion pounds (British Tourist Authority 1985). In recent years inclusive tours have comprised 54 per cent of all holidays overseas, having risen from 2.7 million in 1970 to 7.8 million in 1983. They account for 34 per cent of the total expenditure on holidays abroad. Independent holidays therefore make up 46 per cent of the market but account for 66 per cent of the expenditure.

The Demand for International Tourism

The development and growth of international tourism have been determined by a variety of social and economic factors together with a matching increase in the provision of tourist products and services. Most factors have encouraged growth but a few have acted as a deterrent. Some are general demand factors and others are more specific as they relate to the tourism product and the selection between competing products (for example, see Waterhouse 1975 and Davies 1981).

Social and Cultural Changes

The growth in international tourism, and holidays in particular, has been very much a function of demographic trends and social and cultural elements. These include shorter working hours, longer holidays and increased leisure time; higher levels of education and media exposure to overseas countries and cultures; a more affluent younger generation less inhibited by early families; earlier retirement with more active retirees and a more mobile population. Travel motivations are various, ranging from 'sunlust' to 'wanderlust', and can include the satisfaction of educational, cultural, relaxation, adventure, ethnic and family needs. As each of these are subject to changes in taste the tourism industry may fairly be considered a 'fashion' industry.

Economic and Political Elements

These have far-reaching effects on tourism. Industrialisation, business growth and industrial expansion have contributed to the internationalisation of companies and a resultant demand for international business travel and for overseas conferences. Increasing disposable incomes, combined with decreasing relative prices, have served to fuel the growth in tourism. On the other side of the coin political unrest, strikes, large movements in prices and exchange rates, seasonality with respect to labour and capacity and resentment on the part of the local indigenous population inhibit growth.

Technological Trends

Major technological trends have related to modern transport technology, including increased car ownership, improved roads and railways abroad, modern aircraft, and the introduction of computerised
booking systems and facilities.

Institutional Factors

Governments have traditionally influenced tourism through controls
on modes of travel, transport being highly regulated for both the
safety of passengers and the economic conduct of travel. For
example, international air services operate within air service agreements between countries which determine routes to be flown,
capacity to be provided and fares to be charged—although the 1980s
are characterised by de-regulation in this field. Governments also
place restrictions on tourism through visas and currency allowances
but at the same time encourage tourism through their involvement in
Tourist Boards. Most countries now boast some form of supervision
of tourism via an official National Tourism Office, the objectives of
which are to promote a country as a tourist destination and to
supervise the provision of tourist services and facilities.

The 1970s and 1980s have witnessed a retailing revolution in the
growth of tour operators and travel agents. The Association of British
Travel Agents (ABTA), with its 4,500 retailers, brings some order and
discipline to the tourism market at a time of expansion and protects
the public from less stable tour operators and travel agents.

Products/Services

As in any other industry tourist organisations aim to provide
products and services to meet the needs of defined markets and
market segments. However, tourism services are intangible (one
cannot exchange a product with which one is dissatisfied), heter-
ogeneous (there is little standardisation), perishable (airline seats
cannot be stored), and there is inseparability between production and
consumption. The tourism product is typically defined to comprise
attractions of a destination including images, sites, scenery, events
and weather; facilities including accommodation, catering and entertainment; and accessibility with regard to the time and cost it takes to
reach the destination.

Consumer Satisfaction with Package Holidays

In order to consider consumer satisfaction with package holidays it is useful to look at the consumer purchasing process. The travel decision may involve individuals or families in each of a number of buying stages which lead to decisions on where to go, how to get there, where to stay, travel arrangements and where to book. The process will be influenced by the demand factors already outlined, information and friends and family and commercial sources, and consumer attitudes and needs. Consequently, when a package holiday is finally bought, the tourist can be said to have purchased a set of perceived expectations about the benefits and satisfactions in a tourist product. At this stage the tourist, prior to his or her trip, has expectations about the nature and performance of the package holiday and about the anticipated benefits to be derived from the experience. These can be measured prior to travel. Subsequently, after returning from the package holiday, satisfaction and dissatisfaction can be assessed along with consideration of future similar purchasing behaviour, i.e. is re-purchase likely?

At this stage the reader might not unreasonably suggest that surely the tour operators assess measures of consumer satisfaction and dissatisfaction. Certainly this is the case, but their activities are to some extent limited, and are not usually linked to subsequent purchasing behaviour as revealed by the work of Townsend (1981) who surveyed and interviewed hoteliers, airlines, tour operators and other tourist organisations. He found that American hotel groups are pro-active in trying to assess consumer satisfaction via questionnaires left in guests' rooms, as are some airlines (with on-flight questionnaires for captive audiences). Tour operators were also found to have developed a major interest in consumer satisfaction or dissatisfaction due to the increasingly competitive environment in which they find themselves. Townsend concluded that some tourism organisations do expend considerable effort assessing levels of satisfaction associated with their products, together with customer profiles, but few set out to identify the factors that attracted clients to particular holidays and their subsequent purchasing behaviours. Consequently, the present study was instigated, in liaison with a major tour operator and in turn a travel agent, to examine clients' satisfaction, attitudes and purchase intentions and to ascertain whether or not a relationship exists between clients' satisfaction with their package holiday and the decisions they make concerning the purchase of their next package holiday.

Methodology

It was decided that the most appropriate method of collecting data
would be through the use of a self completion questionnaire. This
was based on pilot interviews with clients of the travel agent who had
recently been on a package holiday. At this stage one is, firstly,
determining the aspects of the holiday to be evaluated, i.e. determinant buying features—as, for example, the influence of choice of
country; and the threshold factors on which organisations will be
expected to perform at a certain level before they will be considered at
all, e.g. comfort, safety, price, reputation. Secondly, pilot interviews
help identify the various dimensions of satisfaction, some of which
will be influenced by the tour operator (food, hotel) and others which
will not (e.g. weather). Together they interact to produce the total
satisfaction with the holiday.

These preliminary interviews were supplemented by 40 pilot
interviews sent to clients together with discussions with market
research staff at the tour operator agency. The sample was initially set
at 1,000, but later reduced by 443 due to practical considerations, and
it covered 17 tour operators—client names for those travelling in
August/September 1983 being selected by the travel agent.

Before their holiday clients were sent questionnaires in which they
were asked about their pre-holiday attitudes towards their package
holiday and their attitudes to package holidays in general. Those who

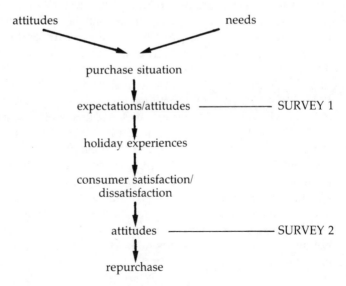

Figure 18.1 *Purchase/Re-Purchase of a Package Holiday*

responded (52 per cent) were also sent a post-holiday questionnaire in which they were asked about their satisfaction with the holiday, post-holiday attitudes towards the holiday, post-holiday attitudes towards their tour operator, and their future purchase intentions with respect to package holidays and travelling with the same tour operator in the future. Eighty-one per cent of the second group replied and the following discussion is therefore based on data from 103 people who completed both questionnaires. Of these, 61 per cent had been on a two-week package holiday. Eighty-seven per cent had stayed in a hotel (13 per cent self-catering) and the most popular destinations were Spain, Italy, Greece and Switzerland.

Clients' Satisfaction With Their Holidays

There was a high level of overall satisfaction among the respondents with their package holidays, 24 per cent being extremely satisfied, 49 per cent very satisfied and 19 per cent quite satisfied. The level of satisfaction with the various aspects of the holiday varied but maintained a high level. Clients were most satisfied with the resort they visited and the cleanliness of their accommodation, and least satisfied with their courier, the food included in the price of the holiday and the service they received in their hotel, apartment or villa.

Table 18.1   *Aspects of a Package Holiday (%)*

	Satisfied			Dissatisfied	
	Very	*Quite*	*Slightly*	*Neither Satisfied nor Dissatisfied*	*Slightly/ Quite/ Very*
The flights to and from the resort	54	34	2	2	8
Situation of accommodation	55	35	5	1	4
Cleanliness of accommodation	65	25	5	1	4
Food in accommodation	47	26	6	8	13
Service in accommodation	49	27	7	9	8
The courier	42	33	4	5	16
Transfer arrangements	56	30	5	3	6
Accommodation overall	51	34	3	5	7
Resort/country	77	18	2	—	3

Clients' Attitudes Towards Their Package Holiday

Again, as can be seen from Table 18.2, the majority of clients'
attitudes towards their holidays were favourable, particularly with
regard to the convenience aspects. In respect of their recent package
holiday, 61 per cent strongly agreed that it was convenient to book
the flight and accommodation together, and 54 per cent said that
having booked the package one had few other arrangements to worry
about. The value aspect of package holidays was not so highly
rated—most probably because package holidays are often seen as
expensive but worthwhile. Further, a package holiday is not seen to
be without its drawbacks, 54 per cent agreeing that there were some
disadvantages to their holiday. A number of people had complaints
and not all would advise their friends to go on the same package
holiday.

Table 18.2 *Opinions of Last Package Holiday (%)*

	Strongly Agree	Agree	Slightly Agree
It was convenient being able to book the flight and accommodation together	61	35	2
Once I had booked this package holiday there were few arrangements to worry about	54	39	2
This package holiday was good value for money	36	40	12
I found that there were some disadvantages to being on this package holiday	19	26	9
I have no complaints about this package holiday	30	25	12
I would advise my friends to go on the same package holiday	33	36	7

On first inspection the figures in Table 18.3 would seem to suggest
that, in general, clients' attitudes towards package holidays appeared
to be very similar to their attitudes toward their recent package
holiday. However, further analysis revealed that a negative attitude
towards a particular aspect of their recent holiday did not necessarily
imply a negative attitude towards package holidays in general.
Specifically, of those clients who thought their recent holiday had not
been good value for money, 80 per cent thought that, in general, most
package holidays do offer value for money; and of those who felt that
there had been some disadvantages with their recent holiday, 44 per
cent thought that, in general, package holidays do not have
significant disadvantages attached to them.

Table 18.3   *Opinions of Package Holidays in General (%)*

	Strongly Agree	Agree	Slightly Agree
Package holidays make it easy to travel abroad	58	38	1
Package holidays have their disadvantages	8	12	7
Package holidays take a lot of the worry out of travelling abroad	53	40	5
Package holidays offer good value for money	39	42	13

Clients' Attitudes Towards Their Tour Operator

Just over half the respondents had a very favourable attitude toward the tour operator with whom they had recently travelled. Fifty-four per cent said they were very satisfied with their tour operator, 55 per cent described their operator as very efficient, 52 per cent described him or her as very good, and 38 per cent described their operator as very caring. Conversely, less than 10 per cent of the clients actually harboured a negative attitude towards their tour operator.

Further, clients did not perceive substantial differences between the tour operator they travelled with on this occasion and other tour operators (See Table 18.4). In particular, 56 per cent thought their operator was completely reliable, but only 20 per cent considered

Table 18.4   *Performance of the Tour Operator You Travelled with on this Package Holiday (%)*

	Completely Agree	Mostly Agree	Agree to a Certain Extent	Slightly Agree	Do Not Agree
Is completely reliable	56	29	7	3	5
Is more reliable than other tour operators	20	26	20	7	27
Gives good value for money	49	28	9	10	4
Provides better value for money than other operators going to similar destinations	23	22	29	7	19
Is the best tour operator	17	17	23	9	34
Gives the highest standard of service	20	22	22	12	24

their operator to be more reliable than others. Forty-nine per cent considered their operator offered good value for money, but only 23 per cent felt that their operator offered better value for money than other operators. Seventeen per cent agreed that their operator was the best and 20 per cent thought their operator provided the highest standard of service. Conversely, 34 per cent did not agree that their operator was the best and 24 per cent did not agree that their operator provided the highest standard of service. These response patterns would certainly seem to be a function of the price clients paid for their holiday and their associated expectations of tour operator performance.

Clients' Purchase Intentions

Respondents expressed a high level of repeat purchase intention concerning the purchase of another package holiday, with short-term repeat purchase intentions being less definite than long-term ones; and a moderate level (lower proportion) of repeat purchasing intentions concerning clients intending to book with the same tour operator, short-term intentions again being less definite (Table 18.5).

Table 18.5   *Future Package Holidays (%)*

(a) Your intentions with regard to:		*Definitely will*	*Almost certainly will*	*Possibly will*
taking another package holiday		54	33	10
choosing to travel with the same tour operator in the future		27	21	33

(b) How likely are you to:	*Certain*	*Very likely*	*Quite likely*	*Slightly likely*	*Not likely*
take another package holiday in the next 12 months	33	27	20	13	7
choose to travel with the same tour operator for your next package holiday	16	21	27	20	16

Clients' Satisfaction and Attitudes Towards Their Tour Operator

When the relationship between client satisfaction and attitudes towards their tour operator was examined, three key findings emerged in respect of respondents' perceived reliability of tour operators, the perceived value of holiday offered, and the perceived standard of service of the tour operator. Firstly, of those clients who said they were either extremely or very satisfied with their package holiday, 69 per cent were of the opinion that their tour operator was completely reliable. However, of those clients who were satisfied to some extent, only 24 per cent considered their operator to be completely reliable. Secondly, of those clients who were satisfied, 63 per cent thought their tour operator gave good value for money, which compares with only 19 per cent of those clients who were less satisfied with their holiday. However, when comparing the performance of their tour operator with others, satisfaction had less of an impact upon this set of client attitudes. Of those clients who were either extremely satisfied or very satisfied, 24 per cent thought their operator was the best, whereas none of the clients with lower satisfaction levels thought this. Again, 27 per cent of clients who were extremely or very satisfied were of the opinion that their operator gave the highest standard of service, compared with none of the clients who were less satisfied.

Client Satisfaction and Repeat Purchase Intention

The key findings from this section of analysis were that satisfaction had a consistent impact on clients' intentions to travel again with their tour operator in both the short and long term. Satisfaction was not found to be highly related to clients' intentions to purchase another package holiday in the long term. There also appears to be no significant relationship between clients' satisfaction and their intention to buy another package holiday within the next twelve months.

Specifically, of those clients who were extremely or very satisfied, 34 per cent said they definitely intended to travel with the same tour operator in the future. This compares with 14 per cent of those clients who were slightly or quite satisfied. Further, 20 per cent of those people who were extremely/very satisfied definitely intended to book with that operator for their next package holiday as compared with 5 per cent of those who were slightly/quite satisfied. Additionally, 60 per cent of those who were extremely/very satisfied with their holiday definitely intended to take a package holiday 'sometime in the future' as compared with only 38 per cent of those who were slightly/quite satisfied. Finally, when asked about their intention to book a package holiday in the next twelve months, 35 per cent of the highly satisfied clients were certain they would, as compared with 33 per cent of the less satisfied clients. Satisfaction does not, therefore, appear to have a significant effect on clients' short-term repeat purchase intentions.

Expectations and Reality

One further revealing analysis is a comparison of responses from the two surveys in respect of features of a package holiday and determinants of enjoyment of a package holiday. Clients were asked in the first questionnaire how desirable certain features of their forthcoming package holiday were to them and how certain they were that these would fulfil their expectations. In the second questionnaire they were asked to indicate whether this actually happened. The results which are set out in Tables 18.6 and 18.7 show

Table 18.6 *Features of a Package Holiday (%)*

	SURVEY 1		SURVEY 2
	Forthcoming package holiday		*Did it happen?*
	Certain/ very likely to happen	*Very desirable*	*YES*
Flights on time	37	68	27
Friendly hotel staff	51	64	94
Efficient service in hotel	45	63	87
Clean hotel	74	86	96
Hotel well situated	59	57	86
Good food	50	74	77
Helpful couriers	58	45	80
Courier readily available	42	44	70
Plenty to do in resort	70	62	77
Good weather	73	86	95

Table 18.7 *Determinants of Enjoyment of a Package Holiday (%)*

	SURVEY 1	SURVEY2
	Major part in forthcoming package holiday	*Contributed a great deal/quite a lot in recent package holiday*
People you meet	88	55
Excursions	85	58
Helpfulness of courier	78	57
People you are/were with	71	68
Facilities in country/resort	69	77
Situation of hotel	63	75
Holiday package	49	85
Efficiency of tour operator	47	76
Comfort of hotel	44	79
Weather	37	96

that people's expectations were fulfilled with regard to most features. There was, however, more variation with regard to expectations of determinants of enjoyment of a package holiday, and the contribution that these factors made in reality.

Summary

The data analysis has indicated a high level of overall satisfaction among the respondents with regard to their package holidays. They were most satisfied with the resort they visited and the cleanliness of their accommodation; and were least satisfied with their courier, their food and the service they received from the staff in their hotel, apartment or villa. They had particularly positive attitudes towards the convenience and value aspects of their package holiday. However, it would seem that clients do not perceive substantial differences in the reliability and standard of service they might receive from different tour operators. Further, they had a high level of repeat purchase intentions concerning the purchase of another package holiday, but only a moderate level of repeat purchasing intentions regarding buying a holiday from the same tour operator. Additionally, a strong relationship was found to exist between clients' satisfaction and their attitudes towards their operator; and satisfaction was related to clients' purchase intentions concerning their tour operator and to their long-term repeat purchase intentions concerning buying another package holiday, but not to short-term intentions.

WATCHDOGS

19

Nationalised Industry Consumer Councils

'The Public be damned.'

Cornelius Vanderbilt

JOHN WINWARD, Director, National Gas Consumers' Council.

The reader could, perhaps, be forgiven for believing that NICCs are a product of the post-war Labour Government which nationalised many of our basic industries. In fact, as will be seen, for many years prior to that a variety of regulatory agencies had existed for ensuring that a range of public utilities were monitored with respect to the service they provided. This would appear to reflect society's belief that many of these companies must necessarily operate in a monopoly situation and as a consequence there is a need to impose an independent assessment of what the customer receives in the way of service. It is of some relevance to record that the work with the American wartime price commission which served to establish Kenneth Galbraith's reputation involved many vitriolic exchanges with industrial representatives opposed to his strongly-held belief that such price controls would only be viable if associated with specified quality standards.

I asked John to provide an overview of the activities of the different NICCs, and this brief he has accomplished admirably. This should have come as no great surprise as he is well equipped for the task, having been the Public Affairs Officer of the National Gas Consumers' Council for five years. He then spent a year as a research officer with the National Consumer Council before returning to the NGCC on second-ment as Director until privatisation. Before this he had followed his first degree at Essex with postgraduate research on energy-related issues at the Universities of York and Nottingham. He has acted as a consultant to the Environment Group at OECD and, from 1982 to 1985, was the Chairman of the National Energy Efficiency Group. Since 1982 he has also been a member of the Council for Freedom of Information.

★ ★ ★

'I take care of my staff first, because without them there would be no business. Then I take care of my customers, because without them there would be no business. When I have taken care of my staff and my customers, I find that taking care of the shareholders takes care of itself.'

The quotation above is attributed to the late Lord Marks. Marks and Spencer, like most service industries, operates in a highly competitive environment, in which the identification and satisfaction of customer demand is an essential defensive tool. Not all service industries are under such pressure. Indeed, some of the largest and most significant industries in the UK fall into the loose category of 'Public Utilities'. These are the bodies that supply commodities or services such as gas, electricity, water, post, telecommunications and rail travel, and they differ from other service industries in a number of ways. As far as customer service is concerned two principal differences can be identified. First, the services provided by utilities constitute 'natural monopolies'. Secondly, they are essential to the well-being of individuals in society, and play a significant role in determining the viability of other industrial sectors. This combination of monopoly power and an indispensable product gives the utilities enormous potential power.

Although the present Nationalised Industry Consumer Councils date back no further than the nationalisation programme following the Second World War, the government has played a role in these industries from their very earliest days. Before the gas industry could come into being, for example, powers had to be secured to break up streets to lay mains. A charter to permit this was granted by Parliament in 1812. Although government was involved in the creation of the industry, it seems not to have felt any compunction to provide special protection for consumers. Presumably it was assumed that competition between gas suppliers would do the job.

However, sustained competition proved impossible. The high fixed costs associated with providing the gas main made the supply market highly unstable. In effect, firms either reached informal agreements with each other to divide their territories and so avoid directly competing, or they fought to the death in local price wars until a single monopolist emerged. Considerable problems were also emerging as roads were continually being dug up to switch customers from one firm's main to another. This actually disrupted not only the traffic but the mains themselves. Firms regularly caused accidental damage to each other's mains—indeed, acts of deliberate sabotage were not entirely unknown.

By 1847 an official report concluded that '. . . the existence in the same town of two rival gas companies does not appear to us at all calculated to benefit the customers'. In the same year, legislation was introduced that granted official local monopolies to individual companies but controlled the rate of return on capital that they were allowed. From the 1860s onwards, increasingly refined price control formulae were introduced, the most common allowing the rate of return to be increased only if prices to consumers fell.

Gas was not unique in this respect. Other utility industries were increasingly subject to the same form of government control so that, although the services were provided by a mix of municipal and private sector undertakings, the industries were already centrally regulated when the nationalisation programme began. According to their architect, nationalised industries were meant to combine '. . . public ownership, public accountability and business management for public ends' and their board members were to be the 'high custodians of the public interest' (Morrison 1933).

To achieve this goal of public service, the government created a series of Consultative Committees. These were intended to provide both a consumer voice against the monopoly power of the industries and a 'grassroots' structure for bringing aspects of the public interest to the attention of the boards.

The Councils

Although the various Nationalised Industries' Consumer Councils (NICCs) were set up to perform a similar range of tasks, there are in fact considerable differences in the structure, staffing and operations of the different bodies. Nor is the definition of what is, and what is not, a NICC entirely clear-cut. The term NICC is used to describe those statutory bodies that represent users of gas, electricity, railways, ferries, post and coal, and whose members are appointed by the Secretary of State. The councils operate with a mixture of full-time staff and part-time members, the great majority of them unpaid.

The Gas and Electricity Consumers' Councils

The Gas and Electricity Consumers' Councils have a regional structure mirroring that of their industries. Both have a national body dealing with policy and strategic issues and regional councils. These take up complaints from individual customers that the industries themselves have failed to sort out. Members of the regional councils are appointed by the Secretary of State and regional councils in turn appoint committees or individuals to act as local representatives.

These local members play a role in handling complaints and may, for example, make visits to consumers' homes to talk face to face about an individual problem, or to inspect a faulty appliance. They do also play a role in deriving policy recommendations from the complaints that they handle. Between two fifths and three fifths of the membership of regional councils must be made up of serving members of local authorities.

The National Councils are made up of the regional chairmen and a small number of other members appointed by the Secretary of State. Between 1981 and 1985, Gas Consumers' Councils handled between 27,000 and 28,000 complaints a year, while Electricity Consultative Councils handled over 24,000 representations in 1984/85. One major difference between the two bodies is that Electricity Consultative Council chairmen are members of the appropriate Electricity Board, while chairmen of Gas Consumers' Councils are not.

Transport

Rail and ferry services are dealt with by the Central Transport Consultative Committee and, at regional level, by a number of Area Transport Users' Consultative Committees (TUCCs). There are no local committees. The London Regional Passenger Committee carries out similar functions in the London Transport area, covering both British Rail and London Transport Services. The committees deal with individual complaints as well as with more general policy issues. In practice relatively few complaints are dealt with directly, though British Rail's own complaints system is available to the committees. The chairmen of the area TUCCs are all ex-officio members of the Transport Users' Consultative Committee, as is the chairman of the London Regional Passenger Committee.

Post Office

The Post Office Users' National Council (POUNC) originally dealt with both postal services and telephones. Since the privatisation of British Telecom, its role has been restricted to postal services. POUNC, which is made up of members appointed by the Secretary of State, deals with both individual complaints and policy matters. There are three country councils for Northern Ireland, Scotland and Wales. At the local level there are a large number of Post and Telephone Advisory Committees. These are not, strictly speaking, NICCs, being voluntary and non-statutory, and are mostly set up by local Chambers of Commerce. They receive financial assistance towards expenses from both POUNC and the Office of Telecommunications (OFTEL)—the body set up to regulate the privatised British Telecom. Although complaints are handled by country councils, the vast majority are dealt with by headquarters staff, which is composed of civil servants seconded from the Department of Trade and Industry.

Coal

The Domestic Coal Consumers' Council is a national body with no regional structure. In the last resort the Domestic Coal Consumers' Council has to arbitrate between an Approved Coal Merchants Scheme member and a complainant, though normally the council does not handle complaints. It will already be clear that the bodies defined as NICCs constitute a rather arbitrary grouping. Although the National Coal Board has a virtual monopoly on the production of coal in the United Kingdom, the final supply to consumers is not a monopoly. It is carried out through the Approved Coal Merchants Scheme, which is administered by the Coal Board, retailers and wholesalers, and a Domestic Coal Consumers' Council representative. Coal supply is not, therefore, a utility industry.

Water

The water industry, on the other hand, is the most complete and unchallenged monopoly utility of them all, yet is not covered by a NICC. Water Authorities themselves have tended to be cast as the representatives of the public interest. Indeed, the Water Authorities are in a rather odd position, being both suppliers of commercial services to customers and regulators on a number of matters, as for example river pollution. The Authorities have now set up a network of Consumer Consultative Committees, though as yet there is no national body, and these committees are relatively powerless compared to the NICCs, lacking even secretarial resources.

Equally, there are a number of other bodies that carry out apparently similar duties but are not considered to be NICCs. For example, the Air Transport Users' Committee was established in 1973 to safeguard the interests of airline users, and handles complaints against airlines by individual travellers. Airport Consultative Committees perform a similar function, representing users of the airports themselves. However, the members of these committees are selected by the Civil Aviation Authority and the British Airports Authority respectively, rather than by the Secretary of State. Neither of these bodies is, strictly speaking, a nationalised industry.

The Goals

The NICCs occupy a unique role in that they have formal, statutory links with the industry's management but are independent of it. In principle, this gives the councils the power to speak out clearly on behalf of consumers, though one of the most persistent criticisms made of them is that they have too cosy a relationship with the industries.

Although complaints handling is a significant part of the work undertaken by most of the NICCs, they are also involved in policy questions and are able to comment on strategic matters. Generally, the NICCs have an extremely wide potential remit, being empowered to consider any matter brought to their attention by consumers. There are some slightly odd exceptions as, for example, the CTCC not being able to comment on rail fares, but on the whole the area of freedom allowed to the NICCs is considerable.

A Department of Trade (1982) discussion paper defined three principal aims for the NICCs:

- Improve the quality of service offered by the industries.
- Ensure that the consumer's view is clearly heard in decisions on costs and prices.
- Ensure that a complaints handling system is provided and that individual customers can obtain redress.

Quality of Service

The NICCs address a wide range of quality of service questions. Gas and Electricity Consumers' Councils, as well as dealing with the problems associated with gas supply, gas tariffs, billing, meter reading, disconnection and so on, also take up a wide range of issues to do with supply of gas equipment, its repair, servicing and installation. Sometimes their work goes beyond the narrow bands of the industry itself, as for example when the councils took up the question of the resale of gas and electricity by landlords to their tenants. The Transport Users' Consultative Committees also deal with a wide range of topics. As well as the direct provision of railway services, for example, they become involved in questions relating to catering facilities on trains.

At times, the councils find themselves caught between the pursuit of costs and efficiency on the one hand and service levels on the other. POUNC, for example, has argued in favour of 'productivity improvements and great efficiency as a means of cost savings' but stresses that they '. . . must not be achieved at the expense of quality of service' (Post Office Users' National Council 1982).

One of the most persistent and obvious of these conflicts arises from the attempted closure of gas or electricity showrooms, post offices and railway stations. These are discussed at local level by the NICC, and PATACs are increasingly consulted about post office counter closures. Although councils do not automatically oppose all such closures, they do often seek to ensure that alternative facilities are provided locally. Often, alternatives are made available, though the CTCC (1985) has recently complained to the Secretary of State that, in a number of such cases, British Rail has given clear undertakings about the level of alternative service to be provided, but has then failed to honour its commitments.

Sometimes the reduction in costs achieved by the industry has a more direct impact on consumers. For example, the CTCC reported that:

> The Consultative Committees have supported the idea of a more efficient railway, but some of the measures designed to achieve greater business efficiency and financial savings are a major source of expressed passenger dissatisfaction. They include, for example, the reduction in the number of through trains, the increasing number of journeys that now have to rely on connecting services, with all the stress and uncertainty that that involves and reduced train formations often resulting in overcrowding. (CTCC 1985)

Prices

Not surprisingly, prices are one of the principal areas of dissatisfaction with nationalised industries. A National Consumer Council Survey (1981) found '. . . tremendous—and growing—concern with nationalised industry prices. Half or more of the users of postal services, electricity, buses and trains said they thought prices were unreasonable, as did two fifths or more of solid fuel users and underground users. . .'

The Department of Trade and Industry (1982) concluded that the NICCs must be consulted about, and must comment on, the policies and plans of the industries to 'ensure that the consumers' views are clearly heard in decisions on costs and prices'—though it was accepted that their views 'cannot be decisive'. The role envisaged for the NICCs in this was to work alongside government in encouraging industries to contain costs and prices, and make an informed contribution to industry efficiency.

This appears somewhat ironic in the light of recent developments in nationalised industry pricing. The major influence on prices has been the government, which has pushed up prices by a variety of means. In the case of the gas industry, the government simply announced its intention that prices should rise by 10 per cent more than inflation in each of three years. It also imposed the Gas Levy—a tax that was supposed to substitute for Petroleum Revenue Tax, but was actually set at a higher rate than PRT would have been (National Gas Consumers' Council 1985). In other industries, including the Post Office, prices were forced up by the setting of 'negative external financing limits'—which effectively forced the industry to loan money to the government.

Government intervention caused the Electricity Council to recommend a 2 per cent tariff increase in 1984/85. A report commissioned by the London Electricity Consultative Committee (1985) showed there to be no economic justification for a price rise in the London Electricity Board area, and it included a Counsel's opinion that questioned the legal basis of the increase. Despite this evidence the board, and the government, pressed ahead with the increase. The LECC then tried to bring a case to court through a pensioner seeking legal aid for judicial review. This also failed, though the LECC did succeed in delaying the board and in generating considerable publicity.

Sometimes, of course, it is the industry itself which raises prices. POUNC (1982) has commented that 'the Post Office finds it easier to generate extra profits from revenue through price increases rather than by significant cost savings within the business'.

Methods Used

The NICCs adopt a variety of methods to pursue their work. They all have a statutory relationship with the industries they serve so that, on day-to-day matters, there is a good deal of contact at middle-management level. This is useful in sorting out consumer complaints. The Councils also hold regular meetings at senior level with the industry to discuss wider policy issues.

Many policy failures are identified from an analysis of complaints received. This is clearly an important, if somewhat negative, measure of the industry's performance. It is, however, useful in identifying detailed matters of policy or practice that are operating against the consumer's interests. Some councils supplement this information with market research carried out through commercial companies. For example, the Gas Consumers' Council (1984 and 1982) has commissioned surveys on general customer satisfaction, and more detailed and comprehensive surveys on the experiences of consumers who have purchased new or second-hand gas appliances. Councils also commission research reports from experts on a wide range of subjects. Both the Electricity Consumers' Council and Post Office Users' Council have lengthy publication lists.

Increasingly, councils make use of quantitative or subjective performance indicators, and publish Codes of Practice. These can give the Consumer Councils a clear idea of the quality of service aimed at and some remedies where such quality is not reached. The CTCC and the TUCCs, for example, use performance statistics supplied by the Railways Board to monitor British Rail's quality of service—particularly with regard to the timekeeping of passenger trains, train cancellations, carriage cleaning and proficiency in dealing with telephone enquiries. These indicators are published routinely in their Annual Report. The CTCC (1985) is now exploring the extension of the performance indicators concept to other areas of service quality, some of which are less susceptible to quantitative monitoring.

POUNC publishes an annual Customer Audit and Review of the Post Office. This examines, from the customer's viewpoint, how the Post Office performed in the previous financial year under a number of headings including the effect of price increases, quality of service performance, the progress of the Mechanised Letter Office Programme and productivity in the mail and counter services. It also makes some comparison with postal services in other countries (Post Office Users' National Council 1984).

The CTCC, in conjunction with the Railways Board, has been formulating a Guide to Customer Service and a Code of Practice for Rail Passenger Travel. The code provides a general guide to rail travel for public bodies, business organisations and individual passengers and sets out the range of services British Rail provides and the standards of service it aims to achieve. It explains the ways in which British Rail tries to lessen inconvenience and describes the arrangements for dealing with passengers' complaints, including an explanation of a simple arbitration procedure for resolution of certain types of dispute between British Rail and its customers.

Some councils also undertake regular 'audits' of more detailed aspects of the industry's performance. For many years all the Regional Gas Consumers' Councils have carried out a monthly inspection of a random selection of disconnection cases selected from the industry's files. The National Gas Consumers' Council, on the basis of these audits, reports each month to the Corporation on any apparent breaches of the Code of Practice that have been identified. These are discussed in considerable detail with the industry.

The councils occasionally undertake straightforward product testing. When the Eastern Gas Consumers' Council (1984) suspected that there was a significant problem with faulty gas meters in 1982, it undertook a programme of testing by the simple expedient of having members send their own meters for testing by the Department of Energy, as all consumers are entitled to under the 1972 Gas Act. This small-scale survey revealed a worryingly high proportion of inaccurate meters, and formed the basis for discussions with British Gas about an accelerated meter replacement programme. The Gas Consumers' Council has also used the Consumer Association's laboratories to carry out safety and performance tests on imported gas cookers.

Powers of Councils

The councils have, on the whole, fairly limited formal powers. All have a statutory relationship with their industries, and cannot be entirely ignored by industry management, though consultation does not always lead to a response that satisfies the councils. The councils can also, as a last resort, appeal to the Secretary of State, though this is rarely done, at least at a formal level. The Electricity Consultative Councils can refer 'defects' in the behaviour of the Electricity Boards to a special panel of the Electricity Council. This provision has been criticised for not meeting the procedural requirements normally expected of tribunals, as it means that the Electricity Council effectively judges complaints against its own members. Over the whole period since nationalisation, the Electricity Council has upheld only two of the 31 representations made against Area Boards (Henney 1986).

The Consumer Councils can, and do, make use of other public hearings. The Electricity Consumers' Council, for example, submitted detailed evidence to the Sizewell Enquiry and TUCCs participate in hearings on railway line closures. All councils frequently submit written or oral evidence to select committees of Parliament.

The Performance of the NICCs

Unlike customer service units operating within firms in competitive industries, the policies recommended by NICCs will not always be in the interests of the industry, however broadly these are interpreted. An example of this is the promotion of energy conservation by the energy NICCs. From the consumers' point of view, an investment in energy efficiency measures might represent a better way of achieving the desired level of comfort than would the buying of more fuel. Broadly speaking, the interests of a fuel supplier lie in expanding sales. The gas and electricity consumers' councils have been active in promoting energy efficiency. At the political level, for example, they submit evidence to select committees and publish critical reports on the government's energy strategy. At the level of the individual consumer, both bodies publish free advice leaflets on energy saving, and have arranged joint exhibitions in shopping centres, etc. Consumer Councils can make a significant contribution on this sort of issue, though they are unlikely to be the most powerful actors, and they may find themselves trying to press their policies on an unwilling industry.

Even when the councils successfully challenge industry price proposals, it is often difficult for them to claim full credit. In 1982, the Gas Consumers' Council held detailed discussions with British Gas about the cost components of the standing charge element in gas bills. The council challenged the figures produced by British Gas, and reported that 'As a result of our arguments, the Corporation abandoned a proposed increase in the standing charge'. In 1983 the Corporation announced that tariffs would be increased in October. Again, after the Gas Consumers' Council challenged this increase, it was postponed until January 1984. However, in neither of these cases is it possible to show that the Council's intervention was decisive (National Gas Consumers' Council 1983 and 1984).

On more specific issues, such as the introduction of Codes of Practice, or the detail of central heating maintenance contracts, the NICCs can demonstrate more palpable success. Equally, the complaints-handling work of the councils provides a clearcut service to consumers, though not all complainants will be happy with the outcome. The councils also provide a good deal of published advice and information, both to individual consumers and in the form of research reports and discussion papers aimed at expert groups.

In the end, though, the success of the Councils must be, at least in part, reflected in the performance of the industries themselves. There is still disquiet about the responsiveness of many of these industries to customers. The National Consumer Council's Customer Concerns Survey (1981) identified a widespread dissatisfaction with low or declining standards. The survey showed that 32 per cent of train users reported problems with comfort and cleanliness and 17 per cent problems with overcrowding; 23 per cent of all respondents reported delays in postal services and 18 per cent of telephone users reported problems with phones going wrong or breaking. Nor do the councils themselves find the services satisfactory:

> . . . the level of punctuality of express trains, especially on the Eastern and Western Regions, leaves a lot to be desired as only a little more than half the number of express trains arrived on time . . . (Central Transport Consultative Committee 1985).

> . . . both the Post Office and its customers have grounds for great disappointment with the quality of mails delivery in 1984/85; both first and second class mail not only regularly failed to meet the targets but performed worse than in the previous year. (Post Office Users' National Council 1985).

The Future

Although the Consumers' Council structure has been the subject of many formal or informal reviews, very few changes have actually been made over the years. A more significant impact is now being made by the Government's privatisation programme.

Telecommunication matters were removed from the remit of POUNC when British Telecom entered the private sector in August 1984. The privatised industry is regulated by a non-ministerial department known as the Office of Telecommunications (OFTEL). This combines both regulatory functions (ensuring that the industry operates within its licence conditions), and specific consumer protection functions, including the handling of individual complaints.

When the privatisation of British Gas was announced, both the National Consumer Council and the National Gas Consumers' Council argued that a separate consumer body should be created to operate alongside the regulator. The Privatisation Bill, published in November 1985, does contain such a provision and the new consumer body looks in many ways very similar to the Nationalised Industry Consumer Council that it is replacing, though the structure of formal regional councils and district committees is not covered by the Bill.

Consumer bodies have argued that there is no reason to expect a private-sector monopoly to be more responsive to consumers than its nationalised equivalent. Fears have also been expressed that the new regulatory bodies are too weak to regulate such powerful monopolies properly, and the consumer bodies have too few powers to defend their consumers properly. It will be some years before it becomes clear whether or not these fears are justified.

20

Community Health Councils

'Better to hunt in fields, for health unbought,
Than fee the doctor for a nauseous draught.
The wise, for care, on exercise depend:
God never made his work, for man to mend.'
Epistle to John Driden of Chester
John Dryden

TONY SMYTHE, Director, Association of Community Health Councils for England and Wales, and **JUDITH COOK.**

Community Health Councils were conceived in Barbara Castle's time at the Department of Health, the idea being to introduce a greater community perspective into the deliberations of the NHS. To say that they were universally welcomed by NHS decision makers would be something of an exaggeration. Each Health Authority is associated with a corresponding Community Health Council, but whereas the health authority is responsible for an annual expenditure running into tens of millions of pounds CHCs manage on 'shoestring' budgets. A recent parliamentary question revealed that the average CHC has a budget of around £33,000 out of which has to come the salary of the full-time secretary. From what follows it is clear that this relatively low level of funding has not stopped many CHCs pushing ahead with exciting initiatives. Not all of these have been directed at opposing hospital closures but where this type of issue has been a major concern it most certainly has had the effect of broadening the resultant debate.

The CHCs collectively and voluntarily fund the Association which, for a short period, had its government grant withdrawn by a government which at the time was questioning the role and contribution of CHCs. Tony Smythe has held the Director's post since that 1983 period of great uncertainty. He, I'm sure, would deny it, but it could reasonably be argued that the stature of the Association owes a good deal to his presence. Before joining the Association he served on two CHCs while he was the Director of MIND for eight years. Prior to that he was General Secretary of the National Council for Civil Liberties. He had also found time to be actively involved, as an officer or on the committees, with an array of voluntary bodies concerned with peace and human rights. He is currently associated with the Markfield project for disabled children and their familes, REACH (the Retired Executive Action Clearing House), the London Brook Advisory Centres and the National Peace Council. Judith Cook is a freelance journalist and author

who has specialised in health and social issues and also health and
safety matters. She has worked with the Association since 1979 and
now writes the Association's monthly newsletter. She is also a member
of the Cornwall CHC.

* * *

Community Health Councils were established under section 9 of the
NHS re-organisation Act of 1973, almost as an afterthought, but with
the support of all political parties. Their job was seen as representing
the interests of the local community in the NHS to those reponsible
for management—a wide brief. Members of the councils are drawn
from all walks of life: one half is nominated by the Local Authority,
one third elected by local voluntary organisations and the rest
nominated by the Regional Health Authority. CHC meetings are
open to the public who are usually invited to voice their concerns.
The character of the districts they cover differs as widely as it is
possible to imagine, from the inner cities to rural areas such as East
Cumbria and Cornwall. The smallest is in the Isles of Scilly. Similar
bodies in Scotland (the Local Health Councils) and in Northern
Ireland (the District Committees for the Health and Personal Social
Services) fulfill the same role.

The hope was that 'in the re-organised NHS, service management
and representation of local opinion will be distinct but complementary functions, entrusted to separate bodies but working in
close relationship. Successful administration of the service will
depend on a continuing and constructive exchange of ideas between
Area Health Authorities and CHCs. The AHA will then be aware of
local opinion on needs and deficiencies in the service and the
community, through the CHC, will know of the actions and
intentions of the AHA and of the problems and constraints with
which it is faced.' Since the first statutory instrument was issued,
AHAs have been abolished leaving the Regional Health Authorities
(RHAs), which are responsible for strategic planning, budgets and
regional specialities and the District Health Authorities (DHAs)
which are responsible for delivering the services. Few suggestions
were given as to how a CHC was to undertake such an all-embracing
task.

The main statutory duty of CHCs is to draw up an annual report,
yet the issues to which a CHC might direct its attention are virtually
limitless. However, the rights of CHCs are constrained. They have
the right to information from the health authorities and to send
observers to DHA meetings and, from April 1985, to those of the

Family Practitioner Committees (FPCs) which were made independent health authorities providing primary health care services. They have the right to be consulted on ward and hospital closures, the change of use of health service buildings, and to visit NHS premises — but not those controlled by private contractors, i.e. general practitioners, dentists and opticians.

In effect, the acquisition of information is more complicated than it sounds. In 1984 the National Consumer Council and the Association of Community Health Councils for England and Wales (ACHCEW) undertook a survey on the information needs of CHCs asking them what they received routinely, what they found difficult to get hold of and what they would like to know. The results were hardly reassuring. While some CHCs received most documents from the health authorities automatically—and it has to be said that some CHC members find a surfeit of information more forbidding than enlightening—some were even refused basic information on topics such as waiting lists. Neighbouring CHCs dealing with different health districts often had conflicting experiences ranging from prompt and friendly co-operation to surly reluctance to disgorge essential information or respond to legitimate enquiries. Many CHCs grumbled about the practice of 'consultation' pointing out that, at best, they were given insufficient time to investigate and consult the public when a closure was proposed and to come up with constructive counter-proposals and, at worst, they only found out about proposals for closures after the event through the local press, often on the grounds that they were temporary or emergencies.

CHCs have the right to appeal against closures or changes of use to the Secretary of State but their success record has not been impressive. Between May 1979 and June 1985, fifty closures had been opposed by CHCs of which only five, and all these before 1983, had been upheld. However, this does not give the full picture. Often, CHCs may be persuaded that a closure or change is appropriate in the circumstances and it is part of their task to explain the reasons to the public. Sometimes initial opposition to a closure leads to genuine negotiation and the modification of health authority plans.

Since few set guidelines were given as to how CHCs should evolve and operate, they have found their own way. It cannot be said that there are any measurements of CHC performance. Some do well due to the flair and energy of the Secretary and Chairperson and an active minority caucus of members. Others manage to involve all their members on special working parties and visits to health service premises and by involving large numbers of people through activating the various community networks. Some of the members can be short on enthusiasm and time, particularly when they are already heavily committed to local authority work or their voluntary organisation. Within certain limits, a CHC can do as much or as little as its staff and membership chooses and little effort has been made to introduce common standards or procedures. It is hardly surprising that a minority seem relatively apathetic and too ready to settle for the easy option. Conscientious monitoring and evaluation of complex health services are forbidding tasks so that a CHC can get bogged down in paper and bureaucracy leaving little time for contact with patients and providers at the sharp end of NHS care. Health authority members may face similar problems: an avalanche of documentation out of which the officers draw attention only to what they want to do.

This picture is probably too bleak. More positively, the scope for an active CHC is boundless. At the most basic level, the CHC is there to deal with consumer needs and to give information and advice. People walking in off the street can ask just about anything from 'Can I have my baby at home?' to 'How can I find a dentist who can take me on an NHS list?' They want to know about facilities for disabled people and their families, starting or finding self-help groups, waiting lists and how to get round them, whether whooping cough vaccines are safe, whether they can be re-housed because of unhealthy conditions at home, and so on.

CHC staff, and sometimes members, can advise patients or relatives on how to set about making a complaint and to whom it should be referred. Unfortunately, the advocacy and representational roles are not included in the Regulations and tend to be frowned upon by health service managers. Yet, Hackney CHC was successful in establishing an advocacy scheme for ethnic minority women dealing with maternity services, and some CHC Secretaries have specialised in advising and representing patients in complaints procedures and up to any subsequent level of appeal. Complaints are self-evidently not popular with those against whom they are made but they can reveal a great deal about the quality of local health services and matters which demand attention. The complaints that come to CHCs vary from poor service by a deputising doctor to delays in getting essential medical treatment for stroke and cancer victims, badly fitting dentures to long waits in out-patient departments. Among the most common is the refusal of a doctor to undertake a home visit when an illness turns out to be serious and the difficulty of extracting from doctors information about what is actually wrong, what is to be done and what are the implications and possible adverse effects from various kinds of treatment.

The aim of the CHC is not to encourage complaining and making a fuss, although this can be necessary, but truly to act as a watchdog and bring to the attention of the appropriate authority or professional body what has gone wrong, and to do everything possible to put it right. The Griffiths Report on health service management placed some emphasis on measuring patient satisfaction and assuring quality of services. Quality assurance managers are being appointed in many districts and they will no doubt concentrate on measuring performance and quality from within and among the professional providers. The CHCs will be increasingly valuable in offering impressions from the consumer's viewpoint and suggesting possible measurements.

The right of CHC members to visit hospitals and clinics is fundamental. This is often exercised through systematic programmes of visiting facilities, discussions with staff and patients, producing reports, making recommendations and submitting these to the health authority for comment or action. The CHC may then go on to monitor progress towards improvement.

Increasingly, CHCs have undertaken surveys of health needs and the facilities available to meet them and many of these have been of an exceptionally high standard. One on the lack of facilities and help available to brain-damaged children and their families led to the Secretary of that CHC being invited to address a meeting of specialists in the subject while the survey was used as a comparison with other areas. Another CHC survey on waiting times at an ante-natal clinic produced little change after the first report. A follow-up one year later which found that conditions were no better produced two immediate results—a decision by the health authority to appoint another consultant and, when it was pointed out to the local transport authority that mothers complained of standing in the cold for buses, the provision of bus shelters and seats outside not only that hospital but all the other hospitals in the area.

To represent the needs of patients fully, CHCs have to extend their knowledge and activity beyond the boundaries of the NHS. Concern over the de-regulation of bus services prompted a number of CHCs to find out how the withdrawal and curtailment of services requiring subsidies would affect people visiting hospitals and clinics. They made representations to the Department of Transport. Health is a pervasive issue which extends beyond the NHS to education, housing, social services, and the whole environment.

New health issues arise. One inner city CHC, which had realised at an early stage that information on AIDS was desperately needed, set up its own information service, started some self-help groups and became so expert that it was able to give effective briefings to the media in a general atmosphere of alarm and hysteria.

Although it is hard to describe the CHC contribution in terms of a national impact, because of the variation in local interests and ways of doing things, it is fair to say that the health needs of women have received the attention they deserve because so many CHCs have contributed to the process. Well Women's Clinics, sometimes on an experimental basis, have surfaced around the country because of CHC pressure. It was the CHCs too which have led the way, with sympathetic MPs, in appealing for a 'no-fault compensation scheme' in cases of medical injuries and accidents. A CHC Secretary dealt with a case of a patient who never recovered consciousness following a routine operation when the Medical Defence Union advised doctors against giving evidence to the Inquiry which had been instituted by the RHA. This battle remains to be won.

If CHCs are to represent the public, they have to communicate with them. As it is physically impossible for an under-resourced CHC to be in contact with everyone, co-operation with the media is vitally important. There are so many good stories with human interest or profound public policy implications. The Cambridge CHC was at the forefront of raising the policy implications at a national level when a private multinational company launched into the business of running a medium-secure nursing home for difficult-to-place mental patients.

Much has been said about the NHS being an 'illness service'. Care and treatment are vital, but in a responsible society the public must be persuaded of its own responsibility to prevent ill health, look after itself and promote healthy social values. The educational system has not been notably successful in making children aware about what they can do for themselves in keeping healthy. The Dewsbury CHC runs an annual 'Children's multi-coloured health week' which tries, very effectively, to fill the gap. Children learn about health and enjoy it.

The NHS is probably the most popular institution we have in the United Kingdom. However, it is complex and ordinary people have the greatest difficulty in getting the best out of the system. Many CHCs issue directories of local services, mostly those within the NHS, but Oxfordshire CHC also produces a guide to private nursing homes for elderly people, leaflets on ante-natal care and abortion facilities, guides to hospital services and services for particular groups of patients such as disabled, mentally ill and mentally handicapped people, and advice to parents on how to deal with drug abuse and glue sniffing.

Many CHCs have become aware of the burgeoning public interest in acquiring more information about health matters and so they hold conferences, workshops and seminars on specific subjects, from the effect of lead in the environment to the problems faced by family carers as more and more elderly and mentally disabled people come out of the long-stay institutions and return to where they belong, in the community.

The very real problems now facing the NHS have brought vastly increased workloads for CHCs. Wards and hospital closures can mean longer waiting times and a desperate shopping around process to get treated or cared for. 'Care in the Community' without sufficient resources to make the transition from institutional to community care properly results in many more people facing such problems coming to CHCs for help. In fact, so heavy has the workload become in some districts that it is not surprising that certain CHCs are adopting a relatively low profile. It would not be physically possible to deal with all the problems brought to them without greatly increased resources.

A combination of a growing number of NHS cutbacks, coupled with poorer transport, can mean increased difficulties for the rural CHC whose remit covers a huge area of small towns and villages, some now entirely without public transport of any kind but with an ageing, unemployed and poor population. One idea currently being considered is a travelling CHC housed in a caravan which could get round to the outlying areas. Another, already working, involves holding monthly CHC meetings in different towns and really drumming up high attendance by the public.

The activity at the interface—bearing in mind that an average CHC office has only one Secretary and an assistant, along with whatever other help it might get on a part-time or voluntary basis—has to be set against all the other demands on time and personnel, the visits, the surveys, the publications, and attendance at countless meetings of health authorities and other bodies. A sudden closure announcement will require the need for fast action, often with insufficient information, to produce an adequate alternative and then follow the suggestions through. There is no question that CHCs are lamentably under-resourced.

The statutory instrument says that CHCs, while giving the consumer's viewpoint to various health authorities, must also understand their problems in the light of resources available. All health authorities are under tremendous pressure to make scarce resources go a long way and may differ from CHCs as to what they consider to be the priorities. The relationship between a CHC and its district or regional health authority varies so much that it is difficult to generalise. The best have a two-way communication, the worst spend their time in a state of armed truce or even in some instances virtually open combat.

Most CHCs have the will to represent the public and press consumer needs constructively. Health authorities vary in their contribution to what should be a reciprocal and mutually sympathetic relationship. One aspect of this is reflected in attitudes to training and resources made available. The West Midlands RHA, for instance, has even sponsored CHC Secretaries to take university degrees while other authorities have put every obstruction in the way of CHC staff being able to increase their knowledge and skill. Collaborative health authorities may provide extra funds for particular surveys, information link-ups and the provision of time-saving equipment. They will listen to what a CHC has to say and act whenever possible.

In a recent study, a number of health service administrators were asked, 'Does the CHC have an impact on decision making in your district management team, regional health authority, district health authority?' 63 per cent of the administrators said 'Yes', they had a definite impact, with only 37 per cent saying that they had not. The study concluded: 'the impact is greatly valued and regarded as a strong and positive advantage by both parties. Regardless of their legitimacy and representativeness, CHCs have clearly succeeded in turning the minds of administrators toward the community and to hitherto neglected groups of patients'. In the same study, administrators saw the most valuable roles of CHCs as 'bringing in new ideas, keeping the management on its toes, commenting on its priorities in service provision'.

It has to be said that many CHC Secretaries are concerned that they have no career prospects. In all but one region they have remained on NHS scale 9, which is no great inducement for well-educated, skilled and experienced people to take on board a job which is pressurised and involves contact with every level of authority within the NHS up to the Secretary of State. If they want to progress, they can only move sideways in the health service, conscious that their prospects will not be good if they have done their job effectively and, on occasions, made a nuisance of themselves. CHCs are, therefore, often presented with problems in recruiting staff of the calibre required.

As already noted, CHCs were introduced with all-party support. Mercifully, the kind of party political combat familiar at national level and in local authorities has not infected either the health authorities or CHCs to any significant degree. The chairpersons of CHCs and DHAs, according to a recent survey conducted by Landsberger, do tend to present a genuine cross-section of opinion of all the major health service issues. They reflect the political and social composition of the district they serve. CHC opinion is vigorously non-partisan but demonstrates a deep commitment to the original principles on which the NHS was founded. If the government of the day or a particular political party strays from these principles, then its own supporters among the CHCs are prepared to join others in opposition.

In 1981 it became clear that the Secretary of State, Patrick Jenkin, someone with enormous commitment to the voluntary sector, felt that CHCs were unnecessary and troublesome. He issued a consultation document to assess whether it was worth getting rid of them and received a very clear answer which had been expressed by the last Royal Commission on the NHS: No, CHCs should stay. Undeterred, he took steps to undermine their credibility and effectiveness. The first of these was to withdraw a grant of £74,000 from their national association ACHCEW. This plunged the national network of CHCs into some confusion and acute financial difficulties.

Fortunately, his successors, without immediately restoring central funding, bailed ACHCEW out from its deficiency crisis. Then, in 1985, a grant, be it on a much lower level, was made. From 1981 it had been the Government's intention to review the role and structure of CHCs when their relations with District Health Authorities had settled down. This was evidently necessary. The variation of performance and effectiveness of CHCs described above demonstrated the need to develop a more coherent and constructive view of their role. There was an obvious need for CHCs to share experience and information and, occasionally, to combine in making representations at the national level. Re-inventing wheels at local level is scarcely the best way of developing patient participation and consumer satisfaction to cope with NHS bureaucracy and professional hegemony. Unfortunately, ministers abruptly abandoned their intentions in April 1985 so that CHCs were left to meander on until the next change of government. The pity of this is that the importance of their contribution cannot be realised throughout the country while government attitudes remain so ambivalent.

At the end of 1985, ACHCEW was left with a membership, on which it depends for its core funding, of 177 CHCs out of a possible 216. Some resigned or refused to join for financial reasons. Some were simply not interested in a national body to represent them.

All CHCs take their remit—that they are representing consumers' *local* interest and needs—very seriously and some see this as their only task. National interests are to them peripheral. Others, however, while keeping their feet firmly on local ground, are intensely interested in what is happening to the National Health Service at the national level and they have a knowledge and commitment to apply their considerable expertise, derived from their local communities, in tackling the genuinely difficult health service issues confronted by the nation.

As well as being watchdogs for the patients, nationally and locally, CHCs are the sounding board which the NHS needs if it is to respond to changing needs, to develop and deal with its many internal contradictions and difficulties. The NHS has been changed, fundamentally, over the last decade. It follows that the role of CHCs has to change, but little or nothing has emerged from government or the health authorities to accommodate this. As we have said, CHC opinion, crossing all the party-political divides, remains committed to the original principles of the NHS. But health care is no longer free, on demand, at the point of need. Those for whom the NHS was responsible—the chronic sick, the elderly, mentally ill and mentally handicapped people—have been transferred, transported or, even, hijacked out of the NHS domain and across administrative boundaries to the alternative systems of care offered by the private and voluntary sectors and by local authorities. If this transformation brings long-stay patients back to their communities it can only be welcomed. But how and by whom is the consumer interest going to be represented?

The resilience of the NHS long-stay institutions, which were attacked by Enoch Powell when he was Minister of Health in 1961, represented a fatal flaw on the landscape of the NHS. Mr. Powell expressed the political will to provide alternatives within 15 years, but that did not happen. It was resisted by professions and unions and tolerated by public opinion which did not get very worked up about citizens who had been put out of sight and out of mind. It needed the pressure of consumer opinion to change all this during the 1970s.

Today, the concept of care in the community is one with which most people agree but, in practical terms, the future will be grim for these displaced or transferred patients unless the alternatives, the better alternatives, are organised, managed and properly resourced. After years of inaction we now face the prospect of some of the long-stay institutions being closed down. The CHC dilemma, expressed vividly at ACHCEW's AGM in 1985, concerns not only the provision of better alternatives in the community, but how to exercise proper responsibility when statutory rights and duties do not cover these. There are fewer and fewer NHS geriatric beds, and particularly psycho-geriatric beds, and there is a definite push towards private residential care for the elderly. There is also greater reliance on self-help groups and dependence on voluntary organisations, private companies and local authorities to do the work which was once done by the NHS. In the inner cities it is now very hard indeed to get on a GP's list if you are old, disabled, mentally ill, chronically sick, homeless or long-term unemployed. Unemployment itself has been shown to provide a higher incidence of mental and physical sickness to which the community and the services must respond.

What place, then, does the CHC have in community care? If the sick, the elderly and the mentally disabled are returned to poor living conditions with inadequate facilities and with insufficient back-up from either the NHS or the local authority, how can a CHC bring pressure to bear to put matters right? There is no provision for all this under the Statutory Instruments which set them up.

Pressure on the services is, in any case, intense and when a mistake happens and there is a tragedy, such as the death of Jasmine Beckford at her stepfather's hands, there is a public outcry, yet very little awareness that resources will have to be increased substantially as more and more people come within the aegis of community care. Cash limits, rate capping, the denigration of social work and the piratical activities of private companies out to make considerable profits from social distress all have a bearing on the monitoring and redevelopment of health services.

A watchdog can patrol the boundaries of a single property. It cannot deal with dispersal unless it is given the remit and the resources to do so. So, while CHCs can visit NHS hospitals and homes and make recommendations for improvements and complain about conditions, they cannot penetrate anything on offer outside the NHS. Possibly, they also need to be able to make some input when the task of caring is put back to families and the community's informal networks. Who cares for the carers? Who looks after their physical and emotional needs? They, like the consumers, need to be represented too. As the DHSS itself has confirmed, care in the community is not a cheap option. If it is properly carried out it is likely to be more expensive than warehoused institutional care, unless the whole burden is lumped on ordinary people.

The rapid, and some say disturbing, growth in the number of private residential homes must be of concern to CHCs, many of which have expressed their fears concerning the maintenance of standards. CHCs have no right to visit private homes and, on the numerous occasions when this has been put to ministers, the reply has been that there is no desire by the private home owners to be monitored by CHCs or that patients want this attention. We have a system of registration and inspection but it is entirely inadequate unless it can be supplemented by bodies such as the CHCs which are prepared to represent effectively the needs of the consumers.

Private hospitals raise the same issues. The case in Cambridgeshire where the health authority gave a licence to a private company while saying that it would not be sending any of its own patients there as it did not necessarily accept the regime, is a glaring example. In this case the CHC has been invited by the company to visit, but the only real monitoring committee has been handpicked by the company itself. If we allow private companies to make money from public authorities by containing people in locked environments, we shall open up the possibility of the sort of scandals which have not occurred since Victorian times but which regularly occur in the USA where private prisons are not unknown.

There are logical extensions to the concept of CHCs becoming involved in care in the community and private homes and hospitals. Could they, should they, will they, have to extend their function to cover military hospitals and prisons? Families of men serving in the armed forces overseas have run into severe problems when they need hospital treatment or when there has been a medical accident; and they virtually have no redress given that a serviceman, working within a disciplined force, may suffer career disadvantages if he dares to make a fuss.

The position in the Prison Medical Service is even worse. The PMS is run by the Home Office, not the DHSS, and there is no-one to represent the views of the prisoner who is in a most vulnerable position. If the concept of a CHC is relevant and useful in the NHS then, surely, it could and should be extended to other such situations.

Our conclusion, as we move to the end of the 1980s and into the 1990s, is that it is surely time to look again at consumer representation and the role of CHCs. Many CHCs have succeeded. Some have failed. Resources and the conceptual framework lie at the heart of the difficulty. There is enough evidence of the effectiveness of the better CHCs during the first decade or so of their existence to suggest that we need to keep them, improve them and extend them.

21

Consumers' Association:
Which? Why and How

'We demand that big business give the people a
square deal; in return we must insist that when
anyone engaged in big business honestly endeavours
to do right he shall himself be given a square deal.'
                    Autobiography of Theodore Roosevelt

MICHAEL WARREN, Head of the Survey Unit, Consumers'
Association.

On both sides of the Atlantic there has been a steady growth in what is
usually referred to as the consumer movement. Never intent on
warming the hearts of manufacturers it has slowly but inexorably
established a high degree of credibility with buyers of goods or users of
services. Certainly this writer is of the opinion that the standing order
to the Consumers' Association is one of his wiser investments which
has repaid itself many times over.

It is hard to imagine that, when that Association was launched 29
years ago from a garage in Bethnal Green, it could have been envisaged
that in 1986 some 700,000 households would subscribe to *Which?* or that
manufacturers would have to be conscious that their products would be
subject to independent appraisals which would invariably feature on
BBC 4's *Today* show on the day of publication. The impact has surely
extended far beyond the readership of *Which?* though. The activities of
the Consumers' Association have undoubtedly had an influence on a
growing acceptance that independent appraisals can and do have a
long-term impact upon product quality.

It seemed natural, therefore, to approach the Association for a
contribution and it was agreed that one outlining the activities of the
Survey Unit would be most appropriate. This is currently headed up by
Michael Warren who took up the position in 1980. He actually started
his working life as a journalist, spent a short period in the theatre, and
moved into survey research in the early 1970s. He spent some ten years
with Research Services Ltd. starting as an interviewer working on
industrial and opinion research. In 1977 he was appointed as an
Associate Director of RSL with special responsibility for social and
public-sector projects.

★ ★ ★

The Consumers' Association is now so much a part of our cultural landscape that it is perhaps difficult to remember how recent and how unlikely were its beginnings. *Which?* is subscribed to by some 700,000 people; it is quoted in the media and at Westminster; it employs 400 people and has a turnover of £18½ million a year. Backed by faith and intellectual vigour, but little else, *Which?* was launched in 1957, by a handful of people, from a garage in Bethnal Green. It was a startling example of an idea whose time had come. Within a week of the launch, 10,000 people had subscribed, and this figure was soon doubled and trebled. And this was without the trailers and pre-publicity that would be the norm in the 1980s, and without anything in the way of precedent, the idea being, to all intents and purposes, totally new to the UK.

Now, nearly 30 years later, the Consumers' Association retains a unique position. CA publishes three subscription-based magazines rather than one, and a range of books, from the Good Food Guide to books on health, DIY, taxation and household emergencies. CA also publishes, for the medical profession, the Drug and Therapeutics Bulletin which is recognised as the definitive independent guide to new drugs. It campaigns and lobbies in Westminster on a variety of subjects from the well-publicised to the relatively obscure, from Sunday trading to the Multi-fibre Arrangement.

CA is not, of course, loved by everyone. For some it is insufficiently radical, for others its advertising methods are suspect, and it is rarely the favourite organisation of the manufacturers whose products it criticises. But for the majority, and demonstrably for the press, radio, television and government it is perceived to be knowledgeable and authoritative.

This has been achieved by the gradual and conscious development of a labour-intensive organisation that is substantial, costly and, in a sense, arrogant too. CA takes on to itself the right to assess, to criticise and to judge. It judges—indeed, it *exists* to judge—manufacturers, service industries and government. CA's approach is perhaps the ultimate example of the position any customer takes up when he privately criticises British Rail, or the toaster that stops working after six months, or the quality of food at a motorway service area. CA's views, however, unlike the views expressed at the drinks or dinner party, or even in the correspondence columns of newspapers, are listened to and are taken seriously. This has been achieved because CA has established, and has maintained, a reputation for independent, thorough and defensible research. This defensibility of CA's work is vitally important. The organisation criticises and judges publicly, and the techniques it uses and the standards it works to must, therefore, be open to examination.

It might be useful if the particular consideration of CA's work in the service sector is linked to a description of the various types of research which the organisation undertakes. It is also worth noting, and this is not simply semantic nit-picking, that CA sees itself very much as a research organisation which publishes its findings, rather than a publishing house which undertakes research.

Laboratory Research

The bulk of the product testing and related activities that CA undertakes is carried out in its own laboratories at Harpenden. The tests that are done there are to establish what the product does: does it do what it claims to do? does it do what it ought to do? The ultimate aim, of course, is to produce comparative data and to advise *Which?* readers on which brand and model does the job best. In particular, the CA looks at such factors as:

- *Safety:*   How safe is it to perform the various operations that will or might be undertaken using the product?
- *Ease of use:*   This may include storage, transportation, the switches, controls, instructions, doors, displays, maintenance, cleaning, etc.
- *Comfort:*   How comfortable are the handles, switches etc. to use?
- *Performance/efficiency:*   How well does it do the job?
- *Adjustability:*   How easy is it to adjust the equipment to fit the user who may be tall or short, thin or fat, and how satisfactory are these adjustments?

It is worth pointing out that many people often use products in ways that manufacturers do not intend. Many people, for example, use a refrigerator top on which to prepare food and the suitability of the top as a work surface must be examined. More difficult to determine, but often of considerable importance, are the ways in which products are habitually *mis*-used. The top of a cooker might be used as a storage surface and a chair may be used as a step ladder. Mis-use of this type is potentially hazardous, but is likely to occur—who among us hasn't done something similar?—and CA tries to consider it. In general, British Standards do not deal with mis-use or abuse. The British Standard on screwdrivers, however, is an interesting exception; a bending test is included which simulates the standard practice, but nevertheless 'abuse', of opening tins of paint with a screwdriver. Other tests which go beyond normal use, but which CA has carried out, include:

- hitting the edges of blades of garden spades with a metal bar to simulate digging stony ground;
- using a saw on wood containing metal pins, simulating nails and screws;
- scuffing car upholstery to simulate dragging a carrycot out of the back seat;
- vibrating calculators, binoculars and cameras to simulate carriage on a car parcel shelf;
- diversion of hot or cold water supply from a mixed-supply bathroom shower, simulating unexpected use of one supply elsewhere in the household;
- dropping pushchairs down simulated kerbs.

It is clear that these tests are intended to ensure that, as far as possible, CA's laboratory work, whilst retaining the discipline that distinguishes scientific from less rigorous research, nevertheless keeps in touch with produce use in the real rather than the clinical world. This emphasis on day-to-day life in the home, the garden, the shop, and in the car or on the train, is also inherent in much of the research carried out by The Survey Unit, CA's survey and opinion research department, which is described in the next section.

Survey Research

The Survey Unit (TSU) is the department of CA responsible for producing survey-research-based data for inclusion in *Which?* and in CA's other publications, and for campaigning purposes. TSU undertakes some 100 separate projects a year and, aside from its work within CA, is also an independent research institute, as too is CA's laboratory. Survey-based projects are undertaken for a variety of government and public-sector clients, though not of course for manufacturers.

The techniques which The Survey Unit uses are those, now fairly familiar, of market and social research. Essentially, a representative sample of people is contacted and asked questions about its experiences, or views, or behaviour. If the correct number of people, selected in the right way, is asked the right questions, the data obtained can give an accurate guide to the total group's attitudes or knowledge. There are two areas amongst many in which CA has found research of this type to be particularly useful:

- For product reliability and servicing—that is, monitoring product performance over months and years rather than hours or days and, increasingly important, monitoring the performance of manufacturers and others in providing after-sales service.

- For examining those things which simply cannot be tested in a laboratory as, for example, the service that is given by insurance companies, British Rail, television, a holiday destination; or to look at what people want rather than what they get.

In the last 30 years the emphasis of consumer research into household durables—washing machines, fridges, televisions, etc—has gradually switched from *performance* to *reliability*. The Consumers' Association tested kettles for the first issue of *Which?* in 1957, and has tested durables of one sort or another for almost all issues since. CA's experience is that, on the whole, products now do what they claim to do. Greater sophistication in manufacturing techniques, strong and international competition, legislation and—perhaps—the impact of the consumer movement itself in increasing purchasers' sophistication, have discouraged the production and sale of rogue products. The occasional new product tested in CA's laboratories may leak, or may be electrically unsafe, but in general the emphasis of the work continues to move from questions like 'Does it work?' to matters of safety and ease of use, and to questions like 'How long does it work for?' and, reflecting this change in emphasis from the product to the service that goes with it, 'If it develops a fault, what happens?'

Information of this type is obtained by Consumers' Association from the *Which?* Monitoring Team which comprises a panel of some 15,000 subscribers. The panel members complete diaries about any problems and faults with their appliances as they happen. They also fill in an additional questionnaire whenever their appliances are repaired. During the past ten years the Survey Unit at CA has also undertaken a monthly 'omnibus' survey amongst a random sample of 2,000 of its subscribers. Such an omnibus consists of a set of small-scale survey projects, usually no more than a dozen questions on each topic, grouped together into a single questionnaire. The covering letter which is sent out with the omnibus questionnaire is also used to recruit members for the Monitoring Team.

Information is obtained regularly from the Monitoring Team. This covers, for example, some 7,000 washing machines, 4,500 colour televisions and nearly 2,000 dishwashers. Whilst the main aim of this project is to obtain data about brand and, if possible, model reliability, it also enables CA to build up data on product repairs. In May 1984 *Which?* noted that its members were 'generally satisfied with the standard of repairs that they had had carried out on their appliances. Where there was some dissatisfaction, the most common reasons were that the repairs took too long, they were too expensive, or that the faults weren't cured satisfactorily.' The February 1986 *Which?* contained the observation that 'although some repairers are pretty efficient, others still have considerable room for improvement.

And repairers of all types could be more specific about when they're going to call.'

There are many occasions on which a single research method is insufficient and a variety of techniques has to be used. An example of this is some work done in 1985/86 by CA to investigate the service given by British Rail. At the time of writing the full data from the study are not available but the techniques used in the study may be of interest. Travellers by rail can be classified in a number of different ways but, for the purposes of their work, CA concentrated on two types, the InterCity traveller and the commuter. It was relatively straightforward, though costly, to contact a sizeable sample of InterCity travellers. Though only 17 per cent of the population travel by InterCity in a year, it proved possible to contact a sufficient number by the same technique used for the study of children in hospital which is discussed later in this chapter. This involved using one of the multi-client surveys carried out regularly by Britain's market research agencies. It was more difficult to contact commuters.

To any rush-hour traveller the supply of commuters must seem inexhaustible, but in fact there are relatively few of them even in, say, Greater London, in comparison with the total population of the area. Interviewing passengers on rush-hour trains would have been impractical even in the unlikely event of BR permitting it and contacting a good sample would be time-consuming and costly using the conventional technique of interviewers knocking on people's front doors. The compromise was to contact commuters as they returned in the evenings at a representative cross-section of stations. The actual interviews were subsequently undertaken by telephone within two or three days of the first contact. To supplement this work, CA sent out inspectors to look at station cleanliness and food specialists to look at—and taste—the food and drink provided by BR. One other aspect of this complex project was to phone a sample of British Rail enquiry offices to find out how easy it was to get through and how comprehensive was the information that was so obtained.

Observation

Observation, whether with the naked eye, through a microscope or a telescope, has traditionally been a prime source of information for scientists. CA also uses observation, and not only in the laboratory. There are a number of types of enquiry, central to CA's work and of particular relevance to this book, where laboratory work is clearly not applicable but where conventional survey research may not be suitable either. The problem for the researcher is that in some circumstances, and with some types of enquiry, we cannot be sure how much we can trust our potential survey informants to tell the truth. Indeed, there are some circumstances in which we can be fairly sure that with a conventional survey research project we will not be told the truth.

In many fields of social research it may be unrealistic—even unfair—to assume that questions will necessarily be answered honestly. Some subjects are so emotive and the social pressures towards a certain type of acceptable behaviour so strong, that the researcher must beware of self-justifying responses. All of us, to a greater or lesser extent, fall below the standards we set ourselves. Perhaps, for example, we drive too fast, or too close to the vehicle in front of us; perhaps we do not teach our children road safety quite as thoroughly as we should; perhaps, just sometimes, we drive when we have had rather too much to drink. Questioned directly and conventionally about these topics and dozens like them informants may well, understandably, give false information.

Some may mislead intentionally, because they do not want to admit to some behaviour or to some attitude about which they feel guilty. Some will mislead because they themselves are not aware of the real situation. The more emotionally charged the field of study, the greater is the possibility that the informant will have rationalised his behaviour or experience. Everyone, to a greater or lesser extent, is subject to 'selective recall'. At its simplest, this means that people remember those things which they want to remember. Of more interest, and of greater significance to researchers, is the corollary— that informants are perfectly capable of forgetting things that may be awkward or embarrassing to answer.

If, for example, one wished to study racial discrimination, it would be unacceptable to collect data only by means of an interview study amongst, say, employers and the ethnic minority population. This would represent an attempt to obtain hard data from sources from which hard objective data may not be available. Clearly, there is the danger of informant rationalisation. If rules have been broken, or a person's experience has been painful or pride has been hurt, how can any conventional interview be guaranteed to obtain factual material? The radically alternative solution of a controlled experiment whereby white people and the ethnic minority are put through potentially difficult situations—job-hunting, house purchase etc.—may well be a more realistic method of tackling the problem.

The Consumers' Association faces a variety of situations in which problems of exactly this type arise. Some involve people and some involve products. Looking first at the people, CA perceived a need in the early 1980s to investigate selling techniques, whether door-to-door or by telephone, adopted by double glazing and insurance companies. Clearly this is not an area where laboratory research is appropriate, nor one where survey research is likely to provide the full story. Accordingly, CA sent anonymous investigators to a number of training courses, some run by insurance companies and some by double-glazing firms. In the course of this investigation CA found, for example, that insurance salesmen with no previous financial know-ledge could be selling to the public after only a few days' training. In three or four days, investigators had acquired only a sketchy knowledge of the basics of life insurance, and did not have much hope of understanding the complexities and the details of the various policies. In one case, CA's investigator was trained to sell only one insurance package. Though the techniques identified by CA were not used throughout the industry, *Which?* suggested that 'so long as disreputable practices are used, and so long as inadequately trained salesmen are let loose on the public, the whole industry risks being tarred with the same brush'. *Which?* also, of course, advised its readers on the pitfalls to avoid when dealing with salespeople.

Turning now to problems with products, it is obvious that the research techniques must vary with the topic being investigated. For a number of years, for example, CA investigated *garage servicing* and its reports spoke of 'an appalling picture of incompetence, wasteful-ness and even dishonesty'. How was the research work underpin-ning such a sweeping conclusion carried out? One problem with studies of this type is that to be fair to the service being investigated— in this case the work done by garages when a car is booked in for service—it is necessary for the vehicles to have a thorough technical examination both before and after the work is carried out. It is not good enough to rely on what people *think* has been done to their cars. This, inevitably, means that only a limited number of vehicles and tests can be included in the study. In 1980, for example, CA decided that 50 tests—five vehicles, each being checked on ten separate occasions—would be sufficient. To be more specific, CA took five cars that had finished their standard *Which?* car test programme—a Datsun, a Ford Escort, a Morris Marina, a Talbot Horizon and a Toyota Starlet. Each vehicle was booked anonymously into ten garages, three franchised for that make of car, three or four franchised but not for that particular make, and the remainder non-franchised. CA asked each garage to carry out a major service as specified by the manufacturer and also to check, and correct if necessary, the wheel balancing and alignment, when this was not already included as a standard service item. Before going for a service, each car was thoroughly checked by the mechanics at CA's Car Test Unit. Certain things were intentionally set up incorrectly. Oil levels and timing, for example, were wrong, and spark plug gaps were too small. CA compiled a full detailed record of the state of all parts of the car included in the service. This careful inspection was repeated when the car came back from the garage. The bill was also checked to see exactly what had been paid for, and how near the bill was to the original estimate.

CA's dramatic conclusions, published in January 1981, were that 'out of 50 garages only two came anywhere near to carrying out a full service in line with the maker's specifications. Of the rest, ten managed to achieve a rating of poor, which meant they got at least a quarter of the service items wrong or failed to do them. Thirty-four were rated as very poor in that only around half the service was done properly if at all, and three were appalling, given that barely one third of the service had been done properly if at all. One garage charged £40 for a full service and did little more than change the oil. It was awarded the accolade of 'words fail us.'

A similar though smaller-scale exercise was carried out in 1980 to look at the servicing of domestic appliances. Analysis of CA's Monitoring Team data suggested that most people are satisfied with the repairs done for them. However, it is difficult for the layman to judge whether a repair has been done well, and whether the charge made for it is fair. To investigate this particular topic, CA set up a small experiment. Faults were introduced into nine washing machines which were installed in different homes and arrangements for repairs were made in the normal way. CA's laboratory checked the machines before and after repair. The type of problems introduced into the washing machines were, for example, placing a faulty gasket on a heating element, jamming an impeller blade with a paper clip and disconnecting a wire from the timer. CA (in *Which?* July 1980) made the point that the sample was not representative in any statistical sense. 'However', said *Which?*, 'out of ten attempts at repairs, only two were completed satisfactorily. The other eight replaced components costing up to £79.50 needlessly. One even reconnected a wire in a way that was electrically unsatisfactory. We don't believe that all the repairmen cheated deliberately, but for the most part, diagnoses seemed skimpy and inaccurate. And five repairmen, who may well have discovered the real fault in the course of replacing an unnecessary component, kept quiet and charged for the replacement anyway.'

Conclusion

This has necessarily been no more than a brief glance at the substantial and complex range of research carried out by CA. In conclusion we present two additional case studies, both coin-cidentally involving children, which further illustrate the variety of research techniques which are necessary for a thorough assessment of the service that the consumer receives.

Children in Hospital

1980 was International Year of the Child. To mark this, CA undertook a study of children in hospital examining, amongst other things, how children are looked after whilst in hospital and what provision is made for parents to visit and stay with the child. Substantial research was undertaken to provide data for this work. More than 13,000 people were contacted, using random omnibus surveys, to identify a representative sample of households having had a child treated in hospital in the six months prior to the interview. Detailed information was subsequently obtained from almost 300 parents. Personal interviews were undertaken with a selection of staff in each of 40 general and 12 children's hospitals.

Two play groups were organised with a sample of children who had been in hospital for at least four days (three nights) in the previous six months. One group involved children aged 4–5 years, the other children aged 6–7 years. Each group contained two boys and one girl, and for approximately an hour and a quarter they played with a variety of toys including a toy hospital. The moderator encouraged the children to play with the toys, and also to express themselves by drawing part of the hospital environment. A selection of photographs, taken inside the children's ward of a typical London hospital, was on hand as stimulus material. Information was obtained through a detailed observation of play and an active dialogue between moderator and children based on the material generated in the group.

Seven in-depth interviews were undertaken with boys and girls of ages ranging from eight to thirteen years, again with the 'four days in hospital' condition. Each interview lasted at least one hour. The hospital photographs mentioned above were used as projective material and yielded interesting pyschological information. This fieldwork was conducted by an experienced child psychologist. In the report on this work published in *Which?* in June 1980, Consumers' Association combined data from the survey with its own views on what should happen. It also referred back to the 1954 report of a Government Committee chaired by Platt, which looked at the welfare of children in hospital (Ministry of Health 1954). Amongst the points that *Which?* made were the following:

CHILDREN'S WARDS, AND THE STAFF

According to the Platt report—and official policy—children should be nursed in separate wards, away from adults. Staff need to be paediatrically trained and overall responsibility for children should rest with a children's physician.

But a third of the adult hospitals we visited trated some child patients in adult wards; another fifth nursed children in a partitioned adjunct to the adult ward . . .

VISITING, AND THE PRESENCE OF PARENTS

According to official policy, unrestricted 24-hour visiting along with facilities for parents to make this possible, should exist everywhere. It has been recognised that this is not simply a social exercise, but a preventative and therapeutic measure. Indeed, Platt put the onus on hospitals to tell parents that visiting was part of the treatment which the child needed.

But only about half the hospitals in our sample had 24-hour open visiting. And a few of those which did, did not do so in all wards which admitted children. The remainder tended to allow visiting by parents until the early evening. But some had other restrictions—no visiting during ward rounds, no visiting before 10 a.m., no visiting just after lunch, for example.

The presence of parents is important to children, particularly at critical times—yet a quarter of adult hospitals contained at least one ward which would bar parents just before an operation. A similar number would not allow parents to stay when the child was coming round from the anaesthetic. And hospital policy on the presence of parents during treatment varied widely—some felt, for example, that it could put the doctor off.

In a follow-up report in April 1985, based in part on additional work carried out by other organisations, *Which?* said:

Since our 1980 report, it seems that the care of children in hospitals has improved. More hospitals now have unrestricted visiting, allow parents to stay overnight and nurse children in children's wards.

Sadly, despite the DHSS recommendations, some hospitals have still not recognised that children and their families have special needs.

But if hospitals are to change, the final push must come from parents. Ask questions, know what's possible and, above all, be persistent.

Children's Playgrounds

The Research Institute for Consumer Affairs, CA's charitable sister organisation, was commissioned in 1981 by the Environment and Consumer Protection Service of the EEC, to undertake a study of playground equipment, concentrating particularly on safety issues. Aside from a substantial amount of desk research, which is a foundation stone of virtually all CA's work, this study involved two

different types of data collection. Firstly, two surveys were undertaken, one with manufacturers and the other with buyers of
playground equipment, and secondly, trained inspectors went out to
look at a sample of playgrounds in Belgium, England and Italy.

In its report to the EEC, RICA recommended amongst other things
that 'the EEC should commission research which aims to develop
safety and performance standards for all the basic, popular items of
playground equipment—swings, slides, roundabouts and rocking
equipment and related surfacing. It is important that this is done with
the aim of eliminating hazards which cannot be foreseen by children,
and reducing the severity of injuries when accidents do occur,
without reducing the "play value" or attractiveness of equipment and
without destroying the element of dare or excitement associated with
successful equipment.'

RICA went on to suggest that the EEC 'should commission and
publish in all EEC languages a book that offers a simple, clear and
well illustrated guide to playground design, installation and operation which should be simple enough to be understood by laymen. All
this information exists. It merely needs to be collected.'

INFORMATION

22

Broadcasting Research— Necessity or Nicety?

'I divide all productions into two categories; those I like and those I don't like. I have no other criterion.'
The *Selected Letters* of Anton Chekhov

PETER MENNEER, Head of Broadcasting Research Department, BBC.*

One Sunday afternoon three years ago a knock on our door revealed a BBC interviewer intent on discovering just which programmes we had been watching over the previous week. I was fascinated by the depth of the questionnaire he was using and, oddly, felt rather guilty that we had not happened to watch much BBC TV, or any other channel for that matter, that particular week. I determined that one day I would find out a little more about what these people were up to and this text provided the ideal opportunity. What will be clear is that the man at the door was but a tip of a quite considerable iceberg of activity which is discussed in what follows. At the time of writing we are awaiting the publication of the Peacock Report on the future of the BBC with interest. Doubtless those in the BBC have a set of anticipatory emotions which go well beyond a neutral anticipation. I cannot resist the opportunity to make my position clear. If the audience research the BBC has conducted over the years has contributed to the quality of the TV programmes we enjoy, then it would appear to be a good investment.

Peter heads up the BBC's Broadcasting Research Department having been appointed to that post in 1979. In this position he is responsible for audience research for the BBC's domestic broadcasting service, the two national television channels, the four national radio stations and the extensive national network of local and regional radio services. He graduated in Politics, Philosophy and Economics from Oxford in 1960 and joined the British Market Research Bureau Ltd. where he was appointed a director in 1970. He left BRMB in 1977 and, between then and joining the BBC, he was joint managing director of Research Surveys of Great Britain Ltd. It could well be that he has actually appeared on one of the various channels, as his principal hobby of singing finds him a Gentleman of the Chapel Royal at Hampton Court Palace.

★ ★ ★

---

*This chapter appeared originally in *Inter Media* (1984) Vol. 12, No. 3.

I cannot help feeling more and more strongly that we are fundamentally ignorant as to how our various programmes are received, and what is their relative popularity. It must be a source of considerable disquiet to many people beside myself to think that it is quite possible that a very great deal of our money and time and effort may be expended on broadcasting into a void. (Val Gielgud, BBC Productions Director, 1930, quoted in Briggs (1965).)

I do not share Gielgud's view on the democratic issue. However complete and effective any survey we launch might be, I should still be convinced that our policy and programme building should be based first and last upon our own conviction as to what should and should not be broadcast. As far as meeting public demand is concerned, I believe that the right way is to provide for a more conscious differentiation of objectives within our daily programme. (Charles Siepmann, BBC Director of Talks, 1930, quoted in Briggs (1965).)

[Audience research] should be related to the needs and requirements of those in the broadcasting organisations whose work could be affected by its results: programme makers, senior management and the Broadcasting Authorities. Audience research is not a substitute for the imagination and creative decisions of producers . . . [and] cannot dictate what a programme should say, but it can tell the producer what people thought it was saying, and how they reacted to the programme. (Home Office 1977)

Audience research has formally existed within the BBC since 1936. The department came into being after a five-year or so debate within the organisation as to whether research was or was not desirable. The 1930 quotations above give a flavour of the arguments deployed on either side at the time.

Today, all European broadcasting organisations actively engage in audience research. The role will usually include that of serving as one instrument of public accountability, in addition to providing a day-to-day information system for programme makers and senior management. But, beyond the routine activities of measuring audience size and audience appreciation of programmes, audience researchers nowadays are actively involved in bespoke studies on particular broadcasting issues of the day. The stature of audience research is (and should be) judged as much by the value of this latter wide-ranging sphere of activity to senior broadcasting management and programme makers.

It often comes as some surprise that all European and many other broadcasting organisations have their own specialist audience research function formally established within their structure. The audience research departments have their own budget for research, in part to monitor audiences on a continuous or intermittent basis and in part to engage in research studies for individual producers on their own programmes.

The existence of such specialist departments has led over the years to their managers seeing a benefit to be gained from discussing issues that are common to most of us. We compare notes and learn from one another. Clearly, on a day-to-day basis we individually attempt to answer the questions posed by both broadcasting management and individual programme makers. There is a potential danger that, as a consequence of heading up specialist and somewhat isolated departments, we fail to recognise that these issues are rarely unique to one's own country and to one's own broadcasting organisation. In fact there is, of course, a great deal in common between countries in what our respective broadcasting organisations set out to achieve.

At a corporate level in any sphere or activity common interests and objectives lead to the rationale for cross-national collaborative bodies: the broadcasters have the European Broadcasting Union. Over time these international associations develop roles beyond those of a narcissistic talking shop. They are required to exercise administrative functions to obtain international agreement on technical standards and a wealth of other, often complex, administrative arrangements.

In our own particular corner, audience research, there is an equivalent need to learn from one another. We benefit from hearing about our colleagues' preoccupations, problems and priorities, and how each country's audience research department has set about tackling what are often very similar objectives. In Europe a special forum, the Group of European Audience Researchers (GEAR), was founded as long ago as 1967. We meet annually, with each country taking it in turn to act as host to a three-day conference. Our current membership includes the heads of audience research in Austria, Belgium, Denmark, Finland, France, West Germany, Hungary, Italy, the Netherlands, Norway, Poland, Portugal, Romania, Spain, Sweden, Switzerland, the United Kingdom and Yugoslavia.

At each meeting we select specific issues, and papers are invited on these subjects. In 1983, for example, the sessions covered a wide range of topics:

- Research for programme development
- Broadcasting developments, including satellites, teletext and video recorders
- Researching children
- Standardisation of statistics

The last was an interesting development. At the instigation of Austria's ORF, a great deal of effort has been put into developing a Euro-standard of research terminology, linked then to a collection of basic broadcasting and audience statistics relating to each country for inclusion in a facts and figures document that we up-date each year. It is useful to have available reasonably authoritative annual statistics for each country on trends or growth in, for example, the number of homes that have more than one TV set; VCR ownership; and the hours and minutes of TV viewing per head per week.

We also exchange information on the proportion of our respective organisations' revenue (whether licence fee revenue, advertising revenue or a mixture of both) that is spent on audience research. The 1983 figures are set out in Table 22.1. These figures include the cost of staff and payments for services such as data collection and data processing, but exclude overheads such as accommodation, lighting, heating, etc. It is remarkable how similar the figures are: the average is 0.4 per cent, that is, for every £100 spent by the average broadcasting organisation, about 40p is set aside for researching its audiences. The clear commitment of broadcasters to audience research raises the basic question of why this should be. At a time

Table 22.1 *Audience Research Budget as a Percentage of Revenue (1983)*

Austria	0.40[1]	Netherlands	0.50
Belgium		Norway	0.14
BRF	0.30		
RTB	0.38		
		Poland	0.37
Denmark	0.11		
		Portugal	0.11
Finland			
YLE	0.13	Spain	0.21
MTV	0.13		
		Sweden	0.55
France	0.40		
		Switzerland	1.53
Germany, FR	0.37		
		United Kingdom	
Hungary	1.17	BBC	0.36
		IBA[2]	0.54
Ireland	0.40		
		Yugoslavia	0.44
Italy	0.46		

1. Some of the figures include external broadcasting services (the BBC figure is for the home services only).
2. Including an estimate of research undertaken by the individual ITV companies.

when most broadcasting organisations are experiencing financial stringency, how is it that in all European countries it is clearly considered important to undertake audience research?

It is not, after all, self-evident that research has to take place—other than perhaps for those broadcast services whose revenue is wholly or partially dependent on advertising revenue and where the advertiser needs to know the size and nature of the audience that his advertising campaign is reaching. The professional drama producer might well argue that he or she knows a good script when he reads it. He knows a distinguished performance of the play when he hears it. What need has he to know the views of his audience? Another devil's advocate position is that, to the extent that audience research is seen as an instrument of public accountability, the role is redundant. Why not rely on unsolicited telephone calls and correspondence from the public or on other more formal consultative gatherings such as advisory councils?

It might be entertaining, and maybe instructive too, if a poll were to be conducted amongst both professional audience researchers and their customers, the senior management and programme makers of broadcasting organisations. How do we see our role? And what difference is there between the functions we actually perform and those we would like to see ourselves fulfilling? And what does the management see as the principal functions of its audience research department? Rather different perspectives might emerge.

To return to our earlier question—how do we justify our existence? As an employee of a broadcasting organisation funded by a licence fee, one can begin by drawing attention to broad but fundamental issues of public accountability. Neither phone calls nor correspondence from the public can represent other than atypical opinions. It is a small and strange minority of listeners or viewers which is ever sufficiently outraged or inspired to pick up a telephone or put pen to paper. Similarly, public meetings and advisory bodies tend to involve those who are in some sense committed to, or at minimum interested in, broadcasting matters. By no stretch of the imagination can they represent the average listener.

Counting the Customers

A broadcasting service is unique amongst the range of goods and services available to the public in that there is no equivalent to sales information. Tins of baked beans can be counted. Theatre ticket sales can be monitored. The use of a motorway service area can be established from the sales of petrol and restaurant services. There is no equivalent source of information readily available on how many people listen to a particular radio network over a period of time, or to a particular programme transmitted on a particular day. (This will not be true of a pay-to-view cable channel—but that is not a conventional broadcasting service.) The audience researcher's basic routine activity must, therefore, include that of audience measurement.

Some reasonable idea of how large or small the audiences are for particular TV and radio channels is required as much for services funded by a licence fee as for those based on advertising revenue. The BBC, for example, sees itself as being under an obligation to produce programmes in which majorities are interested. Otherwise the licence fee becomes a regressive tax. At the same time, however, Parliament may expect the BBC to operate certain minority services that would be impracticable to fund via advertising. One has in mind here, for example, BBC Radio's serious music network, Radio 3. This usually accounts for as little as 2 per cent of all radio listening. Audience measurement enables the BBC to find out and then to demonstrate publicly that both majorities and minorities are being served.

It should, perhaps, be noted in passing that the issue of audience shares is strictly irrelevant to the issue of public accountability. What does matter is that the vast majority of the public views or listens to BBC services—and for a significant period of time. Thus, for example, in November 1983 all but 2 per cent of those who viewed television in the average November week in the UK viewed either BBC-1 or BBC-2 at some time. The average person aged four and over viewed 10½ hours of BBC-TV in that week. It is the absolute audience figures that are relevant to the issue of whether the public is getting value for money.

Also, for reasons of public accountability, most broadcasting organisations want to know in some routine way how the public sees the quality of their programmes—ideally, programme by programme. The combination of quantitative and qualitative information comprises the two currencies of achievement: audience size and audience appreciation. Not least for their own self-esteem, the producer and artists involved in a particular production show more than a modicum of interest (approaching, on occasion, paranoia) in what audience they achieved, and what the audience thought of the show. Bad news on the former can usually be borne if good news emerges from the latter. (But if there is a thumbs-down on both . . .) These two yardsticks of the audience are clearly of value, not just to massage the egos of those concerned, but in a more practical way to influence decisions on whether or not to repeat a series, to commission further series, to review the casting—or for a variety of other professional purposes.

Beyond the Audience

Turning from the routine role of audience research to the overall broadcasting problems of senior management, professional researchers have a major contribution to make. Indeed, given the emphasis on this side of our own work at the BBC, we deliberately have a title for the department that reflects this emphasis: the Broadcasting (not audience) Research Department. We attempt to suggest by this title that audience measurement and reaction represent just the beginning of activity. Each year we currently undertake about 100 *ad hoc* studies which in one way or another relate to specific problems. They can be roughly classified as follows:

- Background strategic research
- Programme development
- Programme evaluation
- Broadcasting developments
- Broader issues of the role of TV and radio in people's lives.

Several examples of each of these kinds of studies are regularly published in our 'Annual Review of Broadcasting Research Findings'. Two examples of strategic research come to mind here. Over the past 30 years the department has regularly undertaken major, and necessarily expensive, studies of how people spend their time. In the trade these are called 'time budget' surveys. A great deal of information has to be collected on a large scale, involving a high quality sample design, on precisely what people are doing—quarter-hour by quarter-hour or half-hour by half-hour. We need to distinguish between different types of people (children vs teenagers vs young adults vs the middle-aged vs those who do not have a paid job, etc.) and we need our findings to be reported separately for weekdays and weekends: when is what kind of potential audience available to view television and to listen to the radio?

This study (of which the most recent, *Daily Life in the '80s*, has just been published) has applications to a vast range of personal behaviour and consumption patterns that extend far beyond our own sphere of broadcasting. When are people at home to have their electricity meters read? When do people have their breakfast? When do people get back from work? When do they go to bed? The cost of the report is therefore in part recouped by sales to advertising agencies, libraries, academic institutions and a wide range of organisations that have a professional need to be well-informed about the population's patterns of activity in and out of the home (BBC 1984).

Secondly, and more parochially to broadcasting, there is the complex subject of households' ownership and use of radio sets. How many radio sets are owned? Do people have a radio in their car? Do people have mains sets or battery sets? What sort of aerial do they have? What frequencies are they capable of receiving? How are the frequencies identified: in terms of metres or kHz? What radio services are listened to on which sets? On which frequency is each station listened to on which sets? On which frequency is each station listened to? And, finally and most fundamentally, what quality of reception is obtained on a particular set, using a particular frequency? Such a study, commissioned by BBC Radio, has recently been completed. It will be a 'bible' for a number of years to come. It will assist the BBC's engineering services in the short term, and more strategically it will influence wavelength policy decisions in the 1990s.

Programme Development

In our programme development work we take pains to make it clear that we exist as a service on which the programme maker can call. It is his decision to seek research to give him broad guidance on alternative editorial strategies. Equally, it is for him to ask for evidence to help resolve an argument that may be raging within his programme department on whether a particular creative approach to the communication of (say) a technical subject is working out. The research method chosen is decided following a full briefing of the research team by the programme-making team. We try scrupulously to enter that discussion without preconceptions of our own. The techniques vary accordingly. They will often involve a relatively small number of in-depth interviews or group discussions. These provide a considerable insight into the nuances of audience response that are difficult to tap via the conventional structured interview. This approach, though, suffers from the disadvantage that conclusions must necessarily be more subjective and more tentative than those obtainable from the more traditional quantitative approach.

Examples of this kind of study have been reported in a number of recent editions of the 'Annual Review of Broadcasting Research Findings'. In the 1983 Review we reported on the work we undertook in advance of the launch of the BBC's breakfast television service, *Breakfast time* (Bristow 1983). We have also carried out work for BBC-TV's Continuing Education Department, associated with the development of the series on computers, *The Computer Programme* (Marles and Radcliffe 1982).

Programme evaluation research is a more familiar, tried and tested territory. Here one is usually concerned with establishing whether or not specific programme objectives have or have not been realised—and, if not, where the problems may lie. Again, the research methodology is chosen to meet particular needs. Account is taken of any special problems of a technical nature which are to be overcome—and it goes without saying that a realistic budget exists for the exercise in question. For example, there was particular interest in the late 1970s in the public's acceptance of, or problems with, drama documentaries. These hybrids had been the subject of extensive debate. The programme chosen for this research was the dramatised biography of Martin Luther King, *King*, a three-part programme transmitted on three successive evenings on BBC-1 in April 1979 (BBC 1979). Other contrasting examples include an examination of a regular radio programme for the visually handicapped, *In Touch*, a weekly magazine programme broadcast on the BBC's principal speech network, Radio 4 (Mitchell 1980). Another was an evaluation of a TV series designed to help smokers give up, *So You Want to Stop Smoking*. This was a major evaluation exercise, involving a panel that was essential to interrelate people's smoking habits over time to their having watched (or not) the six-part series.

Where a study is on an issue of some major significance, part of the funding is obtained from non-BBC sources. This research was sponsored by a combination of a BBC budget and funding from the Health Education Council, the Scottish Health Education Group, and the Department of Health and Social Security in Northern Ireland. It is not the case that such research is limited to the more informational and educational elements of the BBC's output. We have a demand for our services from comedy and light entertainment departments.

New Technologies

One has in mind here the widely-debated issues, opportunities and problems presented by satellites, by cable and the video-cassette recorder. The department has been extensively involved in all these areas. Our role has been to provide a marketing, as distinct from a broadcasting, research insight into alternative scenarios for their development. Some of these skills we cannot claim to possess ourselves and we call on the services of communication consultants. Our principal responsibility then lies in the drafting of the initial formal brief, the choice of consultants, the overseeing of their work and the appraisal of their final recommendations. We have often found such joint enterprises to have been most fruitful, not least because our researchers are able to bridge the private language of broadcasters and of marketing consultants respectively. Problems of communication between client and consultant can otherwise arise— the outcome being a poorly designed and poorly executed study on the wrong subject, and in due course mutual recrimination as the outcome.

In an earlier phase of the UK's cable development, we were concerned with the evaluation of a subscription cable experiment in the London area. This was a joint enterprise between the BBC and Visionhire. For a month's subscription of around £8, Showcable offered three or four films at weekends and during holiday periods. Each film was repeated ten times at a variety of slots over several months. The objective of the research was to evaluate the experiment and help future planning.

There are, finally, the strategic issues of broadcasting: issues of balance and bias, the public's perception of the BBC, its regard for the quality of the BBC's programmes and the relative appeal of particular sectors of the BBC's output. Quite deliberately we tend to delegate such research to outside independent bodies. The object is to ensure independence and authoritativeness—particularly when at the outset it is planned that such studies should be in the public domain and published. In recent years NOP Market Research Ltd. has been commissioned to undertake an image study of the BBC. The Broadcasting Research Unit carried out research on the inner city riots in 1981. This was concerned with investigating, *inter alia*, to what extent TV coverage of the riots played a part in inciting urban violence (the so-called 'copy-cat' phenomenon). It appeared to demonstrate that there was no direct link.

The most ambitious of these research enterprises, though, is the major study currently being conducted by Professors Collins and Jowell of City University and by Gill Courtney of Social and Community Planning Research. They have set out to prove or disprove the hypothesis that one's perception of the fairness or otherwise of broadcast coverage of a major political issue is determined by, or related to, one's own partisan position on that issue. On the subject of unemployment, for example, does the working-class's perception of news and current affairs coverage of unemployment differ markedly from that of the employer—despite the fact that both parties are seeing identical portrayals of that issue on TV? The report on this significant study is due to be completed shortly.

In our experience, broadcasters are in the main positive and committed to research—whether it is on their audiences, on their programmes or on the broader issues they tackle editorially. Of course, research can and is abused on occasion. But that is another matter . . . to do with the human psyche. What is nice is that we rarely encounter apathy in our relationships with professional broadcasters. They are for the most part the most appreciative of clients for whom to work. On occasion the outcome does not suit their purposes. The consequent vigorous debate is rewarding, too.

23

Keeping Customers by Keeping Them Happy— An Example from the Computer Industry

'Nay, madam, when you are declaiming, declaim;
and when you are calculating, calculate.'

Life of Johnson
Boswell

DR MERLIN STONE, Managing Director, Tiba Midas Ltd.

Having decided to include a section on Information, computing obviously entered into my deliberations. Almost as if by fate I then came across a piece produced by Merlin Stone, a colleague from way back, and he agreed to seek the permission of the company involved. This chapter described one very specific project aimed at ascertaining just what exactly customers thought of the maintenance service they were receiving in what is a competitive and, some would even say, a cut-throat business. Star Computers was eager to discover what its customers felt of the service before they became ex-customers. To discover this it turned to Tiba Midas whose team of consultants offers a range of services with the emphasis on training and management development activities projects, usually involving whole teams of staff. Among its many customers over the past two years are many of Britain's leading companies including, among others, British Leyland, Cadbury Schweppes, Grand Metropolitan Hotels, British Telecom, Saatchi and Saatchi and, of course, Star Computers.

Merlin himself is the managing director of the company and was previously, until 1982, business planning manager of Rank Xerox. Prior to joining Rank Xerox he worked as a lecturer, management consultant and marketing manager in the engineering industry. He is a frequent contributor to the computer trade press and has a regular column on marketing and systems management in *Informatics* magazine. He has also written two books and co-authored another on Field Service Management. He graduated with a first class degree in Economics from Sussex in 1969 and went on to secure his doctorate also from Sussex, the topic being product policy.

★ ★ ★

When a customer buys a computer system, he also buys a relationship with his supplier. Once a customer has committed his information to the system and trained his staff to use it, he becomes dependent on the supplier. If the computer fails in some way, he normally relies upon the supplier to rectify the fault, although third-party maintenance now accounts for around 10 per cent of the maintenance market. If the customer is dissatisfied, he cannot suddenly throw out his equipment or software and go to another supplier. The costs involved in switching between suppliers are normally very high and are typically dominated by software conversion and retraining costs. In the case of mainframe computer systems, in which corporate databases are held, these switching costs can amount to millions of pounds.

For the relationship between customer and supplier to survive it has to be seen to be of lasting value to both parties. The value obtained by the customer takes the form of an effective system which performs the desired tasks with minimum failure frequency and a minimum downtime when the system does fail, with problems and queries being resolved quickly. The value obtained by the supplier takes the form of continuing profitable sales, as and when the customer returns for additional or replacement equipment and software, education and training, maintenance contracts and supplies.

This is the ideal picture. Computer system suppliers operate under many commercial and technical pressures which can make it hard to meet customer expectations after the sale. The commercial pressures relate partly to the unpredictable nature of the computer market and in part to the intense competitive pressures that exist within it. Companies in this line of business experience quite wild fluctuations in the level of activity. Often, a company will go through a boom in which it 'acquires' many new customers, and precisely at the time when it should be investing more resources in supporting them, it will economise on support because of a reduction in sales. Under these circumstances, it takes a brave management team to continue committing more resources to post-sales support, even though better support today will bring in more business tomorrow. When the financial pressure is on, jam today has to be the prime objective! Only the largest companies are immune from those pressures. Medium- and smaller-size companies suffer badly from them.

Some technical problems are due to the advanced nature of the technology which is incoporated into computer systems, sometimes only a few years after it has been proven in a laboratory. Engineering problems such as the 'crashes' of disk drive heads may lead to failures which are hard to deal with in the field or which cause customers severe problems such as the loss of data. Although the cost of components is falling and their reliability increasing, the typical item of equipment is becoming more complicated, as more and more features are built into it.

Other technical problems stem from faults in the software. Some may well be faults which are inadvertently built into the original design, but which only manifest themselves when the customer tries to use an obscure combination of facilities. Alternatively, the faults may arise from a modification which has been made to the software, without the modified version having been thoroughly tested. Imperfect software upgrades can make it impossible for customers to perform the routine operations which they were accustomed to carrying out with the unmodified software. For these reasons, most computer suppliers need a very large post-sales support operation, covering both software and hardware. The management process for handling requests for help needs to be very robust if it is to meet customers' needs. Without such a process, service and support staff tend to get tied up in dealing with major problems. As a result, minor problems are not dealt with and they accumulate until they can become a bone of contention between supplier and customer. The largest companies usually invest in sophisticated computerised management systems for support and service, so that every customer fault is recorded and staff allocated to deal with it. Smaller and medium-sized companies often cannot afford such systems, although microcomputer-based systems are now available which, while not offering the complex features available on larger systems, at least allow management to ensure that most faults are rectified within a reasonable time. These systems can also help ensure that the support and service staff are used reasonably efficiently.

Most customers have quite reasonable expectations. They understand that computer systems are liable to failure or substandard performance for a variety of reasons. What they do, quite naturally, demand is that the supplier makes reasonable attempts to deal with problems. In short, they expect value for the money they pay for service and support. But what is 'reasonable'? Aiming for perfection may lead to the supplier investing in so much service and support resource that what should be a profitable operation becomes a drain on the company. The only definition of 'reasonable' that counts must come from the customers. So how do we extract this definition from them?

Happily, the customer is usually prepared to answer questions on this point. One of the quickest and cheapest tools to establish customer perceptions and attitudes is a customer survey. If a company has customers distributed over a wide area, a postal survey is usually the best method. Normally, postal surveys produce low response rates, but if the system is sufficiently important to customers, and if the survey is well researched and compactly presented, the response should be good. It can be raised further by telephone follow-up. This makes the approach particularly well suited to companies which need the results quickly. Costs are low, and smaller companies can, therefore, afford a survey which was once the preserve of larger companies. Another benefit of such a survey is that the mere fact of carrying out the survey can serve to foster a positive relationship with customers, who are likely to feel that their supplier is taking a genuine interest in their feelings and attitudes.

The results of such surveys must, though, be interpreted carefully. Customers may see them as a way of bringing pressure to bear on their supplier. Questions must be phrased carefully so as not to encourage extreme answers by respondents.

The customer survey detailed in Table 23.1 was carried out for Star Computers Ltd during the summer of 1985. Star is a market leader in computerised accounting systems, and has grown rapidly in the last few years. Prior to the survey, Star had begun to experience growing pains in a number of areas, including after-sales service and support. These were partly a result of implementing Star's software, which is recognised by many to be an excellent suite of programs, on a different range of equipment. For strategic reasons, this conversion was carried out very quickly and absorbed critical staff resources which might otherwise have been devoted to after-sales support. Customers were beginning to show signs of unease. The atmosphere at user group meetings was less friendly, and many customers suspected that resources had been diverted from after-sales software support to development work. Star's management at all levels was conscious of this problem. They had already taken a number of steps to ameliorate the situation, but they felt that a survey of customers would help them to identify problems more precisely and to prioritise areas for action.

The first step in carrying out such a survey is, of course, to design the questionnaire. The key ingredient in this process is the conducting of a series of interviews with relevant company staff and with one or more groups of customers. In a company the size of Star, which in 1984 had a turnover of £7.5m and, by 1985, had 1,350 systems installed, the interviews with company staff can be carried out in one day. The staff interviews help to define how company personnel view the problem. They also provide data about how service and support systems work and the pressures felt by support staff. The insights gained from these interviews also ensure that whoever is interviewing

Table 23.1 *Star Client Survey*

Most questions are answered simply by circling the appropriate number.

1. Name_____ Company_____

2. Which Star equipment is currently installed in any location in your company?

		Year installed
	1 Hartley_____	
	2 Auditor_____	
	3 Convergent Technology_____	

3. How often are you in contact with Star personnel, by phone, letter or personal visit? (Note: A call made by yourself and returned by Star counts as one contact)

	Salesman	Client support	Technical support	Engineer	Accounts	Senior managers
Once a week or more	1	1	1	1	1	1
Once every 2 weeks	2	2	2	2	2	2
Once every 3 weeks	3	3	3	3	3	3
Once a month	4	4	4	4	4	4
Once a year	5	5	5	5	5	5
Less often	6	6	6	6	6	6

4. How easy is it to obtain the person you wish to contact?

	Salesman	Client support	Technical support	Engineer	Accounts	Senior managers
Very easy	1	1	1	1	1	1
Easy	2	2	2	2	2	2
Alright	3	3	3	3	3	3
Difficult	4	4	4	4	4	4
Very difficult	5	5	5	5	5	5

5. If you reported a computer printer failure to Star at 10am on Monday, what response time from an engineer do you receive and what do you need?

	SAME DAY			NEXT DAY		LATER
	Before 12	12–2pm	2–7pm	am	pm	
Average achieved	1	2	3	4	5	6
Desirable if failure during critical run (e.g. payroll)	1	2	3	4	5	6
Acceptable if failure during non-critical run	1	2	3	4	5	6

6. How long does it take to repair a printer on site after the engineer's arrival? What time is acceptable?

	Up to 1 hr	1–2 hrs	2–4 hrs	More than 4 hrs
Average time achieved	1	2	3	4
Acceptable time	1	2	3	4

7. If a software problem stops you carrying out an operation, and you contact Client or Technical Support for help at 10am on a weekday, what percentage of problems are solved immediately (i.e. via the coupler)?_____

8. If a software problem is not resolved immediately, when does Star generally have the problem solved? What desirable and acceptable times would you specify?

	SAME DAY		NEXT DAY		WORKING DAYS LATER			
	Before 12	After 12	am	pm	Up to 5	5–10	10–20	More than 20
Average time achieved	1	2	3	4	5	6	7	8
Desirable if problem critical	1	2	3	4	5	6	7	8
Acceptable if problem not critical	1	2	3	4	5	6	7	8

Table 23.1   *Star Client Survey contd.*

---

9. Please rate your Star hardware and software for the following characteristics:

HARDWARE	Very Good	Good	Average	Poor	Very Poor
Reliability	1	2	3	4	5
Overall performance	1	2	3	4	5
Value for money	1	2	3	4	5
Ease of upgrade	1	2	3	4	5

SOFTWARE	Very Good	Good	Average	Poor	Very Poor
Reliability	1	2	3	4	5
Overall performance	1	2	3	4	5
Value for money	1	2	3	4	5
Ease of upgrade	1	2	3	4	5

10. How would you rate Star's maintenance in terms of value for money?

	Very Good	Good	Average	Poor	Very Poor
	1	2	3	4	5

11. Is the £75 'no call' bonus attractive?   Yes: 1   No: 2   Don't know about it: 3

12. What are the implications for your business if your Star equipment fails totally?

No adverse effect	1	Staff idle	2	Revenue loss	3	Cash flow delay	4
Clients lost	5	Goodwill loss	6	Data loss	7	Other (specify)	8

---

13. What is your opinion of the professionalism of Star personnel?

	Very good	Good	Average	Poor	Very poor
Salesmen	1	2	3	4	5
Sales managers	1	2	3	4	5
Client support	1	2	3	4	5
Technical support	1	2	3	4	5
Engineers	1	2	3	4	5
Accounts	1	2	3	4	5
Senior Managers	1	2	3	4	5

14. How good is the service and support you receive from Star compared with the past?

	Much better	Better	Same	Worse	Much worse
Compared with 6 months ago	1	2	3	4	5
Compared with 1 year ago	1	2	3	4	5

15. Would you recommend a Star system to others?

          Yes: 1   No: 2   Maybe: 3

16. If you wish to amplify any of your answers, or comment on other aspects of Star service and support, please do so here, or use an additional sheet of paper.

---

the customers has enough knowledge about the supplier and his staff to interpret the answers given by customers in the postal questionnaires.

The customer interviews which took place in a hotel also occupied a single day. Here, the objective is to generate a relaxed, semi-structured discussion, in which customers are prompted by very general questions in order to ensure that the right issues are covered. Their responses relate to their perceptions concerning the company, the service and support it provides, and what they perceive to be the implications for them. The incentive to attend such a discussion is the opportunity to proffer their views and, in some cases, a buffet lunch! In this particular case two groups of customers (about ten in each) were interviewed—senior customer staff and systems managers—to test whether separate questionnaires were required for the two groups. In this case, attitudes were so closely aligned that one questionnaire sufficed for both.

The customer interviews help focus the questionnaire on critical issues and clarify the language customers use in talking about service and support. This is important in areas such as response time, i.e. how long it takes for an engineer to arrive and failure frequency, where it is necessary to establish the time bands that are used by respondents. Most do not think in terms of hours, but in terms of time bands (e.g. request for service in the morning, response by the afternoon). This paralleled an earlier finding in a study conducted for a photocopier manufacturer, which had always assumed that its customers measured failure frequency by the number of copies made between failures. In fact, customers used broad time bands as, for example, once a week or once a month.

Using the interview information, a draft questionnaire was designed, submitted to Star for approval, and tested face-to-face and over the telephone with customers, to ensure that it could be completed quickly and without ambiguity. The decision was taken at the start of the project to use Star's own systems to record the data. Customers were asked to provide their names, and the survey questionnaire was sent direct to them from Star, with a covering letter from the Managing Director, so there was no issue of confidentiality. This ensured that a valuable database was created which could be used in identifying customers who required more urgent attention.

A key objective was to design the questionnaire so that it covered only two sides of an A4 sheet, ensuring ease and speed of reproduction and completion. The questionnaire could be completed in a few minutes, simply by circling numbers. These could then be entered directly into the computer, thereby avoiding any intermedi-ate coding. The sophistication of computer-read questionnaires was not required. Space was provided for comments and this was used by nearly half the respondents.

Of the 700+ questionnaires sent out, 240 were returned within a month, although little telephone follow-up took place. More came in later. Of the 16 questions, the first two identified the customer and his equipment. This provided a good check on the existing database. The last was the comment space. The check on the database is vital because, despite the fact that computer system suppliers market the idea of holding comprehensive databases to their customers, their own customer databases are often not in very good order. This may be a reflection of their rapid growth and they just might not have the time to install a comprehensive customer database. It is also not uncommon to find the marketing databases of such companies organised by product and not by customer.

The third question covered frequency of contact with staff in sales, service, support, accounts and senior management. This was important for interpreting Question 4, which related to the ease of contact with these staff. The responses to these two questions confirmed management's own view that a major problem lay with support management systems and with restrictions on the number of support staff. Although support staff were the most frequently contacted, these were also judged the most difficult to contact (30 per cent of customers regarded them as difficult or very difficult to contact). This reflected the strong view which had been propounded in group discussions that support staff were hard working and devoted, but needed an improved management system. Individuals performed well, but were too readily tempted to cover for the deficiencies of the management system by working harder. As a result of this finding, considerable management effort was applied to an overhaul and monitoring of support procedures and to ensuring that these procedures were well communicated, to both staff and customers.

Questions 5 and 6 covered response and repair times in the event of printer failure which was, in fact, the most common reason for service engineers being called out.[1] Here, the general situation was good. Customers were asked about achieved, desired and acceptable response times. The average acceptable response time was just under eight hours, as was the average perceived response time. However, both these times were very different from the average response time claimed by the company. This does not imply that the response time was not being achieved, merely that it was not being seen to be

---

1. The aforementioned disk head 'crashes' were also a source of problems, but they are hard to research in a general questionnaire as their low frequency makes responses suspect.

achieved. This problem can normally be solved by making customers more aware of what the response time was at the time of the call. However, in this case, this was not considered to be necessary, as engineering response times were clearly not held to be a significant problem. However, further analysis was carried out to discover just which customers thought they were on the receiving end of a response time which was unacceptable in their eyes.

These answers indicated that customers were in general satisfied, but just under 80 per cent felt that they needed an emergency service during such critical runs as payroll. This suggested the need to investigate some differentiation in the service contract, such as an emergency call allowance, or the provision of back-up equipment. Engineering repair times showed similar results, with an average achieved of just over one hour, with the average acceptable time being a little longer.

As expected, software problem resolution, covered in Questions 8 and 9, was more problematical. The overall situation was not bad, with many customers deeming the solution time acceptable. However, the average achieved solution time of around 24 hours was twice as long as the average time deemed acceptable. The problem here lay mainly with customers who felt that their problems had been outstanding for too long. This indicated a clear need for a formal system for the registration of problems and subsequent progress chasing, rather than leaving the client to do the chasing. It was also clear from comments that customers were often uncertain as to whether their problem was actually being dealt with. It was, therefore, recommended that clients be routinely kept notified of the progress of a problem. This finding reflects one common to many service industries. It is the problem which is long outstanding which is the major source of irritation. It contaminates the relationship between customer and supplier even if overall performance has been reasonable.

In Question 9 customers were asked to rate both hardware and software in terms of reliability, overall performance, value for money and ease of upgrade. Reliability and overall performance were rated highly, with about two thirds of customers rating hardware and software better than average in these respects. However, there was a clear problem with hardware and software regarding value for money and ease of upgrade. These were both rated as poor or very poor by between a quarter and a third of respondents. This was partly related to the problems with support, but the next question (10) also indicated a concern with value for money on maintenance. The group discussions had shown that customers expect to have to pay well for service and support, but in return they expect to receive good value for it. A key justification for price is the quality of the service and support. If customers are of the opinion that the support which they receive is dependent upon the goodwill of a small group of highly motivated individuals, with little management system to back them up, they are unlikely to consider support to be of particularly good value. Poor or low-quality software documentation can generate a similar feeling. Not surprisingly, therefore, a no-claims bonus scheme introduced by Star was found to be far from popular (Question 11). Customers who want quality are not attracted by a discount on a service which they regard as low value for money. In the group discussions, customers had been even more forthright, describing it as a 'sick joke'.

The problem relating to ease of upgrades (i.e. the expansion of capacity in the case of hardware and the implementing of an enhanced version in the case of software) could be traced to two different origins. In the case of hardware, it was traceable to a tendency on the part of salesmen to sell a system of too low a capacity in order to keep within the customer's budget. The upgrade therefore had to be made too soon. In the case of software, the problem was due to the haste with which new revenue-generating versions were released on to the market.

Question 12, which asks about the effects of equipment failure on the customer's business, helps Star's sales and support staff better to comprehend customers' problems. This kind of knowledge will also be helpful should the company try to market an enhanced support contract involving say, very quick response or back-up equipment, as it indicates what benefits the customers would be expecting to derive from it.

Question 13 asked about the perceived professionalism of different categories of Star staff. Here, the general situation was remarkably good, but some indications of the training that might be required were obtained, particularly with respect to sales staff. Nearly a quarter of customers judged their professionalism to be poor or very poor. Poor performance on this front undoubtedly related to a particularly difficult period that the sales force had been through. However, a more fundamental issue was touched upon in the group discussion which probably had a direct bearing on this issue. As a supplier of accountancy systems, Star had always recruited sales staff with some knowledge of accountancy. Many customers were of the opinion that the salesmen should have a better appreciation of how an accountancy (or any) business runs, since this was more critical for the selling of a computer system.

Question 14 asked about the change in the quality of service and support over time. This was inserted to check whether perceptions were improving or not. Obviously, if the questionnaire were to be sent out on a regular basis, such a question would not be necessary; but this was the first questionnaire. The responses showed that over half the customers thought that it had remained the same. Of the rest, more thought it was improving than thought it was deteriorating.

A critical question (15) sought to ascertain whether the customer would recommend the system. This is an oblique way of testing customer loyalty. It is not wise to ask whether the customer would buy again, as it is not certain whether the respondent has purchasing authority, or whether he bought it in the first place. More importantly, he may not want to be completely open or he may simply fear commitment in the face of such a direct question. The responses obtained in answer to this question revealed that some work needed to be done to improve loyalty, as just under one fifth of customers indicated that they definitely would not recommend a Star system, and only just under one third said that they definitely would.

The comments space was used by just under a half of the respondents. Typically, negative comments emerge, which is normal in a survey of this kind. The main criticisms related to maintenance costs and software and support. There were, though, many positive comments which would seem to indicate that there was ample opportunity for improving the situation by improved management. Indeed, some of the criticisms displayed a high degree of awareness by customers of internal management process problems associated with resource allocation, scheduling, communication, etc.

The overall conclusion of the survey was that the general situation was not too bad. The main problems related to the extremes or 'tails', namely the problems that had been outstanding for a long time, or to the customers who were very dissatisfied.

As a result of the survey, several changes have been introduced and others confirmed. The Technical Support department has been centralised in Birmingham, where software version control has also been overhauled and centralised. This should have the effect of substantially reducing the incidence of perceived upgrade problems. The upgrade procedure has been improved by strengthening testing and documentation standards (a subject of frequent comment by customers). An error report form has been introduced to enable users to report and log bugs. The Quality Assurance Department has been expanded, and it will now be very much more difficult for any defective software to reach customers. Training for Client Advisors has been set up and an on-line software notice board set up on Telecom Gold. Management systems are under review. Star is also arranging further training of support staff in their techniques of handling customers over the telephone, as many software faults are solved on-line from the Star office. Although the results of the first survey are still being digested, Star plans to monitor customers routinely in this manner. The information gleaned from such surveys will serve to supplement the frequent feed-back via sales, service and support staff and the User Group. There is also some feeling among customers that Star's efforts to understand its customer needs in depth is a positive indication of an emerging maturity in a company famed for the speed with which it grew to be one of the 'stars' of the Unlisted Securities Market.

24

The Quality of Library Services

'If I borrow a book, I cannot abstain from reading it without a pricking of conscience every time I see it and I cannot help seeing it every time I am looking for something else.'

The Blue Lion
Robert Lynd

DAVID YORKE, UMIST.

While 'information' in 1986 conjures up images of computers, it is still a fact of life that the overwhelming majority of people will look to the printed page for the bulk of their reading matter. For a large proportion of the British public, a substantial part of this reading matter is secured from our public library services. Until recently though, libraries had made little, if any, effort to determine what the public thought of the service being offered. Given the current concern with the cost-effectiveness of local authority services there is an imperative need for studies aimed at plugging this gap if only to protect this particular form of community interest.

David has been actively involved in investigating the way in which marketing concepts can be used in libraries for well over a decade. It is not inconceivable that this represents a continuation of an interest in the printed word which found him operating in market research with the Liverpool Daily Post group of companies. He has also operated in a market research capacity with Joseph Lucas (Electrical) Ltd. His work in libraries has involved a range of projects with both the City of Manchester and Cheshire County Council and out of this work have emerged a number of articles and a monograph. This interest in local authority affairs has broadened out to encompass the marketing of public sector leisure services. He is currently acting as a consultant to a large local authority's Community Leisure Department and is a Principal Tutor to courses mounted by the Local Government Training Board.

★ ★ ★

Public sector organisations, and particularly local government, are currently much more accountable for their activities than heretofore. Cutbacks in government expenditure are the backcloth against which public sector organisations are now operating. More legislation as, for example, the 1980 Local Government Planning and Land Act which calls for greater disclosure in local authority reports, including the use of performance indicators, has put such organisations on the defensive, resulting in administrators being required to cope with limits on their expenditure plans. The emotive phrase 'Value for money' has become commonplace in most of the town halls in the UK.

But what is 'Value for Money?' Who measures it and for what purpose? Butt and Palmer (1985) suggest that it covers three basic elements: economy, efficiency and effectiveness. The introduction, use and evaluation of each are clearly interrelated, but there are important differences depending upon whether they are being viewed from the standpoint of the supplying organisations or from that of the user. *Economy*, they suggest, is the practice by management of the virtues of thrift and good housekeeping. An economical operation acquires resources in appropriate quality and quantity at the lowest cost. *Efficiency*, they argue, is making sure that the maximum useful output is gained from the resources devoted to each activity, or, alternatively, that only the minimum level of resources is devoted to achieving the given level of output.

Both these measures essentially represent the supplier's point of view of the situation but it is equally vital that the needs of the user, or maker, are incorporated. Accordingly, they go on to define *effectiveness* as 'ensuring that the output from any given activity, or the impact which services have on a community, is achieving the desired results'. Likewise the Chartered Institute of Public Finance and Accountancy (CIPFA) in the UK has stated in its Standards that 'Economy and efficiency in the execution of programmes are of small consequence if the programmes are not meeting the authority's objectives and no assessment of value for money is complete without regard to effectiveness'.

Effectiveness, however, is notoriously hard to measure. In some instances it may be possible to produce quantitative data as, for example, an increased number of users, but even here the number of users may be a reflection of increased patronage by existing users rather than any net increase in the persons involved. In other cases, resort may have to be made to a proxy measure of the perceived value of a service amongst current users and possibly even among non-users. Inevitably there will be some conflict and misunderstanding, not only between suppliers and users but, also, within suppliers and users. The provision of any public service is the responsiblity of both politicians and officers. Politicians, with re-election always in mind, tend to adopt a short-term perspective, whereas officers should be more concerned with longer-term success. Users are faced with a dilemma of, on the one hand, constantly demanding a wider range of services and a high standard of personal service whilst, on the other hand, being somewhat reluctant to make increased financial contributions.

Finally, there may be traditional barriers to the adoption of any new philosophy. The dominant qualification for a local government officer was traditionally that of being a sound administrator, attending primarily to the satisfactory achievement of budgets. These may or may not have been established on 'management' grounds, and might or might not have involved an input from users. A secondary qualification was that of technical competence, although very rarely has technical competence included any ability to measure effectiveness through user satisfaction research. This contribution has led to an 'empire-building' ethos and the preservation of inward-looking standards, rather than the adoption of a more user-oriented approach.

Value for Money in Libraries

Libraries and library services are big business. In Table 24.1 the 1985 income and expenditure of libraries are contrasted with those of some other forms of education and entertainment in England and Wales. The average library expenditure figure of £6 per head poses a number of interesting questions relating to whether or not the library service is giving value for money. These may include—'Who is the target market?' (Users or non-users?)—'How should the results be assessed?' (In terms of users or non-users or both?)—'What is meant by a user?' (Once a year or twice a week?)—'What should be measured?' (Satisfaction with obtaining what was required, or staff attitudes, even if unsuccessful?)

Table 24.1 *Annual Income or Expenditure on Various Public Services in 1985 (£m)*

BBC TV	410
BBC Radio	150
Local Authority Recreation Services	270
Penguin Books	100
Mirror Group	220
Public Libraries	330

Source: Banham (1985)

From the supplier's point of view, rows of empty shelves would seem to indicate that the service is being used 'efficiently' whereas users, on entering the library, expect to see as wide a choice as possible. Furthermore, different users expect to find fundamentally different products and services.

In a previous paper (Yorke 1984), it was postulated that the challenge facing local authorities in the provision of discretionary services, such as leisure activities and library services, is one of giving the 'best possible' service to as many members of the community as possible and as frequently as is possible given the potentially limited resources available. Taking these three variables, namely 'services', 'community' and 'frequency', the eight possible states set out in Table 24.2 present themselves as assuming that the terms 'nothing', 'nobody' and 'never' do not enter into consideration!

Table 24.2   *A Typology of Service Strategies for Libraries*

	Services (Things)	Community (People)	Frequency (Times)
1	All	All	All
2	All	All	Some
3	All	Some	All
4	All	Some	Some
5	Some	All	All
6	Some	All	Some
7	Some	Some	All
8	Some	Some	Some

Quite clearly, within a service such as public libraries, there is the major problem of trying to be all things to all people all of the time. Notwithstanding the lack of resources, there will be those members of the community who, for one reason or another, do not wish to use a public library, preferring to use their discretionary resources of time and money in some other way. At the opposite end of the spectrum, the provision of some things to some people some of the time may convey a perception of not trying too hard, particularly with respect to certain target groups within the community. To pour all the available resources into the provision of a mobile library service for the housebound might well, for example, meet the needs of the individuals involved, but would leave others decidedly unsatisfied.

A socially successful strategy, it is argued, ought not deliberately and permanently to exclude any one group within the community and, therefore, options 3, 4 and 7 must be rejected. Of the remainder, strategy 6 is inferior to that of 5 in that similar resources are being deployed to meet community needs, but at less frequent intervals. The redeployment of these resources could well result in increased user satisfaction but at no extra cost.

The choice between strategies 2 and 5 is a difficult one, particularly in trying to measure the effects in the longer term. To offer 'some things all of the time' may alienate sections of the community who feel that their particular needs are never likely to be met, yet to offer 'all things some of the time' implies that there will be periods of time during which certain services may not be offered, which again may alienate custom. The last-named strategy also implies a flexibility of organisation offering services a rotation over a given length of time. However, such flexibility enables the provision of services to meet ever-changing needs, preferably in advance of their occurrence and resources may be concentrated relatively more on those target groups which, it is thought, currently need them (note that the targets, however, are not necessarily based on a high level of demand, but on criteria which the library service may choose).

Such a macro approach may help to give answers to the problems of achieving economy and efficiency, but what of effectiveness? Actual measures of satisfaction obtained may be sought from current users, but can any such measure be generated from those who do not? For this latter group, resort may need to be made either to previous usage or even to perceptions where the service has never, or at best infrequently, been used.

Studies of levels of general satisfaction with the library service amongst the community abound and most libraries will have attempted some work on it. A recent MORI survey showed that satisfaction with the library service in Lewisham ranked second behind refuse collection and ahead of the police, health services, schools and leisure. However, the percentage which expressed itself 'very satisfied' with libraries was only 25 per cent, presumably indicating that the other 75 per cent were, at best, only partly satisfied and, at worst, dissatisfied.

However, even this approach gives no detail on satisfaction with individual library services, nor does it illustrate differences between users and non-users. The need for more detail has been pursued with a number of studies beginning as long ago as 1947 and reviewed by Moore (1979). Early projects were concerned mainly with discovering whether people used, or did not use, libraries and books. Later studies were concentrated on the attitudes of users and non-users towards particular aspects of the service.

The best known of such attitudinal studies is that by Totterdell and Bird (1976) which became known as the Hillingdon survey. This was probably the first attempt to measure, on any large scale, user satisfaction with the public library service. It revealed that a great deal of information could be relatively easily collected which would provide indications of future strategies. The writers distinguished between 'user success' and 'user satisfaction', the latter being the broader term because it includes both success and subjective feelings of satisfaction. User success means that the user succeeded in finding what he wanted on a particular visit to the library, whereas user satisfaction encompasses not only success but perception of the service being offered.

One major feature of the survey was that it recognised that a number of diverse groups existed in the community and it was clearly stated that essential information for any librarian trying to assist or improve service effectiveness was a detailed knowledge of the composition of the community that he actually served. Consequently the analysis included a number of cross-tabulations in respect of a wide range of essentially demographic groups which reveal certain differences in their attitudes towards the service.

The basic premise was that 'the effective library', as opposed to a merely efficient one, was always required. Effectiveness was defined as 'the extent to which a library service satisfies the needs of its community and how far it promotes itself as a means of so doing' and total effectiveness must therefore involve the development of hitherto unactivated needs. Specific conclusions were that:

- Particular services are judged to be effective rather than the whole library. Any attempt to add total performance to arrive at some aggregated measure of satisfaction would be meaningless.
- The effectiveness of a service must always be treated as a relative concept, the user subjectively measuring such effectiveness.
- Current measures of output are inadequate as they rarely relate to the total community served.
- Certain libraries deliberately avoid any consideration of user needs and are consequently not in a position to translate knowledge of such needs into the correct output and fail to inform the public of the existence of such output.

More recently, extensive work has been undertaken by Cheshire Libraries and Museums on measuring the degree of satisfaction experienced by users and perceived by non-users in an area of the county where a new town and a new public library have recently been established (Cheshire County Council 1985). An initial survey, conducted in 1977, set out to determine the needs of potential users of a new district library to be constructed at the heart of Runcorn New

Town. The study sought to ascertain the size of the latent demand for library services, the characteristics of the proposed users, what facilities would be required, which location would maximise use, how the library should operate when opened and what effect it would have on existing libraries in the area. Data were gathered from four sources: a survey of residents in the community; a survey of current users of both the old library and mobiles; a survey of organisations in the area; and from discussions with selected groups of potential users.

The study revealed the nature of leisure activities pursued in the four weeks prior to interview, the nature of reading habits (both books and magazines) and the source of such reading, the type of music listened to, and membership of organisations. Current levels and patterns of library usage were examined together with user attitudes towards libraries and levels of satisfaction with the facilities provided. Some data were also gathered on attitudes towards libraries by non-users, together with the overall image of the library service. Finally, many of the data were cross-tabulated by demographic values. A summary of attitudes revealed the following:

- Only 11 per cent of current users expressed themselves as 'dissatis-fied' with the facilities provided and marginally more (16%) with the range of books available.

- 'Inadequate facilities' (14%), 'No time' (13%) and 'Not interested in reading' (30%) were the principal reasons non-users proffered for never using a library.

- Libraries were judged to be relatively easy to find one's way around and the overall atmosphere presented was favourable. Staff were considered to be easily approachable and services, especially those for business information, were deemed satisfactory.

- 74 per cent of residents supported the construction of a library in the centre of the New Town and 61 per cent felt that there should be facilities provided other than the loan of books.

The issues, and some specific recommendations which emerged in relation to the proposed operation of the new library, included:

- the problems associated with weekly and daily peaks and troughs;
- a grouping of services for clients in different age groups;
- an association of audio-visual facilities, film shows and magazines aimed at teenage usage;
- the provision of space for musical performances, lectures or meetings for the over 45s;
- the provision of a newspaper reading area for the elderly;

• the need for study space adjacent to reference material and information.

This detailed analysis enabled the practical planning of the proposed
facilities in the new library to proceed in the expectation of meeting
the needs of specific user groups in the pursuit of not only an
efficient, but also an effective, operation.

The 1984 follow-up survey revealed the value of such detailed
planning and provision. There had been major environmental
changes in the previous seven years, including an increase in the
overall population, and the proportion of that population in the
younger age groups and, above all, a massive increase in unemployment, leading to a need for people to fill more discretionary time.

The results were very encouraging. Based on a matched sample of
respondents (users and non-users, individuals and organisations),
the usage of the library facilities in Runcorn had more than doubled
since 1977 to the extent that 67 per cent of the residents had used the
library at least once in the previous 12 months. This high level of use
was reflected in all sections of the population, but was particularly
pronounced among the under-18s age group and intermediate and
former non-manual workers who had previously been relatively low
users of the service. Overall, one third of those interviewed visited a
library at least once a week.

Attitudes amongst users were very positive. Table 24.3 shows the
degree of satisfaction expressed by users towards both the range of
services provided and the books available. For the last two figures in
the table those who were dissatisfied compare with the corresponding figures for 1977 of 11 per cent and 16 per cent. This would lead
one to believe that the effectiveness of operation has increased
notwithstanding an overall increase in efficiency. In fact, existing
users expressed little need for the improved services.

Table 24.3 *Percentages of Respondents Who Expressed Satisfaction with the
Services Provided at Libraries and the Books Available*

	Services	Books
Very satisfied	62	47
Quite satisfied	31	41
Neutral	5	7
Fairly dissatisfied	2	4
Very dissatisfied	1	1

Attitudes within the community as a whole were equally favourable,
although direct comparisons were not always possible because the

statements in the questionnaire had been altered between the two surveys. The image of staff had improved, with 71 per cent of respondents stating that 'librarians are easily approachable', as against 63 per cent in 1977. Indeed, 91 per cent of users were of the opinion that staff could not be more helpful.

The figures in Table 24.4, for which there are no directly comparable 1977 data, show the importance of recognising the perception of the wider role of the public library service within the community both in terms of the provision of a range of facilities and in meeting the needs of disadvantaged groups. However, from the point of view of trying to meet the needs of all people some of the time, there may have been some failures. Among the reduced number of non-users, opinion against using the library appears, if anything, to have hardened (see Table 24.5).

Table 24.4   *Attitudes Towards the Library: Respondents' Replies (%)*

	Favourable		*Neutral*	*Unfavourable*	
	Very	*Fairly*		*Very*	*Fairly*
'There should be more things going on in libraries than just lending books'	66	23	5	4	3
'Libraries provide a good service for the unemployed'	61	19	16	3	1

Table 24.5   *Reasons for Never Using Public Libraries (%)*

	1977	*1984*
'Not interested in reading'	30	31
'No time'	13	20
'Too young'	20	27

The conclusions of the 1977 survey stated that 'the provision of adequate and convenient library facilities should enable the generally favourable attitude towards libraries to considerably increase the level of library use from only one third of residents to one half. The new users should come mainly from the New Town area, from clerical, semi-skilled, manual and personal service socio-economic backgrounds.'

The results of the 1984 survey would seem to indicate that the service has more than met this target. The survey concludes: 'The libraries in Runcon, therefore, can now be considered to be providing a much appreciated service to the community with little indication of dissatisfaction with present provision or demand for new.'

There would, therefore, appear to be a strong case for local authority library services to attempt to implement not only an economic and efficient service, given reduced real resources, but also, with the aid of survey techniques, to discover the needs of users within the community and to offer an effective service in meeting those needs. Constant monitoring of needs and the setting of realistic attainable targets by the supplier should ensure that a high level of user satisfaction is maintained. By such actions, the provision of a range of library services for the community (all, or some, things to all people some of the time) may be a step nearer to the ideal where every member of the community perceives he or she is adequately provided with the facilities needed.

Epilogue

'Why beholdest thou the mote that is in thy brother's
eye, but considerest not the beam that is in thine own
eye?'

St. Matthew, vii.3

It is an occupational hazard facing those of us who choose to teach in
the field of management that we are inevitably and not infrequently
confronted with the observation that, perhaps, we ought to examine
our own practices before quite so readily criticising those of others.
The outsider could well be very surprised at the amount of time that
we in universities devote to discussing the content of courses or the
design of degree programmes, as the popular perception is that we
are pretty well able to teach what we want and how we want.

In fact, the situation has changed dramatically even since I first
joined academia in the early 1960s. Almost all university departments
now feature some form of student representation and a proportion
of the associated discussions invariably focuses on the content
of courses and their presentation. Many student unions produce
'alternative' prospectuses which can make for salutory reading.
At a different level league tables are regularly produced in, for
example, *The Times Higher Education Supplement* in which are displayed
the assessed standings of departments in specific fields. These peer
ratings do, of course, incorporate considerations not only of course
content but also of the perceived academic standing of staff and
the research activities pursued by the staff. Additionally, sixth-formers
can now consult guides in which they can gain an independent
assessment of the various departments offering undergraduate
courses in their chosen field.

In short, universities, in common with the other service organisations featured in this book, are confronted with the need to improve
the quality of their offerings. This has been exacerbated by the recent
swingeing cuts in the funding of universities which have seen whole
departments under threat, and it has culminated in the University
Grants Committee opting for a funding policy whereby universities
will be on the receiving end of a series of further percentage cuts
based on an appraisal of the status of the component departments.
This, coupled with the eminent sharp decline in the 18-year-old

288

population, is forcing an ever greater introspection on what we do and how we do it.

In the particular field of management education most university staff have found themselves at one time or another mounting post-experience courses for outside organisations. There the buyer calls the tune and, quite sensibly, those responsible for the courses have increasingly insisted on some formal assessment of the tutors. Unusually, only a few of the more enlightened also demand a formal assessment of the students. In the early days the assessments, not surprisingly, focused on what might loosely be termed 'circus performance' criteria. This early concentration on whether the lecturer was amusing, etc. eventually gave way to more insightful assessments which focused on the more constructive features of the anticipated educational experience.

Eventually, these two themes came together and very gradually assessment of lecturers has been introduced into universities, albeit on a voluntary basis. No-one should claim that it is, as yet, a routine procedure but the pressure for some formalised assessment is building up from students at one end of the spectrum to the Secretary of State for Education and Science at the other. In the middle, a substantial proportion of academics would, I suspect, welcome such a development in the belief that such feedback will, in all probability, serve to enhance teaching performance. At UMIST we talked about the possibility for years but it was only upon the return of Len Goldstone from a sabbatical in Texas, along with his 'best-rated teacher' plaque, that we put our minds to work as to how we could solicit insightful evaluations. The document we devised is shown overleaf. Suitably modified, it can and has been used on post-experience courses. Whatever the setting, I have always found it takes a couple of stiff drinks to recover from the initial shock of receiving such specific feedback, particularly when one always assumed, quite naturally, that no-one else comes close to reaching one's own standard!

This form of feedback is invaluable. As with the patient questionnaire, the questions are pretty specific and, as a consequence, the responses reveal where improvements can be affected. My own scores for a recently completed course are shown and from these it is clear that I have some way to go on several of the parameters. You can rest assured that the high scores on several others have stemmed directly from earlier evaluations which have served to identify rectifiable deficiencies.

With this final exposé of the editor's teaching weaknesses, we have almost come to the end of the book. All that remains is for him to add a few final observations based on his multiple reading of the text.

Table 1 *Lecturer Evaluation Questionnaire*

Name of Lecturer_____

Course_____Date_____

The primary purpose of this questionnaire is to give me the benefit of the opinion you have formed from your participation in this course. Please indicate your response for each item by circling the most appropriate number on the horizontal line provided. At the end space is provided for any general comments you consider appropriate. Your completed questionnaire will remain in my possession, and I will use it to improve future courses.

1. MASTERY OF SUBJECT

   10   9▼   8   7   6   5   4   3   2   1

Appears to possess good mastery of subject	Occasionally displays limited grasp of subject	Often gives impression of inadequate mastery of subject

2. PREPARATION AND ORGANISATION OF LECTURES

   10   9   8   7▼   6   5   4   3   2   1

Lectures well prepared and organised	Lectures usually well prepared and organised	Lectures frequently ill prepared and organised

3. PERSONAL MOTIVATION AND INTEREST IN SUBJECT

   10 ▼ 9   8   7   6   5   4   3   2   1

Enthusiastic about his subject	Displays some interest in subject	Usually appears indifferent and bored with the subject

4. ABILITY TO MOTIVATE OTHERS

   10   9 ▼8   7   6   5   4   3   2   1

Arouses interest and enthusiasm of students	Students only mildly interested	Students in general disinterested or bored

5. CONFIDENCE AND SELF-RELIANCE

   10   9▼   8   7   6   5   4   3   2   1

Always well poised and assured	Occasionally lacks poise and assurance	Usually appears ill-at-ease

6. PERSONAL MANNERISMS

   10   9   8▼   7   6   5   4   3   2   1

Pleasing manner, free from annoying or distracting mannerisms	Mannerisms sometimes annoying or distracting	Mannerisms often annoying or distracting

7. ABILITY TO COMMUNICATE

   10   9   8▼   7   6   5   4   3   2   1

Has ability to get across ideas in an effective manner	Sometimes fails to get ideas across	Usually unable to communicate ideas clearly

Table 1 *Lecturer Evaluation Questionnaire contd.*

8. CONTROL OF CLASS

10	9	▼8	7	6	5	4	3	2	1

Always in control of class	Sometimes lets class get out-of-hand	Usually not in control of class

9. ATTITUDE TOWARDS STUDENTS

10	9▼	8	7	6	5	4	3	2	1

Courteous; easy to approach; welcomes differences of opinion	Sometimes indifferent or impatient	Unapproachable; sometimes unpleasant

10. ATTAINMENT OF SPECIFIED COURSE OBJECTIVES

10	9	8	▼7	6	5	4	3	2	1

Subject matter always pointed toward attaining course objectives	While occasional deviations occur, subject matter usually in line with objectives	Subject matter and course objectives usually not compatible

11. SUITABILITY OF ASSIGNED TEXTBOOK(S) (if text assigned)

10	9	▼8	7	6	5	4	3	2	1

Clearly written and compatible with course	Some parts of course not covered by textbook	Textbook poorly written or incompatible with course

12. EFFICIENCY IN THE USE OF CLASS TIME

10	9	8	7▼	6	5	4	3	2	1

Class time extremely well used	Class time sometimes well used and sometimes wasted	Class time frequently wasted

13. LECTURER'S PERCEPTION OF WHEN STUDENTS DID NOT UNDERSTAND MATERIAL

10	9	8▼	7	6	5	4	3	2	1

Lecturer fully aware of students' backgrounds and limitations	Lecturer oblivious to students' backgrounds and limitations

14. LECTURER AND THE HANDLING OF MAJOR POINTS

10	9	8 ▼	7	6	5	4	3	2	1

The lectures were well structured with summaries and emphasis on major points	The lecturer did not summarise or emphasise important points

15. FAIRNESS IN MARKING OF TESTS AND COURSE WORK (if applicable)

10	9	8	7	▼6	5	4	3	2	1

Completely fair	Sometimes unfair	Frequently unfair

16. WILLINGNESS TO HELP STUDENTS OUTSIDE CLASS

10	9	8	7	▼6	5	4	3	2	1

Always willing to assist outside class	Usually willing to help	Generally inaccessible or aloof; unwilling to assist students

Table 1   *Lecturer Evaluation Questionnaire contd.*

17. SUITABILITY OF CLASS SIZE

10	9	8	▼7	6	5	4	3	2	1

Class size suitable for this course	Size of class sometimes too large to allow class discussion/participation etc.	Excessive size of class detrimental to course

18. SUITABILITY OF ASSIGNED COURSE WORK

10	9	8	▼7	6	5	4	3	2	1

Assignments given clearly and co-ordinated with lectures	Sometimes indefinite or unrelated to lectures	Usually unclear or unrelated to lectures

19. AVAILABILITY OF LECTURER OUTSIDE CLASS HOURS

10	9	8	7	▼6	5	4	3	2	1

The lecturer specified when he would be available and kept to it	Lecturer specified when available but did not keep perfectly to it	Lecturer did not specify availability but was frequently available	Lecturer did not specify availability and was extremely difficult to catch

20. SCOPE OF THE COURSE

10	9	8	7	6▼	5	4	3	2	1

Far too much work to do (in relation to other courses)	Not enough to do

21. COMPARED WITH OTHER LECTURERS IN THE DEPARTMENT, HOW GOOD HAS THE LECTURER BEEN?

10	9	8	7▼	6	5	4	3	2	1

In the top 10%	In the bottom 10%

If there are any other general comments you wish to make about the course, please detail them below.

The reader will, hopefully, by now have an appreciation of the level of concern with quality in the service sector. Commercial organisations in the service sector increasingly appear to take it for granted that future business is dependent on the return of satisfied customers. The cost of flying from one part of the world to another is, in many cases, so fixed that airlines can only really compete on the customer's anticipated level of service. Relying on one's own nationals would certainly not keep most of them solvent. When a businessman travels abroad on expenses the cost of the hotel room is unlikely to be a major determinant of where he stays. What matters to him is whether he receives the level of service he expects. On the retailing front we have witnessed a shopping revolution, during my lifetime at least, which has reflected changing employment patterns. Many people now look on shopping, even for groceries, as an experience which, if not enjoyable in the normal sense of the word, can be pleasant. Sainsbury's knows this only too well and organises its supermarkets accordingly. As was evident from its contribution, it invests many man-hours of senior executive time and effort ensuring that what it offers continues to meet enhanced customer expectations.

From Ron Mortiboy's opening piece and on throughout the text this theme of top-level concern with quality has been either clearly evident or implicit in what was happening in a range of organisations. Such a concern has certainly come too late for many of our manufacturing organisations which might well have benefited from an earful from Frank Price. Fortunately for Britain, while we will undoubtedly continue to impact on the world's manufacturing scene, we will almost certainly continue to earn substantial revenues from the service sector. Financial services and tourism are two obvious areas where the quality of the 'product' on offer will determine the size of these revenues. It is also somewhat sobering to reflect on the fact that the fee income and associated living expenses of the overseas student population in British universities generates well in excess of £250 million annually. I came to the end of editing this text feeling optimistic that a greatly increased quality consciousness pervades this expanding part of our economy.

There is absolutely no way in which we can stop the inexorable move towards an economy in which the service sector plays an ever-increasing part. We will expect ever more things to be done for us, thus allowing us the selective pursuit of those activities which give us greatest satisfaction. Some authors even go so far as to suggest that work itself might be sought after as a means of occupying one's time. Such a scenario overlooks the fact that the new services are labour-intensive. Around a million people will probably continue to be involved in the delivery of health care, dustbins will still need to be emptied, and hotel guests pandered to. Service industries are here to stay, as is quality consciousness.

One manifestation of this growing concern, in addition to the aforementioned top-level involvement, is an interest in the measurement of the quality of service being delivered. In several of the chapters we have heard of organisations tackling this issue. In some cases the approach has been fairly low-key whereas in others it has been a full-blown attempt to measure what customers or patients think of the service provided. It will be obvious that this writer favours the latter approach provided, always, that it is well founded or, dare I say, well researched. The resultant specificity of the approach does enable the identification of areas of concern and the eventual eradication of that concern.

I fervently hold to the view that it behoves those in education and those in health to make a genuine effort to ascertain how our clients rate our efforts on their behalf. By the time a student wakes up to the fact that he is in a mediocre department it is too late. For a patient to become conscious of deficiencies in his care might be considered even more serious.

On the commercial front the attempts at measurement are obviously predicated on the belief that only by knowing in what ways potential customers, actual customers or lost customers see the company meeting their needs and expectations does it have any real chance of matching them. What I do find surprising is that in a number of service industries some form of centralised and independent customer auditing has not emerged. The responses to our patient satisfaction surveys only take on any real meaning when the results emerging from one hospital can be set against those from another. I would have thought that the same story holds true in the travel industry, the hotel industry etc, etc. The data collection is easy, the computing is trivial and the insights to be gained would surely justify the pooling of information.

This inter-unit comparison brings me to my penultimate point. Customers and suppliers alike owe a tremendous debt to those agencies which have, by their pioneering efforts, striven to impact positively on the quality of service we have come to expect. The consumer movement is another of those unstoppable forces. Given the upward trend in disposable incomes and the increasing number of people engaged in the service sector there was, to some extent, a certain inevitability in the rise of this phenomenon. We have, though, been well served by it. We can now purchase goods and services more confident than ever before that they will do what they are supposed to and, if they do not, we have redress. Companies which have found themselves unable to live with this changing reality have gone to the wall and those that survive are ever more sensitive to the quality dimension. This, then, contributes to those goods or services being able to hold their own in an ever more competitive world. We still have an awful lot of catching up to do, but the open sharing of experiences typified by the contributions in this book would suggest that the concern for quality is contagious.

And that, in turn, brings me to the final point. Perhaps more so than any other topic, quality appears to act as a commitment producer. People like to be associated with success and it transpires that for a large proportion of the work force success is synonymous with quality. Producing what are palpably shoddy goods or delivering what one knows is a poor service must be soul-destroying. Being in a position to impact on the quality of the product being made or the service delivered quite clearly provides a good deal of satisfaction. This point has come across in several of the contributions and it is that, as much as normal commercial pressures, which will guarantee that, unlike other supposed panacea, quality consciousness and all that it brings with it will not go away. It touches a sensitive nerve and is here to stay. It has certainly got me excited and already I'm lining up contributions for the second edition which will have an international orientation.

Bibliography

Abdellah, F.G. and Levine, E. (1957) 'What patients say about their nursing care', *Hospitals*, Vol. 31, pp. 44–48.

Ball, J.A., Goldstone, L.A. and Collier, M.M. (1984) *Criteria for Care: The Manual of the North West Nurse Staffing Levels Project*, Newcastle-Upon-Tyne Polytechnic Products Ltd.

Banham, J. (1985) *Securing Value for Money in Libraries*, The Public Library Authorities Conference, Peebles, October.

BBC (1979) *King: A Drama Documentary*, Broadcasting Research Department Annual Review of BBC Audience Research Findings, No. 6.

BBC (1984) *Daily Life in the '80s*, Broadcasting Research Department Data Publications.

Briggs, Asa (1965) *The History of Broadcasting in the United Kingdom, Volume 2*, Oxford University Press.

Bristow, R. (1983) *Appetite for Breakfast Television: A Pre-broadcast Study of Awareness and Interest*, Annual Review of BBC Broadcasting Research Findings, No. 9, BBC Data Publications.

British Tourist Authority (1984) *British National Travel Survey*.

British Tourist Authority (1985) *British National Travel Survey*.

Burkart, A.J. and Medlik, S. (1981) *Tourism: Past, Present and Future*, 2nd edn, Heinemann.

Buswell, D.C. (1983) 'Measuring the quality of in-branch customer service', *The International Journal of Bank Marketing*, Vol. 1, No. 1, pp. 26–41.

Butt, H. and Palmer, R. (1985) *Value for Money in the Public Sector*, Basil Blackwell.

Byrne, P.S. and Long, B.E.L. (1977) *Doctors Talking to Patients*, HMSO.

Cartwright, A. (1964) *Human Relationships and Hospital Care*, Routledge and Kegan Paul.

Central Transport Consultative Committee for Great Britain (1985) *Annual Report of the Official National Committee Representing Rail Passengers 1984/85*, HMSO.

Cheshire Country Council (1985) *The Cheshire Library Survey*, Cheshire Libraries and Museums Committee, Chester.

Collard, R. and Dale, B.G. (1986) 'Direct Participation', in K. Sissons (ed.) *Personnel Management in Britain*, Basil Blackwell.

Crosby, P. (1985) *The Quality Man*, BBC Education and Training.

Dale, B.G. and Lees, J. (1984) *A Study of Quality Circles in the UK Service Sector*, Occasional Paper 8406, Department of Management Sciences, UMIST.

Daniel, D. (1975) 'What the patient thinks', *Nursing Mirror*, Vol. 141, No. 23, p.73.

Davies, A.H.T. (1981) 'Strategic Planning in the Thomas Cook Group', *Long Range Planning*, Vol. 14, No. 5, pp.27–38.

Department of Trade (1982) *The Nationalised Industry Consumer Councils: A Strategy for Reform*, Department of Trade.

DHSS (Department of Health and Social Security) (1983) *An Enquiry into the Management of the NHS*, HMSO.

Eastern Gas Consumers' Council (1984) *Annual Report*, 1983–84.

Economist Intelligence Unit (1984) *International Tourism Quarterly*, Nos. 2 and 3.

English Tourist Board (1983) *British Home Travel Survey*.

Goldstone, L.A., Ball, J.A. and Collier, M.M. (1983) *Monitor: An Index of the Quality of Nursing Care for Acute Medical and Surgical Wards*, Newcastle-Upon-Tyne Polytechnic Products Ltd.

Gregory, J. (1978) *Patients' Attitudes to the Hospital Service*, Royal Commission on the National Health Service, Research Paper 5, HMSO.

Halpern, S. (1986) 'All in the name of money', *Health and Social Services Journal*, Vol. 96, No. 4987, pp.250–251.

Hayman, D.J. and Spurrell, G.L. (1975) *Quality of Care: A Pilot Study*, Unpublished dissertation for a Diploma in Management Sciences, Department of Management Sciences, UMIST.

Hayward, S., Dale, B.G. and Frazer, V.C.M. (1985) 'Quality circle failure and how to avoid it', *European Management Journal*, Vol. 3, No. 2, pp.103–111.

Health Advisory Service (1983) *The Rising Tide — Developing Services for Mental Illness in Old Age*, DHSS.

Henney, A. (1986) *Regulating Public and Privatised Monopolies: A Radical Approach*, Public Finance Foundation.

Hertzberg, F. (1966) *Work and the Nature of Man*, World Publishing Co.

Home Office (1977) *Report on the Committee of the Future of Broadcasting*, HMSO.

Jelinek, R.C., Haussman, R.K.D., Hegyvary, S.T. and Newman, J.F. (1974) *A Methodology for Monitoring Quality of Nursing Care*, Department of Health Education and Welfare, Washington, D.C.

Jelinek, R.C., Haussman, R.K.D. and Hegyvary, S.T. (1977) *Monitoring Quality of Nursing Care. Part 3: Professional Review for Nursing: An Empirical Investigation*, Department of Health Education and Welfare, Washington, D.C.

Kinston, W. (1983) 'Hospital organisation and structure and its effect on inter-professional behaviour and the delivery of care', *Social Science and Medicine*, Vol. 17, No. 16, pp.1159–1170.

Lees, J. and Dale, B.G. (1985) *A Further Study of Quality Circles in the UK Service Sector*, Occasional Paper No. 8511, Department of Management Sciences, UMIST.

Ley, P. and Spelman, M.S. (1967) *Communicating with the Patient*, Staples Press.

Lockyer, K.G., Oakland, J.S. and Duprey, C.H. (1982) 'Quality control in British manufacturing industry: a study', *Quality Assurance*, Vol. 8, No. 2, pp.39–44.

London Electricity Consultative Committee (1985) *Speaking Out for London Electricity Customers: A Report on the Council's Policies and Activities for the Period 1981/85*, LECC.

Marles, V. and Radcliffe, R. (1982), *The Role of Research in the Production Process: The Computer Programme — A Case Study*, Annual Review of BBC Broadcasting Research Findings, No. 8.

Martin, J.D. and Evans, D. (1984) *Hospitals in Trouble*, Basil Blackwell.

McGhee, A. (1961) *The Patient's Attitude to Nursing Care*, E. and S. Livingstone, Edinburgh.

Mitchell, K. (1980) *In Touch*, Annual Review of BBC Broadcasting Research Findings, No. 7.

Moore, N. (1979) *Investigating Public Library Users*, Paper delivered at the Anglo-Scandinavian Public Libraries Conference.

Moores, B. and Thompson, A.G.H. (1985) 'From the patient's mouth', *Health and Social Service Journal*, Vol. 95, No. 4962, pp.1040–1042.

Moores, B. and Thompson, A.G.H. (1986) 'What 1,357 hospital inpatients think about aspects of their stay in British acute hospitals', *Journal of Advanced Nursing*, Vol. 11, pp.87–102.

Morrison, H. (1933) *Socialisation and Transport*, Constable.

National Consumer Council (1981) *Summary of Findings on Issues of Consumer Concern Based on a Survey of Consumers in the United Kingdom: the Nationalised Industries*, Occasional Paper 2, National Consumer Council, London.

National Gas Consumers' Council (1984) *Research Survey: Gas Consumers and Gas Appliances*, NGCC, London, 3 volumes.

National Gas Consumers' Council (1983) *Tenth Annual Report*, year ending March 31, 1983.

National Gas Consumers' Council (1984) *Eleventh Annual Report*, year ending March 31, 1984.

National Gas Consumers' Council (1985) *Twelfth Annual Report*, year ending March 31, 1985.

Natioal Economic Development Council (1985) *Task Force on Quality and Standards, Quality and Value for Money*, National Economic Development Council, London.

Post Office Users' National Council (1984) *Customer Audit and Review of the Post Office 1983–84*, POUNC, Report No. 35.

Post Office Users' National Council (1985) *Annual Report, 1981–82*.

Price, F. (1984) *Right First Time*, Gower Press.

Raphael, W. (1967) 'Do we know what the patients think? A survey comparing the views of patients, staff and committee members', *International Journal of Nursing Studies*, Vol. 4, pp.209–223.

Raphael, W. (1969) *Patients and their Hospitals: A Survey of Patients' Views of Life in General Hospitals*, King Edward's Hospital Fund for London, London.

Raphael, W. (1974) *Survey of Patients' Opinion Surveys in Hospitals*, King's Fund Project Paper 9, King's Fund Centre, London.

Research Surveys of Great Britain Limited (1982) *NGCC Awareness Study*.

Skeet, M. (1971) *Home from Hospital*, Dan Mason Nursing Research Committee, London.

Slack, W.P. (1985) 'Standards of care', *Nursing Times*, May 29, pp.28–32.

Swan, J.E. and Combs, L.J. (1976) 'Product performance and consumer satisfaction: a new concept', *Journal of Marketing*, Vol. 40, No. 2, pp.25–33.

Thompson, A.G.H. (1983) *The Measurement of Patients' Perceptions of the Quality of Hospital Care*, Unpublished doctoral dissertation, University of Manchester.

Thompson, A.G.H. (1986) 'A patient's eye view', *Nursing Times*, Vol. 82, No. 10, pp.30–32.

Totterdell, B. and Bird, J. (1976) *The Effective Library*, The Library Association.

Townsend, D.W. (1981) *An Examination of Consumer Satisfaction in the Tourist Industry with Particular Reference to Airlines, Hotels, and Tour Operators,* Unpublished dissertation for a diploma in Management Sciences, Department of Management Sciences, UMIST.

Waterhouse, E.C. (1975) 'Tourism' in M. Goldsmith (ed.) *Forward Planning in the Service Sectors,* Macmillan.

Yorke, D.A. (1984) 'Local authorities and the marketing of leisure services', *The Service Industries Journal,* Vol. 4, No. 3, pp. 151–165.

Index